STRAIGHT OUTTA DUBLIN

James Joyce and
Robert Anton Wilson

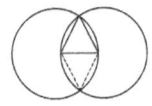

STRAIGHT OUTTA DUBLIN

James Joyce and Robert Anton Wilson

Eric Wagner

More Notes by R. Michael Johnson

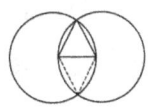

Straight Outta Dublin
Copyright © 2025 Eric Wagner

All rights reserved. No part of this book, in part or in whole, may be reproduced, transmitted, or utilized, in any form or by any means, electronic or mechanical, including photocopying, recording, or by any information storage and retrieval system, without permission in writing from the publisher, except for brief quotations in critical articles, books and reviews.

Print ISBN: 978-1-952746-41-3
eBook ISBN: 978-1-952746-42-0

Print Edition 2025, Hilaritas Press
eBook Edition 2025, Hilaritas Press

Cover Design by Richard Rasa
eBook design by Pelorian Digital

Hilaritas Press, LLC.
P.O. Box 1153
Grand Junction, Colorado 81502

www.hilaritaspress.com

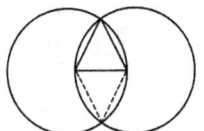

To Debbie, my Wife and Muse,
you make all the nonsense worth it.

Editor's Note

Oz Fritz and Tom Jackson offered extensive notes while proofing Straight Outta Dublin, which added greatly to the final edited version. Hilaritas Press has benefitted repeatedly from their scholarly contributions to our publishing efforts, and we are eternally thankful.

"Oz and Tom, MVPs of Wilsoniana, improved the text with their caring, thoughtful attention."
– Eric Wagner

"Yeoman copyediting service was provided by Oz and Tom. Thanks guys: you saved our entire side of bacon."
– R. Michael Johnson

The vesica piscis glyph found throughout this book is a nod to the diagram Joyce included in Finnegans Wake that represents geometric metaphors.

This book, among other things, explores the influence of James Joyce on Robert Anton Wilson and uses Wilson's books as a lens to examine Joyce's work. I patterned it after the five-fold structure of Joyce's *Portrait of the Artist as a Young Man* and the five-fold model of history in Robert Shea and Robert Anton Wilson's *Illuminatus!*, which consists of Thesis, Antithesis, Synthesis, Parenthesis, and Paralysis. (Bob Wilson later renamed the divisions as Thesis, Antithesis, Synthesis, Paralysis and Paresis.) A portion of the Thesis section appeared in my *An Insider's Guide to Robert Anton Wilson* as an appendix, "*The Influence of James Joyce on Robert Anton Wilson's* Masks of the Illuminati." I greatly expanded this appendix for my master's thesis for the California State University at San Bernardino, "The Influence of Finnegans Wake on Robert Anton Wilson's *Masks of the Illuminati*." December 2004 marked the publication of both *An Insider's Guide* and my master's thesis. A modified version of that Thesis appears as the Thesis section of this book. This book concludes with a commentary on the exercises in Wilson's *Prometheus Rising*, focusing on the Joycean elements of those exercises.

This book seems cursed
(with appreciation for the church in Rennes-le-Château).

I had an email exchange with Robert Anton Wilson shortly after the publication of *An Insider's Guide* about what I should write about next. I had several ideas, and he liked the idea of expanding my thesis about Joyce's influence on his writing. About a year later I rejoined Weight Watchers, and I had the idea of magickally linking my writing with my weight loss journey. I would write a page for each pound I lost for a section of about sixty pages.

Well, after some initial success, I started to regain the weight I had lost. I didn't have as much skill in metaprogramming my nervous system as I thought I did. I kept researching Joyce and his influence on Wilson as my weight yo-yoed from 2006 to 2020. In March 2020 all three of my teaching jobs switched to distance education because of the Pandemic. I feared my weight would go up due to staying at home, but surprisingly I had the greatest weight loss success of my life, and I finished writing this book.

Rereading the book, I think it deals with two areas important to Bob Wilson. He wanted people to know how much Joyce's writing had influenced his own, and I think I address this issue thoroughly. Also, over and over again during the last twenty-four years of his life, Wilson referred readers back to the exercises in *Prometheus Rising*. Wilson thought these exercises would help readers loosen the imprints in their nervous systems. Joycean threads run through that book and through those exercises. I have spent decades doing those exercises, and this book contains my experiences with those exercises, and I trace the Joycean trajectories though that book and through Bob's life work.

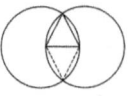

Table of Contents

Thesis 15
  1) Introduction 16
  2) The Techniques of *Finnegans Wake* 22
  3) The Influence of *Finnegans Wake* on
      the First Four Sections of *Masks of the Illuminati* 38
  4) The Final Section of *Masks of the Illuminati* 49
  5) Conclusion of Section I 54

Antithesis 55
  6) Springtime for Hitler 57
  7) Joyce and *The Wizard of Oz* 60
  8) Page 109, Etc. 63

Synthesis 71
  9) Psychedelic Howth Castle Music 73

Parenthesis and/or Paralysis 82
  10) The Sisters and/or Ode to Joy 84
  11) An Encounter and/or:
      On Robert Anton Wilson and Misunderstanding
      Finnegans Wake 87

Paralysis and/or Paresis 89
  12) Araby and/or *Coincidance* 91
  13) Evaline and/or *The Earth Will Shake* 94
  14) After the Race and/or *Prometheus Rising*, Chapter 1 .. 104
  15) Two Gallants and/or *Prometheus Rising*, Chapter 2 118
  16) The Boarding House and/or *Prometheus Rising*,
      Chapter 3 122

17) A Little Cloud and/or *Prometheus Rising*, Chapter 4 .. 128
18) Counterparts and/or Did Pink Floyd Play
    Woodstock Europa? 133
19) Clay and/or *Prometheus Rising*, Chapter 5 135
20) A Painful Case and/or *Prometheus Rising*, Chapter 6 .. 141
21) Ivy Day in the Committee Room and/or *Prometheus Rising*, Chapter 7 145
22) A Mother and/or *Prometheus Rising*, Chapter 8 147
23) Grace and/or *Prometheus Rising*, Chapter 9 151
24) The Dead and/or *Prometheus Rising*, Chapter 10 153
25) *Prometheus Rising*, Chapter 11 157
26) *Ulysses* at 100 160
27) *Prometheus Rising*, Chapter 12 162
28) *Prometheus Rising*, Chapter 13 166
29) *Prometheus Rising*, Chapter 14 171
30) Neo-Decembrist Ramblings 175
31) *Prometheus Rising*, Chapter 15 177
32) *Prometheus Rising*, Chapter 16 181
33) *Wilhelm Reich in Hell*, Questions from Tom Jackson .. 184
34) *Prometheus Rising*, Chapter 17 191
35) *Prometheus Rising*, Chapter 18 201
36) *Prometheus Rising*, Chapter 19 203

Coda 205

Appendix 1: The Dogon Age of Music 208

More Notes on the Influence of James Joyce
    on Robert Anton Wilson
    – by R. Michael Johnson 214

Selected Bibliography 326

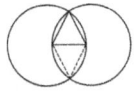

Thesis:

The Influence of *Finnegans Wake* on *Masks of the Illuminati*

FW is what I call "The Good Book", and I'm only half joking. To me it's not only the greatest novel ever written, it's the greatest poem ever written, the greatest detective story ever written, and the most entertaining work in all literature, and as William York Tindall of Columbia says, "it's the funniest and dirtiest book in the world." People are intimidated by it. If the publishers just had the sense to put on the cover, "the funniest and dirtiest book in the world – Tindall, Columbia", it would sell a lot better, and people would make the effort to decipher it.

- Robert Anton Wilson

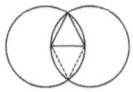

1) Introduction

According to Michael Powers, "The formation of subjects, and especially the ways in which language and history affect that process, is a central theme of *Finnegans Wake*" (102). David Hayman has discussed a number of experimental writers who have continued along the path forged by James Joyce in the *Wake*. In fact, *Finnegans Wake* in its collision of "language and history" has exerted considerable influence over Irish-American novelist Robert Anton Wilson.[1] The first section of this book will illustrate how one contemporary novelist, Wilson, has used the techniques of the *Wake*, and integrated them with other narrative and rhetorical strategies, such as those developed by William S. Burroughs and Ezra Pound. Jean-Michel Rabaté writes, "Joyce's systematic creation of an ideal audience has first and foremost a defensive function: the 'common or neuter' reader is less educated than critics might wish, yet he or she (he-she) can read the book and derive 'lots of fun' from it" (58). Wilson does indeed "derive 'lots of fun' from it," and he uses Joyce's means to his own ends.

~•~

1) Wilson's books have influenced a variety of contemporary subcultures. *Illuminatus!*, co-authored by Wilson and Robert Shea, won the Prometheus Hall of Fame Award in 1986 as a "classic" of science fiction. *Changing Times* magazine listed Wilson's *Cosmic Trigger* in first place among recommended books on the New Age. As of 2002, *Illuminatus!* became the best selling science fiction paperback in the U.S. and held 10th

place among the top 100,000 science fiction novels sold by Amazon (Wilson, *TSOG*, 215-216).

~•~

The traditional Irish drinking song "Finnegan's Wake" tells of a hod carrier named Tim Finnegan who liked to have a pint of the creature (Guinness Stout) each day to help him with his work. One day he falls from his ladder and passes out. His friends and family assume he has died, and they give him a funeral and a traditional Irish wake. A fight breaks out, and someone spills a drink on Tim Finnegan, awakening him. Joyce sees this as paradigmatic of the dream/waking cycle, as well as a model for the fall of man and redemption in Catholic theology, Humpty Dumpty's fall from the wall, etc.

Robert Anton Wilson has written a number of novels and nonfiction works, which some readers classify as postmodern. I find Wilson's work explores a number of areas typical of post-colonialism and postmodernism with great wit and insight. Joyce scholar John Bishop writes that Robert Anton Wilson "has discovered in *Finnegans Wake* both the formula for the hydrogen bomb and the molecular structure of the double helix of DNA" (Bishop, Introduction to *Finnegans Wake*, xii). Wilson delights in making these sorts of connections, following in the Joycean tradition, although he does not really make the claims Bishop ascribes to him. Rather, Wilson finds isomorphisms between processes in *Finnegans Wake* and processes in physics and genetics. He discusses these at great length in his book *Coincidance*, and he also taught about them in a class called "The Tale of the Tribe" at the online Maybe Logic Academy. Wilson also seems particularly interested in the multiple viewpoints used by Joyce, which he sees as parallel to the multiple observers in modern physics and the multiple perspectives in cubism, etc. Wilson wrote, "I bought the Wake on my 16th birthday, in 1948, started reading it, and haven't stopped yet" (*Illuminati Papers*, 31). In *Prometheus Rising* Wilson writes about "the multi-level language of *Finnegans Wake*, where Finnegan is Finn-again, Finn Mac

Cool of Irish legend reborn and Huck Finn again also, sailing down 'Missus Liffey,' both the river Anna Liffey in Ireland and Huck Finn's Mississippi" (ibid., pg. 201). He has written frequently about *Finnegans Wake* in his non-fiction, explaining some of what he considers Joyce's methods in the book and the ideas underlying the text.

I will examine how Wilson has deployed the techniques of *Finnegans Wake* and its covert rhetoric in explaining his own work from a post-colonial perspective. Wilson views Joyce's writing as part of a tradition of covert writing, going back to Oscar Wilde's essay "The Truth of Masks." Wilson contends that this essay conceals its meanings in part due to the British colonial control of Ireland. (Note: Wilson calls the Wilde essay "The Reality of Masks.")

On the surface Wilde's essay discusses the importance of costuming in Shakespeare's plays, but Wilson reads the essay as a discussion of the necessity for covert behavior, or mask wearing, by some groups in society. (I wrote this originally around 2003. Rereading it in 2024, I think about the changing role of masks in our society due to the Pandemic.) At first, Wilson felt that Wilde's essay dealt with the masks worn by gay men in Victorian England, hiding their sexual identities. However, over time Wilson came to believe that one could also read the essay as dealing with the masks worn under the oppression of English colonialism. Wilde himself suggests that the essay may contain more than appears on the surface. In "The Truth of Masks" Wilde cryptically comments, "Not that I agree with everything that I have said in this essay. There is much with which I entirely disagree" (pg. 1078). In an essay on *Finnegans Wake* in Wilson's *Coincidance*, he refers to "the Irish people's (or any colonial people's) obsession with hiding what they are doing" (ibid., pg. 14). Wilson reads Wilde's essay "The Truth of Masks" as working on at least three levels: the importance of costuming in Shakespeare; the masks worn by homosexuals in Victorian England; and the masks worn by those under colonial oppression. Wilson sees this tradition of multilevel writing continuing in Irish writing, particularly in Yeats and Joyce. I contend that Wilson himself continues this tradition in his writing. In the first section of this book I will focus on *Masks of the Illuminati*, which includes Joyce and Yeats as characters.

Wilson next traces this tradition to Yeats' concept of Mask in his book *A Vision*. Yeats wrote that automatic writing by his wife provided the basis for this text. In *A Vision* Yeats provides a complex model of the self, but Wilson sees Yeats continuing in the covert writing tradition of Wilde.

Wilson sees these ideas continuing to develop through the various stages of Joyce's career, from the "silence, exile and cunning" of *A Portrait of the Artist as a Young Man* to the concealing word games of *Finnegans Wake*. My contribution is to show precisely how Wilson employs the word games of *Finnegans Wake*, along with other devices, to depict dreams, drug states and stream of consciousness, etc., in his novels, as well as to conceal and reveal a variety of levels of meaning.

This thesis will offer a close reading of Wilson's use of a variety of narrative techniques, integrating those of the *Wake*, including multiple viewpoints, combined words, multi-lingual puns and webs of allusions, in his novel *Masks of the Illuminati*. I will examine where Wilson deploys the Wakean devices, and to what end he uses them in the novel. I will examine how he uses these devices to reveal the nature of the characters, as well as lampoon the power structure which gave rise to Irish-English tensions. My research will demonstrate the continued relevance of the *Wake*, as well as display the various colonial tensions in the book. I contend that Wilson utilizes many of the stylistic devices of *Finnegans Wake* in *Masks of the Illuminati* and puts them to new and creative use. The small amount of existing critical work on Wilson has not shown his tremendous debt to Joyce.

The critical tradition of *Finnegans Wake* has reached little consensus. Even before the publication of the complete novel in 1939, many voices had chimed in either condemning or championing Joyce's book of the night. Even old friends such as Ezra Pound thought Joyce had gone too far in his final novel. In subsequent years, a great deal of scholarship has outlined a variety of interpretations of the novel such as that of Campbell and Robinson (1944), Tindall (1969), McHugh (1980), Bishop (1986), and Kenner (1987). Wilson has studied Joyce a great deal over more than fifty years, and he has also read a great deal of the Joyce literature. He tends to see *Finnegans Wake* as a dream where some (such as Bishop) might disagree. (Bishop sees *Finnegans Wake* as presenting the whole sleep experience, with dream as one component of that experience.) Wilson mentions Hugh Kenner more than any other Joyce scholar. Kenner has given a great deal more attention to *Ulysses* than to *Finnegans Wake*, but I suspect part of Wilson's interest in Kenner's writing comes from their shared deep interest in the work of Ezra Pound, whom both Wilson and Kenner admire much more than most other Joyce scholars do.

Masks of the Illuminati includes Joyce and Albert Einstein as major characters just before the outbreak of World War I. (Ezra Pound also appears as a minor character in the novel.) At this time Joyce had begun thinking about the writing of *Ulysses*. In the novel Joyce and Einstein meet in a bar in Switzerland, and while there they meet an Englishman who believes in an occult conspiracy trying to kill him. Joyce and Einstein then attempt to discover the truth behind this man's fears. Using the techniques of the *Wake*, Wilson shows in *Masks of the Illuminati* how some of the new literary ideas arising in Joyce's mind blend as he prepares to write *Ulysses*. My research will show how Wilson has deployed Joyce's own devices to portray Joyce developing those very devices. Wilson also uses the techniques of the *Wake* to illustrate the English-Irish tensions in the novel. Wilson employs the techniques of the *Wake* to draw parallels between Einstein's theories of relativity and the multiple viewpoints deployed in *Ulysses* and *Finnegans Wake*. In personal interviews with Wilson for my book *An Insider's Guide to Robert Anton Wilson* (New Falcon Press 2004), Wilson told me how Joyce's techniques helped him to add layers of depth to the meaning of his novels and to reveal the kinds of realities not accounted for by conventional thought.

Although Wilson's work has not received a great deal of critical attention, I will attempt to show the continued relevance of *Finnegans Wake* to his work, as well as analyze the tools Joyce developed to express some of the more repressed aspects of the human experience. I also hope to demonstrate that Robert Anton Wilson's work deserves scholarly review for its wit, its vision, and its humanity.

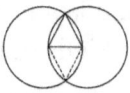

2) The Techniques of *Finnegans Wake*

When Joyce published *Ulysses* in 1922 at the age of forty, he found himself at a crossroads. Some of his peers, such as T. S. Eliot and Ezra Pound, saw him as having written a masterpiece, perhaps the greatest novel ever written. Where should he now turn his attention? Well, he decided that since *Ulysses* told the story of a day, he ought now to tell the story of a night. He spent most of the rest of his life attempting to do so, finally publishing *Finnegans Wake* in 1939, just two years before his death. Many of those who had praised *Ulysses* so highly had reservations about *Finnegans Wake* and the huge amount of effort Joyce put into its creation. Pound felt that Joyce had gone too far from comprehensibility and dwelt too much on scatology. This chapter will explore some of the techniques Joyce developed for the shaping of this unique narrative and hopefully will help to illuminate why he would devote so many years to the creation of such an odd book.

The sixth chapter of *Finnegans Wake* provides an interesting starting point for discussing the text. This chapter takes the form of a radio quiz show, with twelve questions and/or riddles and their answers. The ninth question and answer pair seems to provide a general introduction to the book. William Tindall suggests that "Jimmy MacCawthelock" "quizzes Shaun, letter carrier for 'Jhon Jhamieson and Song'" (111). Humphrey Chimpden Earwicker, or HCE, whom most commentators see as the dreamer of the book, or one identity of the dreamer of the book, has two sons, Shem and Shaun, also known as Shem the penman and Shaun the postman. These paired opposites run throughout the text.

> 9. Now to be on anew and basking again in the panorama of all flores of speech, if a human being duly fatigued by his dayety in the sooty, having plenxty off time on his gouty hands and vacants of space at his sleepish feet and as hapless behind the dreams of accuracy as any camelot prince of dinmurk, were at this auctual futile preteriting unstant, in the states of suspensive exanimation, accorded, throughout the eye of a noodle, with an earsighted view of old hopeinhaven with all the ingredient and egregiunt whights and ways to which in the curse of his tory will had been having recourses, the reverberration of knotcracking awes, the reconjungation of nodebinding ayes, the redissolusingness of mindmouldered ease and the thereby hang the Hoel of it, could such a none, whiles even led comsilencers to comeliewithhers and till intempestuous Nox should catch the gallicry and spot lucan's dawn, byhold at ones what is main and why tis twain, how one once meet melts in tother wants poingings, the sap rising, the foles falling, the nimb now nihilant round the girlyhead so becoming, the wrestless in the womb, all the rivals to allsca, shakeagain, O disaster! shakealose, Ah how starring! but Heng's got a bit of Horsa's nose and Jeff's got the signs of Ham round his mouth and the beau that spun beautiful pales as it palls, what roserude and oragious grows gelb and greem, blue out the ind of it! Violet's dyed! then *what* would that fargazer seem to seemself to seem seeming of, dimm it all?
> (Joyce, *Finnegans Wake* pg. 143)

This question (yes, it consists of one rather elaborate sentence) suggests beginning again, "be on anew", using all the flowers of speech, "flores of speech," to tell the tale of a person duly fatigued by his day in the city, "if a human being duly fatigued by his dayety in the sooty." Note that "sooty" suggests both the griminess of daily toil plus "dear dirty Dublin," as many inhabitants referred to Dublin in Joyce's day. When this person falls asleep, they will have plenty of time (as well as "off time") to dream about the concerns of their life. As well, they will have virtual time and space within their dream worlds to act out those concerns, "having plenxty of time on his gouty hands and vacants of space at his sleepish feet." In *Ulysses*, and to a limited extent in *Portrait of the Artist as a Young Man*, Joyce had associated the sense of vision with perception of space and the sense of hearing with the perception of time. Joyce expands these perceptions in *Finnegans Wake*. In the *Wake* he links them as space-time, taking Einstein into account. As space becomes time in the *Wake*, s becomes t, and a sailor becomes a tailor. Joyce frequently makes reference to Thomas Carlyle's *Sartor Resartus* in this regard. One can see a bit of this play in the above passage about space-time. The hands have become "gouty" through the inactivity of sleep. In *Time and Western Man* Wyndham Lewis criticized Joyce for too great an interest in time rather than space, and he said of *Finnegans Wake*, "You must draw the line somewhere" (Tindall 179). Joyce incorporated Lewis's criticisms in the *Wake*, showing via language how space and time flow into each other in a relativistic, post-Einsteinian world, sailor becoming tailor.

    In the question Joyce refers to "camelot prince of dinmurk." This phrase appears in the context of explaining the experience of dreaming, showing how different literary and mythical figures can blend in the dream world. Here Joyce conflates the Arthurian legends of Camelot with Shakespeare's Hamlet. One can see parallels between the infidelity between Guinevere and Lancelot and the possible infidelity between Gertrude and her dead husband's brother, or with the King Mark, Tristan and Isolde triangle. The "portmanteau" expression "dinmurk" suggests dim and murky, for the nighttime dream world of the *Wake*, as well as the synesthesia of din and murky, sound and sight. The din suggests the sound of thunder that terrifies the dreamer in the *Wake*, as well as Vico's theory of thunder as the origin of religion (Tindall 166, McHugh 143).

The dreamer, in a state "of suspensive exanimation" uses his "noodle" for "an earsighted view of old hopeinhaven." Joyce thus creates this synesthesia of "earsighted" to show how all borders dissolve in the dream state. John Bishop has observed the importance of the role of sight and hearing in the *Wake* (*Joyce's Book of the Dark*, pg. 216). The dreamer with his eyes closed becomes effectively blind, but the ears continue to function, at least in a limited fashion, throughout the night. "Hopeinhaven" in this passage combines the Copenhagen of Hamlet's Denmark with a "hope in heaven."

"Erregiunt" suggests the medieval philosopher Scotus Erigena who greatly influenced Ezra Pound. Pound attributed to Erigena the quote, "*quae sunt, omnia sunt*," which means "all things that are, are lights" (Terrell, pg. 143). This metaphysical model fits in with the *Wake*'s dreamworld, even with its lack of external light. "His tory" suggests the dreamer's history as well as the domination of Ireland for 700 years by Tory England. This whole question suggests a model of the nature of dreams, as well as a model of the structure of *Finnegans Wake*.

I read "knotcracking" as suggesting the difficulties the noggin (or brain) encounters dealing with these riddles, as well as the Nutcracker ballet, another dreamstory whose magical mice and dancing candy fits in with the *Wake*world. (The later "hang the Hoel of it" continues this Christmas theme, along with the holistic idea that the whole of our perceived world hangs from our models of the world.) "*Nox*," Latin for night, fits in with the sexual bedroom references to "comeliewithhers," which also suggests Christopher Marlowe's *carpe diem* poem "Come Live with Me and Be My Love," although of course Joyce suggests that we rather seize the night (McHugh, pg. 143).

"Reconjungation" suggests conjugal love, as well as the conjugations of language ("all flores of speech"). This word also contains the name of Carl Jung. Joyce took his mentally ill daughter Lucia to see Jung. Joyce commented to Jung that he played the same sort of games with language that Lucia did. Jung responded that Joyce "was diving, while she was drowning." On reading Joyce's *Ulysses* Jung responded that this seemed the evidence of a mentally ill mind or of a whole new kind of sanity. Jung found Joyce's insights into female viewpoints in the final section simply amazing (Maddox, pg. 398). "Reconjungation" also suggests "recirculation," a term which appears in the first sentence of *Finnegans Wake*.

> riverrun, past Eve and Adam's, from swerve of shore to bend of bay, brings us by a commodious vicus of recirculation back to Howth Castle and Environs.
> (Joyce, *Finnegans Wake*, pg. 3)
>
> "Recirculation" in conjunction with "vicus" suggests the cyclic philosophy of Giambattista Vico, whose thought greatly influenced Joyce
> (Wilson, *Coincidance*, pg. 7).

The water imagery also ties in with Jung's comment about diving and sinking.

To return to riddle nine, "why tis twain" suggests the division between all the dyads of *Finnegans Wake*, male and female, day and night, light and dark, etc. Robert Anton Wilson has suggested that each paragraph of *Finnegans Wake*'s hologrammatic prose contains the essence of the whole novel (*Illuminati Papers*, pg. 33). "Twain" suggests Mark Twain, who plays many roles at the *Wake*. He of course wrote about Huck Finn, and married a woman named Livy, whom Joyce associates with A. L. P., the "heroine" of *Finnegans Wake*, the goddess Anna Livia Plurabella and the river Liffey in Dublin. Twain wrote about the Mississippi, which becomes Mrs. Liffey in *Finnegans Wake*. Plus Mark suggests one of the *Wake*'s four old men: Marcus Lyons, Matt Gregory, Luke Tarpey and Johnny MacDougal. These four old gossips also associate with the four evangelists, the four bedposts of the dreamer's bed, the four men carrying Tim Finnegan's casket, the four animals in the vision of Ezekiel, etc. (Wilson, *Coincidance*, pg. 166). Medieval Irish Catholics associated the evangelists with these animals from the Old Testament: Mark with the lion, Luke with the bull ("taur" in Latin), John with the eagle and Matthew with the angel or human (Gregory contains "ego"). Again, quiz question nine connects with many of the major themes and characters of the entire book.

Continuing with question nine, "wrestless in the womb" suggests parallels between the experience of the sleeper and of the infant in the womb. The ego dies at night, and then after the Dark Night of the Soul and/or nine months in the womb, gets reborn with the dawn as in "lucan's dawn" from the question. The seven colors of the rainbow accompany this morning resurrection, "what roserude and oragious grows gelb and greem, blue out the ind of it! Violet's dyed!" John Bishop suggests that *Finnegans Wake*'s frequent rainbow references refer to the color spectrum, the palette available to the essentially blind sleeper (*Joyce's Book of the Dark*, pg. 230).

Joyce gives as an answer to the riddle, "A Collideorscape" (*Finnegans Wake*, pg. 143). One can see *Finnegans Wake* as a collision of all the stuff in the dreamer HCE's head[2] and/or as an attempt to escape from history, what Stephen Dedalus in *Ulysses* calls a nightmare from which he is trying to escape. This collision and/or escape becomes a kaleidoscope. Of course, as McHugh points out, one can also see these "flores of speech" as flaws (McHugh, pg. 143). McHugh's *Annotations to* Finnegans Wake reveals how multivariate Joyce made *Finnegans Wake*. Each passage lends itself to interpretation after interpretation. Joyce said it would take the professors a thousand years to figure out the novel. In over eighty years we've only begun to scratch the surface.

~•~

2) "Mind and its contents are functionally identical" (Wilson, *Prometheus Rising*, pg. 222).

~•~

Finnegans Wake's resistance to interpretation ties in with Joyce's persistent water imagery. Joyce makes many parallels between the nature of water and that of dream. Both of them escape the easy grasp, flowing away easily. An expression such as "gouty hands" suggests fleshy hands afflicted with gout, but it also suggests "weekends" by its sound (McHugh 143), and "gouty" and "sleepish" suggest goat and sheep, a fundamental Christian duality. One can see why John Bishop sees *Finnegans Wake* as the fountainhead for much modern critical theory. Bishop discusses "the *Wake*'s interest in the utter arbitrariness of language as a sign-system infiltrated with insidious patterns of 'awethorrory,' so to show how Joyce anticipated by decades one current academic interest in theory" (*Joyce's Book of the Dark*, pg. 299). Even all the flowers or flaws of speech cannot capture the watery nature of the sleeping state in any way simpler than the text of *Finnegans Wake* as a whole, even though each part of *Finnegans Wake* gives a semblance of the text as a whole, of the night as a whole (or a hole). Shakespeare's Bottom had a dream, but dreams have no bottom (Zukofsky, pg. 15). Bishop continues, "As those most influential in advancing the importance of theory have attested, Joyce was light-years ahead of attempts now being made to theorize him" (*Joyce's Book of the Dark* 299).

Returning to the first line of *Finnegans Wake*:

> riverrun, past Eve and Adam's, from swerve of shore to bend of bay, brings us by a commodius vicus of recirculation back to Howth Castle and Environs.
> (Joyce, *Finnegans Wake*, pg. 3)

"riverrun" begins with a lower case r, suggesting that this connects with the last line of the book, "A way a lone a last a loved a long the" (Joyce, *Finnegans Wake*, pg. 628). All of the A. L. initials suggest the return of Anna Livia Plurabella (Tindall, pg. 140). One can see *Finnegans Wake* as having a great cycle and a lesser cycle.[3] The large cycle consists of the rain falling from clouds in the mountains, flowing downstream in the river Liffey, "from swerve of shore to bend of bay" (Joyce, *Finnegans Wake*, pg. 3), eventually reaching Dublin Bay and the Irish Sea, only to evaporate into clouds, which float back over the mountains to begin the cycle again and again. One can see the book cycling this way, with the connections between the final "the" and the initial "riverrun" in that opening sentence.

~•~

3) This discussion of the cycles in *Finnegans Wake* owes a great deal to a conversation I had with Robert Anton Wilson in 1988.

~•~

The lesser cycle of *Finnegans Wake* consists of an interlude where the Guinness brewery uses water from the Liffey to make the beverage beloved by Tim Finnegan. Various Dubliners have a pint of the usual (or two or three). They eventually urinate this out, and it eventually gets evaporated up again into clouds which drift back towards the mountains, world without end.

The first sentence of the book also introduces the reversal of patriarchy explored by the novel. Note the capital letters which occur at the end of the first sentence of *Finnegans Wake*, H. C. E. This stands for Humphrey Chimpden Earwicker, perhaps the dreamer of the book and husband to A. L. P., father to Shem and Shaun and Isabelle. Also, the River Liffey passes the Church of Adam and Eve. In the *Wake* this becomes "Eve and Adam's." Following Freud, Joyce suggests that whatever dominates during the day becomes dominated during the night,

Adam and Eve's becomes Eve and Adam's and the goddess Anna Livia Plurabella rules the night. This expands Freud's concept of the return of the repressed.

In a similar vein chapter five of *Finnegans Wake* begins with the prayer to HCE's wife Anna who has become the river goddess Anna Livia Plurabella:

> In the name of Annah the Allmaziful, the Everliving, the Bringer of Plurabilities, haloed be her eve, her singtime sung, her rill be run, unhemmed as it is uneven!
>
> (Joyce, *Finnegans Wake*, pg. 104)

I find it interesting that so many writers of the modernist period wrote about the return of goddess worship, from *Finnegans Wake*'s Anna Livia Plurabella, to Kupris Aphrodite in Ezra Pound's *Cantos* whom critic Hugh Kenner sees as the most important figure in the poem,[4] to nearly all of Robert Graves' work,[5] and such oddities as the writings of Aleister Crowley.[6] Even Jung wrote about the return of the goddess.

~•~

4) Aphrodite permeates *The Cantos*, from her appearance in Canto I to Pound's vision of her eyes in *The Pisan Cantos* and throughout the poem.
5) Graves built his whole concept of poetry around historical notions of the Muse. He wrote at length about this, especially in *The White Goddess*.
6) Crowley wrote poems to a variety of female deities, especially the Egyptian Nuit. He saw prehistory dominated by female deities, the Age of the Mother Isis, and the last four thousand years dominated by male deities, the Age of the Father Osiris. He thought the future would see a union of these forces, the Age of the Child Horus.

~•~

In this prayer Joyce combines the Muslim prayer "To Allah the All-Merciful" with the "Our Father," "Hallowed be Thy Name, Thy Kingdom come, Thy will be done, on Earth as it is in heaven." Joyce even included a reference to the Native American maize goddess in "maziful." The "unhemmed" reference fits in with the tailor theme elsewhere in the novel.[7] Joyce wanted to show that the unconscious processes revealed through dreams relate to all human belief systems.

~•~

7) In the eleventh chapter of *Finnegans Wake* a sailor becomes a tailor. This s-t transformation corresponds with the space-time transformations in Einstein (Tindall, pg. 189).

~•~

One can see Joyce's particular interest in the goddess theme in the Anna Livia chapter. Joyce devoted the whole eighth chapter to Anna Livia, the final chapter of the first book of the *Wake*. This chapter begins with the shape of the Greek letter delta, which also suggests the delta of a river and Goethe's Eternal Feminine.[8] "The flowing of the river is to carry us forward to a new book and a new age" (Campbell and Robinson, pg. 133). The river provides a model of the dream process as well as the twists, turns and flow of the novel itself.

~•~

8) In *Faust* Goethe personifies the Eternal Feminine as the Queen of Heaven.

~•~

O
tell me all about
Anna Livia! I want to hear all
about Anna Livia. Well, you all know Anna Livia?
Yes, of course, we all know Anna Livia. Tell me all. Tell me now.
(Joyce, *Finnegans Wake*, pg. 196)

Joseph Campbell and Henry Morton Robinson call this chapter "The Washers at the Ford" (Campbell and Robinson, pg. 10), picturing women washing laundry in the River Liffey, gossiping about Anna Livia, essentially washing dirty linen in public in two ways. They physically clean the dirty linen, and, in their gossip, they figuratively wash their dirty laundry in public (McHugh, pg. 196). Note that Joyce does not give the chapters actual titles in the book itself.

    Joyce plays a bit with the poetry of numbers here. The first line has one word, "O." This 1 (the one word) and 0 make up the binary number system, as well as suggesting the male and the female. I don't think Joyce believed in the numerological systems favored by some of his contemporaries like Yeats, but he knew about them and played with them. The Golden Dawn, an occult organization which included William Butler Yeats, Arthur Machen and Aleister Crowley as members, associated the twenty-two trumps of the Tarot deck with the twenty-two letters of the Hebrew alphabet. They associated the first trump "The Fool" with the Hebrew letter aleph, which has the value of 1, although if you add up the Hebrew letters which spell aleph, you get 111. The Hebrew letters which spell aleph have the following values: Aleph (1) + Lamed (30) + Peh (80) = 111. Of course this also gives another A. L. P. Joyce weaves the number 111 throughout *Finnegans Wake*. (Recall that even T. S. Eliot included tarot images in *The Waste Land*.) Joyce uses numbers kabbalistically to emphasize the difference between waking logic and dream logic (Wilson, *Coincidance*, pg. 159).

    As seen above, the second line of this chapter "tell me all about" contains four words, suggesting the four old men, the gospels, the four seasons, the four bedposts, etc. The third line contains seven words, suggesting the seven colors of the rainbow, the seven dancing girls who appear throughout the novel, the seven days of the week, the seven planets of medieval astrology, etc. The delta which begins the chapter thereby contains within it some of the other systems of *Finnegans Wake*: the zero, unity, the four function and the seven function. These different functions reappear over and over again in Joyce's dream novel, functioning in a way analogous to characters in an ordinary waking world novel.

One plus four plus seven yields twelve, another system of *Finnegans Wake*, associating the member of a jury, a dozen eggs (remember Humpy Dumpty), the months of the year, the twelve signs of the zodiac, the twelve customers in H. C. E.'s pub, etc.

One times four times seven yields 28, the number of classmates of A. L. P. and H. C. E.'s daughter Isabelle. It all seems "as semper as oxhousehumper" as Joyce puts it elsewhere in the *Wake*. The first three letters of the Hebrew alphabet, aleph, beth and gimel, mean "ox," "house" and "camel." "Semper as oxhousehumper" becomes "simple as A, B, G." Of course, *semper* means "always" in Latin, suggesting "always as A, B, G," suggesting the Golden Dawn's insistence on associating everything with their own Christianized kabbalah, in the tradition of Raymond Lull and Giordano Bruno (Bishop, *Joyce's Book of the Dark*, pg. 269).

This chapter contains hundreds of river names. John Bishop suggests that Joyce intended this chapter to suggest the sounds perceived by the ear in what might seem total silence. Composer John Cage, a *Finnegans Wake* enthusiast, once visited a soundproof room at Harvard. When he came out he commented that he had heard a low thumping sound and a high whining sound inside the supposedly soundproof room. His scientist friend told him he had heard the thumping of the blood in the circulatory system in his ear and the whine of his nerves firing. Bishop suggests that Joyce conceived of the sound of the sleeping body, particularly the pumping blood, as similar to the sound of waves, and that Joyce tried to capture that sound in the watery language of this chapter (*Joyce's Book of the Dark*, pg. 279). Bishop writes:

> "[L]yne" after "lyne" in the washerwomen's dialogue simply means what the sound of human bloodstream also "meyne[s]," both as it streams through "the presence (of a curpse)" and as it moves right now, "in the present, of course" beneath

consciousness and the visible surface of the world in the mind of the sympathetic reader.
(Joyce's Book of the Dark, pg. 346)

Elsewhere in the dream H. C. E. hears ten thunderclaps, yielding the ten thunder words, each of which has 100 letters, except for the last one which has 101 letters. This adds up to 1001, suggesting another book of the night, *The Arabian Nights*. Joyce weaves this number into his tapestry as well, because he wanted to include *The Arabian Nights* as another book of the night. His play with the number 1001 complements his kabbalistic play with 111 and other numbers.

Interestingly, Sir Richard Burton translated *The Arabian Nights* in the nineteenth century. He married a woman named Isabelle and had a near obsession with a river, the Nile, whose headwaters he sought. References to him and his work crop up from time to time in the *Wake*. From Burton Joyce gained many uncommon terms as well as some linguistic strategies (Yared, pg. 166).

The thunder words also relate back to Giambattista Vico, who suggested that human religion began with a fear of thunder, noting the role of thunder gods in many cultures, from Yahweh to Zeus and Jupiter. The novel as a whole has four books which correspond with the four cycles in Vico's philosophy (Tindall, pg. 8). In the dream H. C. E. also hears the sound of a branch tapping against his window at various points in the book, especially in the first chapter when he has not yet entered deeply into sleep, and so pays more attention to external sounds than he will later in the night. Joyce indicates this by the word "tip" which frequently interrupts the text. (Joyce, *Finnegans Wake* 9, etc.) (Note that some Joyce scholars completely disagree with this interpretation of the word "tip" in the novel.)

Reading an extraordinary book such as *Finnegans Wake* calls for extraordinary reading strategies. In discussing the

Anna Livia chapter, John Bishop relates it to a later passage in the book.

> -When your contraman from Tuwarcathay is looking for righting that
> is not a good sign? Not?
> -I speak truly, it's a shower sign that it's not.
> -What though it be for the sow of his heart?
> (Joyce, *Finnegans Wake*, pg. 490)

Bishop comments of this passage:

> These lines finally suggest that not simply "looking for writing," but falling into language generally is a "sure sign" that one is badly misreading the wet and "showery" "sanscreed" (215.26)[9] of which "Anna Livia" is composed (it's like "looking," rather than listening, for "the sound of your hear"). Where the effect of "writing" is to "right" things, by defining and limiting them according to known and "creeds" (hence "writing"), "Anna Livia's" "sanscreed" is "without creed" altogether (hence the Fr. *sans*, "without") and does exactly the opposite.
> (Joyce's Book of the Dark, pg. 346)

~•~

9) Page 215, line 26, of *Finnegans Wake*.

~•~

This final "opposite" suggests the "coincidence of opposites" which Giordano Bruno thought made up our world, as the "contra" at the beginning of the passage from page 490 of *Finnegans Wake*. Bruno's philosophy also played a central role in Joyce's conception of *Finnegans Wake*. Samuel Beckett[10] wrote about the role of Vico, Bruno and Dante in the creation of *Finnegans Wake* (Beckett, pg. 1).

~•~

10) Beckett interacted with James Joyce for a few years during the 1920's in Paris while Joyce worked on the *Wake*.

~•~

This coincidence of opposites also corresponds with the "O" which begins the Anna Livia chapter suggesting both 0 and 1, both female and male. Elsewhere in the novel Joyce suggests this by writing "O!," combining O with the phallic exclamation point. This also suggests zero factorial, 0!, which mathematicians define as having the value of 1.[11] This provides Joyce another opportunity for relating one and zero, the male and the female, day and night, presence and absence, etc. He uses this to illustrate Bruno's dicta of the coincidence of opposites.

~•~

11) A factorial gives the multiple of all the integers up to and including the indicated number, so $1! = 1$, $2! = 1 \times 2 = 2$, $3! = 1 \times 2 \times 3 = 6$, $4! = 1 \times 2 \times 3 \times 4 = 24$, etc. By convention, mathematicians have set $0! = 1$.

~•~

Joyce's use of "sanscreed" also echoes T. S. Eliot's use of Sanskrit in *The Waste Land*. John Bishop emphasizes the importance of the absent sense of sight and the dampened sense of hearing in decoding Joyce's text. Like Eliot and Pound, Joyce uses radical juxtapostions of a wide variety of materials from dozens of languages, using myriad viewpoints. One can see all of the concerns of modernism manifesting in the *Wake*, in its own mutated way. The horrors of war appear over and over again, such as in the "cashels aired and ventilated" (Joyce, *Finnegans Wake*, pg. 4), which suggests a castle with walls "ventilated" by cannonballs, as well as the old Irish capital of Cashel. Again like Pound and Eliot, Joyce shores up the ruins of the past in this novel. He does this through the dream of a publican in the Dublin suburb of Chapalizod. Joyce shows how the past and present flow into each other in our dreams, like Bruno's coincidence of opposites, which Joyce turns into a "coincidance."

Finnegans Wake abounds with "coincidances" of opposites, of female and male, irrational and rational, night and day. Joyce does this to illustrate his conception of the logic of dreams. The reader of the *Wake* will also encounter varying extremes, the delight of discovery and a sense of becoming totally lost; a feeling of uncanny familiarity might collapse into a sense of the utterly unknown and perhaps unknowable. Joyce spent seventeen years shaping this peculiar novel, which continues to find new readers despite its formidable difficulties. The book unwinds like the River Liffey, and repeated reading allows greater familiarity, but the willful obscurity of much of the text remains. Hopefully this section of my book has illuminated some of the devices Joyce used to craft his book of the night, as well suggested some avenues for reaching at least a tentative understanding of the shape of the novel and some of its minute particulars. Joyce scholarship has uncovered various layers of meaning in the text of *Finnegans Wake*, but they have only just begun their task. Each new generation of readers will cycle through the *Wake*'s many cycles and uncover new ways of reading and understanding this formidable text.

In the following two chapters I will describe how Robert Anton Wilson makes use of various techniques developed by Joyce in *Finnegans Wake* in his novel *Masks of the Illuminati*.

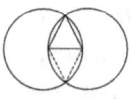

3) The Influence of *Finnegans Wake* on the First Four Sections of *Masks of the Illuminati*.

James Joyce has exerted considerable influence over novelist Robert Anton Wilson. Wilson writes, "My style derives directly from Ezra Pound, James Joyce, Raymond Chandler, H. L. Mencken, William S. Burroughs, Benjamin Tucker, and *Elephant Doody Comix,* in approximately that order of importance" (*Illuminati Papers*, pg. 66). Wilson frequently mentions Joyce in his nonfiction as well as in his fiction. He even made Joyce a major character in his novel *Masks of the Illuminati,* and Joyce shows up in various guises in other of Wilson's novels. Wilson has used stylistic devices from *Finnegans Wake* and elsewhere in the Joyce corpus, as well as structural devices from *Ulysses* and the *Wake*.

I first read Wilson's *Masks of the Illuminati* in 1982. At the time I knew next to nothing about James Joyce. Wilson's books introduced me to Joyce's personality, his techniques, and his work, all at the same time. Over the last 42 years I have continued to read Wilson's work with a great deal of pleasure. In addition, I have delved deeper and deeper into the worlds of James Joyce, Ezra Pound and others whose work has influenced Dr. Wilson. Wilson has served as a constant mentor. As Hugh Kenner said about *Ulysses*, "A mentor is advisable: not an unreasonable prerequisite for one of the key books of the space-time age" (Kenner, Intro to Budgen, pg. ix). Robert Anton Wilson has mentored me and many others through the worlds of *Finnegans Wake*, *Ulysses*, Ezra Pound's *Cantos* and beyond.

Wilson's non-fiction over the last forty years has frequently focused on Joyce. These interests carry over into his fiction. Wilson has looked at Joyce's work through the lenses of various psychological theories, from those of Freud and Jung to those of Wilhelm Reich and Timothy Leary.[12] For Wilson, Joyce brings Einstein's relativity to literature. Joyce provides a kaleidoscope of viewpoints and uses a variety of techniques in his novels, eliminating the single viewpoint narrator of nineteenth century realistic fiction. Joyce moves from the Newtonian paradigm to one more in tune with the umwelt of Einstein and quantum mechanics. Like the multiple viewpoints of the cubists, Joyce presents incidents and characters from multiple viewpoints, revealing them in a dynamic ever-changing universe through literary parallax. Wilson uses these techniques in *Masks of the Illuminati* to reflect on the characters of both Einstein and Joyce, as well as to present multiple views of all of the novel's characters.

~•~

12) Wilson has also mentioned a variety of writers on Joyce, from Samuel Beckett to Hugh Kenner and Richard Ellmann.

~•~

Hugh Kenner, discussing *Ulysses*, commented:

> But toward the end, working on 'Penelope' and 'Ithaca' together, James Joyce seems to have gone farther, divining – no, not the cosmos of Picasso, Einstein, Heisenberg and Gödel, his visual taste being banal, his science but a smattering of terms, his very arithmetic deplorable – divining rather something of what they intuited and modeled in their own idiom, their own arts; for that the human experience is homogenous, that innovators in diverse

fields are assuredly one another's contemporaries without necessity of interaction, is one of the exhilarating truths of history.
(Kenner, *Ulysses*, pg. 153)

Wilson illuminates this in his novel *Masks of the Illuminati*. He makes Einstein, Joyce, Aleister Crowley, Carl Jung, Ezra Pound, William Butler Yeats, and Lenin, et al., characters whose fictitious and actual interactions reflect the parallels between their innovations. Wilson describes his "major theme . . . Relativity as illustrated by Einstein's physics, Joyce's art and Crowley's 'magic'" (Wilson, 10/20/2001 email). The title itself links the book with Wilson's vision of Joyce's Irish tradition. Wilson has frequently discussed Oscar Wilde's essay "The Truth of Masks," which he links with the notion of Mask and Counter-Mask in Yeats' *A Vision*, which Yeats saw as components of the self. Wilson even called the two parts of his *Cosmic Trigger Volume III* "The Masks of Reality" and "The Reality of Masks." Wilson links Wilde's concept of mask with Stephen Dedalus' "silence, exile and cunning." Silence seems a powerful Joycean mask, the "presence of the absent" (Wilson, *Coincidance*, pg. 87).

In his 1986 Introduction to a new edition of *Cosmic Trigger*, Wilson says:

> "Reality" is a word in the English language which happens to be (a) a noun and (b) singular. Thinking in the English language (and in cognate Indo-European languages) therefore subliminally programs us to conceptualize "reality" as one block-like entity, sort of like a huge New York skyscraper, in which every part is just another "room" within the same building. This linguistic program is so pervasive that most people cannot "think" outside it at all, and when one tries to offer

a different perspective they imagine one is talking gibberish.

(Wilson, *Cosmic Trigger*, pg. iii)

Wilson presents myriad relative realities in *Masks of the Illuminati*, using methods derived from the relativities of Einstein, Joyce, Crowley and Pound while incorporating Einstein, Joyce, Crowley and Pound as characters. In addition, Wilson makes Einstein and Joyce into amateur detectives. Wilson had commented on the similarities between Joyce's method of almost obsessive observation with that of Sherlock Holmes in his *Schrödinger's Cat* trilogy, a work of fiction that deals with parallel worlds and includes Wilson's usual fascination with Joyce. Hugh Kenner refers to Sherlock Holmes as "our mentor" in his book on *Ulysses*, since Holmes also serves as a model for the observer looking at Joyce's fictional worlds (Kenner, *Ulysses*, pg. 143). Leopold Bloom had an overdue library book by Conan Doyle, which the "real" Dublin library declared "missing" in 1906 (ibid.).

Masks of the Illuminati tells of a young man, Sir John Babcock, who becomes interested in the Kabbalah. He eventually joins a secret society interested in Kabbalistic matters and undergoes initiations into their mysteries. He becomes convinced he has become the center of a murderous conspiracy and flees from London to Zürich, where he meets Einstein and Joyce. He tells Einstein and Joyce about the supposed conspiracy, and they attempt to understand what has happened to him.

Masks of the Illuminati begins with a newspaper article dated April 23 (perhaps Shakespeare's birthday), 1914. Numbers play a poetic role in Wilson's work, especially the number 23 which haunts this and all of his novels. Using methods learned from Aleister Crowley, William S. Burroughs and Joyce (*Finnegans Wake*'s 1132, 111, 1001, etc.), etc., Wilson almost makes the numbers characters in the book. Emerson once said every word contains a fossil poem, and

Joyce allowed the poems in certain numbers to blossom in the *Wake*. Similarly, Wilson uses 23 as a leitmotif in *Masks*. The news article that launches *Masks of the Illuminati* also mentions Conan Doyle, anticipating Joyce's role as a detective in the novel and evoking Wilson's comparison of Joyce and Sherlock Holmes in *Schrödinger's Cat*, wherein Joyce in a parallel universe becomes Pope Stephen and an obituary compares him with Holmes. Of course, Joyce made use of a journalistic style in one section of *Ulysses*, the first of many parallels between *Ulysses* and *Masks*. The opening section of *Masks* concludes with a fragment of a film script, a style of writing or genre Joyce didn't include in *Ulysses*, although he did write the Nighttown chapter in the form of a play. This film script fragment includes the acrostic "I nearly reached India" (Wilson, *Masks*, pg 6), a play on the Christian I.N.R.I. Acrostics figure largely in *Finnegans Wake*, especially the interplay of the initials H.C.E. and A.L.P.

One could see *Masks* as the portrait of a magician as a young man. Sir John Babcock, the main character of the novel, becomes fascinated with the occult and eventually ends up interacting with members of the Golden Dawn such as Yeats and Crowley. Wilson uses devices from *Ulysses* and *Finnegans Wake* to bring to life various altered states of consciousness Babcock encounters and endures during his occult adventures.

In the novel, Babcock arrives in Zurich, pursued, he thinks, by Satanists. He bursts into a bar where he coincidentally runs into Joyce and Einstein. They play the role of Good Samaritans and Babcock tells them about his initiation into a secret society and how his life has turned into chaos. (Incidentally, Wilson sees the parable of the Good Samaritan underlying *Ulysses*, with Samaritan Leopold Bloom rescuing Stephen Dedalus in the Nighttown episode.) Joyce and Einstein bring their considerable observational and reasoning powers to bear on Babcock's conundrum that night and over the next two days. When they finally reach the conclusion that his nemesis Aleister Crowley has manipulated all the events which have terrified Sir John, supposedly for Sir John's own benefit, Aleister himself shows up at the door. He congratulates the scientific detectives with champagne. Then Einstein comments:

> I imagine, Einstein said staring fixedly at his pipe ash glittering, that your original plan for Sir John's rite of passage had some dramatic climax. I hope we haven't ruined it by explaining the tricks to him prematurely. Have some more wine, Babcock, Crowley said pouring. As a matter of fact, the climax of the drama will be much as I planned except of course that there will be three candidates instead of one.
>
> (Wilson, Masks, pg. 320)

Of course, Aleister has spiked the champagne with a psychedelic drug.

Wilson patterned the scene in the Zurich pub in which the reader first encounters Einstein and Joyce after the opening of the first chapter of *Ulysses*. "Stately, plump Albert Einstein" plays the role of Buck Mulligan while Joyce once again plays Stephen Dedalus. While the first sentence in Ulysses begins with "Stately" and ends with "crossed," indicating the two tyrants Dedalus must escape (the state of England and the Catholic Church), *Masks* gives us Einstein who "came from the gloom-domed Lorelei barroom bearing a paleyellow tray on which two mugs of beer stood carefully balanced, erect" (Wilson, *Masks*, pg. 12). This suggests the more frankly sexual nature of this book, as well as the particular concerns of both the characters Joyce and Sir John. The first sentence of *Ulysses* has 22 words, suggesting the number of letters in the Hebrew alphabet and the number of trumps in the tarot deck. Wilson's parallel sentence has 24 words.[13] The word "paleyellow" in the Wilson sentence suggests the style of the first chapter of *Ulysses*. Wilson has Joyce use "yellowbrown" a few pages later. (Wilson, *Masks*, pg. 15)

13) In *The Game of Life* Wilson and Timothy Leary add two new trumps to their post-modern tarot deck.

In the next section Wilson provides a series of questions and answers about Joyce and Einstein's conversation in the style of the Ithaca chapter of *Ulysses*. Wilson suggests that

> Joyce had escaped from the normal constrictions of ego by pondering deeply what it feels like to be a woman. Einstein had escaped from the normal constrictions of ego by pondering deeply what it feels like to be a photon. Joyce approached art with the methodology of a scientist; Einstein practiced science with the intuition of an artist.
> (Wilson, *Masks*, pg. 14)

Wilson draws a similar parallel between Beethoven and Einstein in his *Illuminati Papers*, calling Beethoven the "World's Greatest Sound Engineer" and Einstein the "World's Greatest Intuitive Artist" (Wilson, *Illuminati Papers*, pg. 143). Joyce achieved a deeper understanding of human nature through his contemplation of life as a woman, enabling him to write Molly Bloom's section of *Ulysses*. Einstein reached a deeper understanding of the nature of physics through his contemplation of life as a photon, enabling him to develop his revolutionary theories.

Throughout the novel Wilson has Joyce think about the possibility that his mistress Nora Barnacle had had an affair with his brother Stanislaus. In the Scylla and Charybdis chapter of *Ulysses* Joyce has Stephen Dedalus present the case that Shakespeare thought his wife had cuckolded him with his brother. Wilson presents an obsessed Joyce similar to the obsessed Shakespeare Joyce himself has Stephen Dedalus present. This theme occurs in the internal monologue of the character Joyce throughout *Masks of the Illuminati*, just as Leopold Bloom's thoughts return again and again to Blazes

Boylan and Molly Bloom in the Leopold Bloom chapters of *Ulysses*. However, where Leopold avoids the thoughts of the (probably actual) infidelity of Molly and Blazes, the character Joyce dwells on the (probably false) infidelity of Nora and Stanislaus. This theme of Joyce's fear of Nora's infidelity first appears in the mock-Ithaca section of *Masks of the Illuminati* and continues to reappear throughout the book. Wilson models his presentation of Joyce and his jealousy on Joyce's own presentation of Bloom and his jealousy.

Also in the mock-Ithaca section of *Masks* Wilson writes a passage locating Bahnhofstrasse in space-time, similar to a passage locating Stephen Dedalus in space-time in *Portrait of the Artist as a Young Man*. Wilson provides a few more scientific details in his version of this locating motif, fitting with the plethora of scientific details in the novel. The mock-Ithaca pattern of questions and answers in the text of *Masks* recurs several times in the novel. Following the Ithaca-like passage, Wilson has Joyce suggest that "all work in progress was always followed by work in regress" (19), suggesting *Work in Progress*, Joyce's working title for *Finnegans Wake*. Wilson uses these Joycean techniques to illuminate Joyce himself developing those very techniques.

Many details of the novel illuminate coincidences. Samuel Beckett saw coincidence as the main theme in *Finnegans Wake*. Wilson even brings Carl Jung as a minor character to the novel. Jung writing with physicist Wolfgang Pauli called some coincidences "synchronicities," and Wilson combines the notion of synchronicity with Joyce's ideas of coincidence in *Masks*. Jung thought patients going through periods of radical change tended to experience more coincidences than average. Wilson uses Jung's notions of synchronicity to complement his use of Joyce's techniques. Joyce came to coincidence from an angle suggested by Giordano Bruno. Bruno saw reality as a coincidence of opposites. Joyce constructed the world of *Finnegans Wake* (and to a lesser extent *Ulysses*) from these coinciding opposites. Wilson combines the Jungian and the Joycean views of coincidence. As the character Sir John Babcock in *Masks* gets deeper into his personal transformation, he encounters more and more coincidences. Babcock has become involved in a secret society similar to the Golden Dawn, which included William Butler Yeats and Aleister Crowley as members. This society aims to help him come into contact with his higher self, to awaken his inner potentials. He also comes to see the world more and more in a Brunoesque fashion, as a deeply interrelated web of coinciding opposites. However, the character Einstein discovers at the end of the novel that Babcock's initiators (those above him in the hierarchy of the secret society) have manufactured many of these coincidences. This undercutting of the proliferation of coincidences by human agency suggests the central role of human intelligence in the process of perception, one of Wilson's central themes. Wilson uses Joyce's techniques to attempt to explicitly demonstrate the processes of perception. Of course, this also demonstrates Bruno's ideas. A web of spontaneously occurring, interrelating synchronicities coincides with a net of manufactured coincidences.

Following Joyce's example of playing with form in *Ulysses*, Wilson includes the forms of radio broadcasts, game shows and film scripts at various times in the novel. Like Joyce, Wilson brings together the ridiculous and the sublime in his novel. This use of fragments of various genres follows and expands Joyce's example. Wilson even includes four pictures of tarot cards on pages 72 and 73, and a drawing of an alien (or perhaps a time-traveler) on page 165. This use of graphic images in the novel breaks the linearity of conventional narrative, as well as introducing the reader to visual representations of images described in the text of the novel.

All of the forms Wilson uses help to reveal the different perceptions his characters have from their own perspectives. When Joyce hears Sir John Babcock's narrative about his adventures with the occult, Joyce contemplates "the historical and temperamental abyss between the Anglo-Saxon and Hibernian mentalities" (45). Sir John, "a member of the conquering and therefore probably loathed English race" (49), represents the English colonial reality while Joyce represents the Irish/Hibernian.

Among the many types of writing included in his novels, Joyce liked to make use of lists in his novels, transforming them with ludic wordplay. Similarly, when describing the contents of Sir John's library, Wilson refers to "an ova of Bacons" (54), meaning the works of Francis Bacon. The "ova," an egg, makes a bacon and eggs joke. *Finnegans Wake* contains many jokes about ham, eggs, Shakespeare's HAM-let, the theory Bacon wrote Shakespeare's plays, Shakespeare's son HAM-net and the presence of a boar on Shakespeare's coat of arms, etc.

At various points in *Masks* Wilson includes Sir John's dreams, always written in a style reminiscent of *Finnegans Wake*. This blossoms into the full blown Wakean-style prose which represents altered states of consciousness in the drug scene at the end of Wilson's novel. Of course, Wilson does not limit himself to a Joyce pastiche. He combines Joyce's use of portmanteau words, lists, puns, jokes and acronyms with Crowleyean Golden Dawn kabbalah, Burroughs' cut-up technique and Wilson's unique sense of humor.[14]

~•~

14) The cut-up technique involves taking pages of text, cutting them up and rearranging the pieces. Then the writer can take passages from the cut up text and use them as they see fit. Artist Brion Gysin invented this technique, and Williams S. Burroughs developed it over several decades.

~•~

In this chapter I have demonstrated Wilson's extensive use of Joycean techniques in the first four sections of *Masks of the*

Illuminati. In the next chapter I will focus on Wilson's use of techniques from *Finnegans Wake* in *Masks of the Illuminati*'s final section.

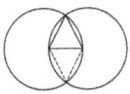

4) The Final Section of *Masks of the Illuminati*

Using a variety of Joycean techniques, Wilson presents the climactic drug scene of *Masks of the Illuminati* in language reminiscent of *Finnegans Wake*, although Wilson does not limit himself to Joycean techniques. As the next step in Sir John Babcock's initiation, Aleister Crowley (now revealed as a high ranking member of the same secret society as Sir John) had intended to surreptitiously give Sir John a hallucinogenic drug. When Crowley discovered Sir John in the company of such remarkable minds as Einstein and Joyce, Crowley decided to drug all three of them.

In writing about a psychedelic drug experience, Wilson has the opportunity to bring all of his tools to bear, especially those derived from the techniques of *Finnegans Wake*. Joyce developed these techniques to present the shimmering and ever changing details of the unconscious processes of the sleeping mind. Wilson now brings these techniques into play to present the altered states of mind encountered and endured by his characters under the effect of the drug. This scene in the novel provides a climax to the ordeal and initiation of Sir John Babcock. Wilson uses the opportunity of the drug session to examine the character, not only of Babcock, but of Einstein, Joyce and Crowley as well.

Wilson uses the drug scene to explore Joyce's jealousy and other emotions, as well as to reveal the kaleidoscopic nature of his consciousness. Wilson shows Joyce coming to understand the shifting nature of his perceptions, and Wilson then shows Joyce integrating these perceptions with his still unformed ideas about how to write *Ulysses*. Wilson uses the drug scene to present a fictional picture of the genesis of Joyce's massive, rule-breaking novel.

> Hawk-like man, Joyce reflects. Ascending from the labyrinth old father old artificer the moocow in the beginning the Goat.
> Come back to Erin, mavourneen.
> *Merde*, said General Cambronne. A toll telled of shame and scorn.
> (Wilson, *Masks*, pg. 325-6)

The "labyrinth" points to its builder Daedelus, who of course links with Stephen Dedalus. The "old father" suggests the Christian God as well as Daedalus' relationship with Icarus. It seems to me the "moocow" points to the first line of Joyce's *Portrait of the Artist as a Young Man*: "Once upon a time and a very good time it was there was a moocow coming down along the road and this moocow that was coming down along the road met a nicens little boy named baby tuckoo . . ." (*Portable Joyce*, pg. 245) Of course, the character Stephen Dedalus hallucinates the beginning of *Portrait* while sick in the hospital, whereas the character James Joyce hallucinates this allusion to the *Portrait* while intoxicated at the end of *Masks of the Illuminati*.

General Cambronne replied *"merde"* when asked to surrender at Waterloo. This anecdote recurs many times in *Finnegans Wake*, illustrating the link between Freud's anal stage and fights over territory. "A toll telled of shame and scorn" echoes the *Wake*'s refrain "a tale told of Shaun and Shem." This climatic drug scene lasts thirty pages, filled with this sort of Joycean wordplay.

Part five of *Masks of the Illuminati* begins with the quote "All material things are but masks" (317) from *Moby Dick*. Wilson has a fascination with the ideas associated with masks.

In *TSOG: The Thing That Ate the Constitution* he writes,

> After all, modernism really dawned with Wilde's "The Reality of Masks"[15] and Yeats's hermetic mystique that the world we know emerges from interactions of Mask, Anti-Mask, Self, and Anti-Self: which may or may not fit all of us or all the world but certainly fits the world of spooks and snoops that Angleton[16] created.
>
> (pg. 35-36)

~•~

15) Wilde actually called the essay "The Truth of Masks."
16) James Jesus Angleton, director of counterintelligence for the CIA from 1954 to 1974, who appears in many contemporary conspiracy theories (Wilson *Everything Is Under Control,* pg 42).

~•~

Wilde's essay "The Truth of Masks" dealt with costuming in Shakespeare, but Wilson also reads it as a commentary of the double life Wilde led as a homosexual in Victorian London. On another level Wilson reads Wilde's essay as a commentary on the masks worn by colonial people to hide their reality from the colonizers. In the final section of *Masks of the Illuminati* he peels away the masks of day to day existence. He peels away the masks of Irishman, Englishman and German, poor novelist, nobleman, and physicist to reveal the human beings underneath. Wilson demonstrates the dynamics involved in the interactions of all the different masks maintained by the characters and the difficulty of maintaining them. The above quote refers to James Jesus Angleton, head of counter-intelligence for the C.I.A. for many years. In *TSOG* Wilson wrote, "modernist tendencies, which also appeared in science and philosophy at the same time, blossomed into obsessions and, perhaps, raging madness when Angleton systematically applied them to the spy-game" (Wilson, *TSOG,* pg. 35). Spying, which attempts to penetrate the masks put forward by foreign governments, seems one model for the behaviors provoked by the post-colonial realities of oppression and intrigue, or as Stephen Dedalus observed in *A Portrait of the Artist as a Young Man*, "silence, exile and cunning" (Joyce, *Portrait* 247).

In hierarchical structures, people at the bottom sometimes withhold information from those above them. Wilson sees this communication jam as typical of colonial situations, where the colonized individuals do not communicate in total honesty with the colonizers. The colonized individuals develop masks to facilitate their existence under the oppression of the colonial rule. Wilson traces the idea of mask from Wilde to Yeats and to Joyce as a description of the sorts of false identities Irish people have had to develop over the centuries of English oppression. In their work on *Finnegans Wake* Derek Attridge and Marjorie Howes refer to "the variety of binary oppositions that divide human communities" (pg. 1). Joyce developed the language of *Finnegans Wake* to demonstrate these oppositions and, following Giordano Bruno, attempt to unify them. Vincent Cheng calls late-colonial Ireland "a culture of imposture, adulteration, and inauthenticity" (pg. 258), or what Wilson might call a culture of masks.

As a grand finale, the novel ends with Einstein looking at his watch when asked the time, replying, "Exactly thirty-two minutes after eleven" (Wilson, *Masks*, pg. 355). Of course, the number 1132 will show up over and over again in *Finnegans Wake*, giving rise to dozens of theories over the decades. [17] Here Wilson gives a fictional origin to the mystery which also corresponds with all the discussion of time, clocks and relativity in his novel. The novel began with the date April 23, often regarded as Shakespeare's birthday and the day on which Robert Anton Wilson and Robert Shea's novel *Illuminatus!* begins as well. (Wilson and Shea filled *Illuminatus!* with numerical play around the number 23, influenced in part by *Finnegans Wake*'s 1132s and 111s.) Wilson bounds *Masks of the Illuminati* with a date and a time, tying in the Einsteinian themes of the measurement of time and pointing hypertextually both to his own fiction with the 23 at the beginning and to *Finnegans Wake* with the 11:32 at the end. Of course, Wilson learned many techniques of using numbers poetically in the body of a text from *Finnegans Wake*.

~•~

17) One can find some theories about Joyce's use of 1132 in Tindall page 41, McHugh page 13, and Wilson's *Coincidance* page 10. Wilson hypothesizes the number refers to the time 11:32 A.M. when the dreamer retired to the bushes in Phoenix Park and two young girls accidentally saw him there.

~•~

Wilson uses this poetry of numbers to show how the human correlates things by methods other than the ordinary sense of rationality. The mind sometimes functions by irrationality like that of dreams, which Wilson sees as parallel to the odd processes of the mind undergoing hallucinogenic drugs or initiation by an occult society.

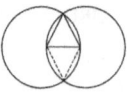

5) Conclusion of Section I

At the novel's end the character Joyce feels he has a better idea of the huge novel he wants to write, patterned on the *Odyssey* and *Hamlet* as well as the Bible story of the Good Samaritan (*Ulysses*). Wilson has employed Joyce's methods to help him shape his narrative, incorporating various Wakean devices into his own prose style. Wilson has also created the character Joyce in the novel to unravel those narrative strands of Sir John's initiation and the apparent conspiracy to kill Sir John, and to piece together the underlying patterns. Wilson has taken and expanded Joyce's methods to present the character Joyce, and he has presented the character Joyce to better understand the writer James Joyce, both as an artist and as a human being.

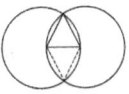

Antithesis

Everybody just relax, man; we have ya all night long.
> – Jerry Garcia, May 2, 1970 C.E.

Everything has an antithesis.
> – Yu Shu Lien

A carnival is feral; another carnival ship shows up and is pitted against the first one; and the antithetical interaction is preplanned in such a way that the first carnival wins. It's as if the two opposing forces that underlie all change in the universe are rigged; in favor of thanatos, the dark force, yin or strife, which is to say, the force of destruction.
> – Philip K. Dick, 1978 C.E.

Shakhisbeard, either prexactly unlike his polar andthisishis
> – *Finnegans Wake*, pg. 177

To arrive at a cultural turning point where you decide that all human conduct can be classified in one of two categories, good and evil, is what creates all sin – plus anxiety, hatred, guilt, depression, all the peculiarly human emotions. And, of course, such a classification is the very antithesis of creativity.
> – *Illuminatus!*, pg. 248

Wagner's loopy howls.

— ibid., pg. 292

Paris was Dublin's antithesis.

— Richard Ellmann,
James Joyce, pg. 111

Holy Out – or Joe Smith – told me he *enjoyed* working for a living. "It gives your days a pattern," he said, "and without pattern, life is a bore." I thought this was an interesting antithesis to the notion held by many acidheads that in the perfect society of the future, all work would be done by machines and people would be free to devote themselves to love, head games and art. Addicts, and even ex-addicts, tend to regard life as a problem either to be evaded (by down drugs) or solved by effort of will; but psychedelic people see it as a sport to be enhanced (by up drugs) or observed in meditative tranquility.

— Robert Anton Wilson,
Sex, Drugs & Magick, pg. 207

James Card, in his book *Penelope,* postulates that for Joyce Gibraltar represented the antithesis of Dublin and also the city guarding the Pillars of Hercules, the gateway separating Odysseus's known world, the Mediterranean, from the abyss beyond. Card also saw in Gibraltar the symbolic geography of female organs.

— Brenda Maddox,
Nora: A Biography of Nora Joyce, pg. 277

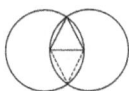

6) Springtime for Hitler

Many Joyce scholars refer to Leopold Bloom as Jewish, but Robert Anton Wilson more subtly outlines five different models of Jewish-ness, two of which fit Leopold, and three of which don't[18].

~•~

18) Leo Bloom appears as an accountant in Mel Brooks' *The Producers*. Note the two and three in the above discussion.

~•~

> Rabbinical law defines Jewish-ness as having a Jewish mother, which Bloom didn't have. The Nazi's defined Jewish-ness as having a Jewish ancestor, which he did have. Some would define Jewish-ness as practicing the Jewish religion, which Bloom doesn't do, and others would define Jewish-ness as perceiving oneself culturally as a Jew. Bloom only does this when confronted by the anti-Semitic Citizen, but generally he doesn't refer to himself as a Jew. Lastly, Jewish-ness can mean one lives in a society where, for any one of the above reasons, people regard him as a Jew, and he perforce has to recognize this "Jewishness" as something – even if only a spook – that people usually "see" when they think they see him.
>
>   (Wilson, *Quantum Psychology*, pg. 103)

In Bloom's words:

> He called me a jew, and in a heated fashion, offensively. So I, without deviating from plain facts in the least, told him his God, I mean Christ, was a jew too, and all his family, like me, though in reality I'm not.
>
> (Joyce, *Ulysses*, pg. 643)

Joyce created ambiguousness around Bloom's "Jewish-ness." Wilson suggests "Joyce gave Bloom a very tangled genetic/cultural background just to create this ambiguity and thereby satirize anti-semitism more sharply" (*Quantum Psychology*, pg. 103). In some ways *Ulysses*, first published February 2, 1922 C.E., years before the Holocaust, reads like a commentary on the Holocaust and the horror and absurdity of anti-Semitism, at least to some post-1945 C.E. readers. Joyce's rejection of anti-Semitism stands out in stark contrast to the anti-Semitism of his friends Ezra Pound and T. S. Eliot.

Wilson has commented on this eerie trans-time of Joyce's writing in *Coincidance*. He discusses *Finnegans Wake*'s references to television and the apparent pairing of Nagasaki and nuclear explosions. Philip K. Dick discussed the seeming prescience of the *Wake* in *The Divine Invasion*.

In *Email to the Universe*, Bob comments that his 1958 article "Joyce and Daoism" "sure sounds like an Acid Head wrote it" (pg. 87), even though he didn't try LSD until 1962. Timothy Leary said Joyce's prose prepared him for psychedelic space.

In the "Joyce and Daoism" article Wilson mentions how Shem the forger in *Finnegans Wake* wants "to utter an epochal forged check on the public" (pg. 91), while Stephen in *Portrait of the Artist as a Young Man* seeks to "forge in the smithy of my soul the uncreated conscience of my race" (ibid.). These quotes bring to mind one of Wilson's favorite films, Orson Welles' *F for Fake* about the fakers and/or forgers Elmyr and Clifford Irving (and Orson Welles). In *Prometheus Rising* Bob advises those trying to temporarily change their belief systems to, "as Jazz musicians say," 'Fake it until you make it'" (Wilson, *Prometheus Rising*, pg. 29). In the "Joyce and Daoism" article Bob emphasizes the fluid, watery values of Daoism and *Finnegans Wake*. "Forging" seems an opposite process, that of solidifying, similar to Leary's ideas of "imprinting" the nervous system. According to Wilson and Leary, the nervous system tends to impose its own imprinted structure on the world it perceives. Bob quotes Thomas Huxley on the method of science, to "follow humbly wherever and to whatever abysses Nature leads" (Wilson, *Email to the Universe*, pg. 89). If one could reimprint the nervous system with more fluid imprints along the lines suggested by Huxley, Joyce, Wilson and Leary, one might have a better opportunity to perceive the process world around one instead of believing dogmatically in the model of universe forged by the nervous system. Of course, William Blake writes about "Mind forg'd manacles." Bob calls Shem in *Finnegans Wake* a forger (ibid., pg. 91) which suggests *F for Fake*, a fake documentary about a fake biographer of a fake painter, the forger Elmyr. (All forgers in the *Wake* also suggest Pigott, who forged a letter implicating Parnell in the Invincibles murder.) Bob says, "Probably everyone who ever gains any experience of the Dao begins by faking a little" (ibid.).

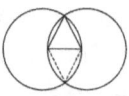

7) Joyce and The Wizard of Oz

On page 91 of *Email to the Universe* Bob mentions the hen Belinda in *Finnegans Wake*. Belinda refers, in part, to the Belinda in Pope's "The Rape of the Lock." Bob's wife Arlen thought this hen might also refer to the hen Billina in *Ozma of Oz*, the third of the Oz books by L. Frank Baum. For decades I have searched through books on Joyce and found no explicit reference to Oz or Baum, but I wonder. Bob said he didn't know. Joyce scholar Riverend Clarence Sterling used to think Joyce knew of Oz, but shortly before he died he told me he no longer thought so. (You can check out the Riverend's terrific writing on the *Wake* at http://rosenlake.net/fw/index.html.) The Riverend even discouraged me from exploring the Joyce/Baum connection, considering it a dead end, but the idea of the possible connection kept coming back to me in some vague Lovecraftian manner. When I got the chance to attend the International James Joyce Conference in Pasadena in 2011, I decided to give a talk on the possibility that Joyce put a bit of Oz into the *Wake*. I read *Finnegans Wake* a few more times seeking some definitive reference, but I remained and remain uncertain.

Various passages of the *Wake* make references to oil cans and tin men and cyclones and witches, but I've yet to find definite proof that Joyce knew of Oz. I've discussed this with Vincent Cheng, Margot Norris, and other Joyceans, and no one seems sure one way or another, which seems very Joycean, doesn't it?

The song "Woodman, Spare That Tree" shows up a bunch of times in *Finnegans Wake* (for example "Spare, woodman, spare!", pg. 42, "wouldmanspare," pg. 77, etc.). This could refer to the Tin Woodman, but I haven't seen this interpretation in any books on Joyce. It could also suggest the occultist Austin Osman Spare, a reference I found in a discussion of Oz and *Finnegans* Wake on an online Aleister Crowley forum (Zardoz). I find it interesting that I've encountered many interpretations of the *Wake* online that acknowledge the possibility of the influence of Baum on Joyce (or even insist upon it) but none on paper. Online Joyceans sometimes seem to think that Joyce read everything.

The passages of the *Wake* which most suggest an Oz influence occur in the footnote chapter. Footnote seven on page 290 includes "I'm blowed if I knowed who the slave is doing behind the curtain" which could suggest the Wizard behind the curtain. Three pages later (page 293) the expressions "Ante Ann," "aunty anna live," and "Antiann" which might combine Oz's Auntie Em with the *Wake*'s Anna Livia Plurabella. I think of Heisenberg's Uncertainty Principle here. For me the question of whether Joyce knew anything about Oz remains open. I bet he had heard of it, but I don't know if he intended to put it in *Finnegans Wake*.

The next page (page 294) has "cyclone" and "galehus". This could refer to Dorothy Gale and the twister that took her to Oz. *Alice's Adventures in Wonderland* influences every page of *Finnegans Wake*, and according to Wikipedia, the character of Alice influenced Baum's creation of Dorothy ("Dorothy"). The Alice books and the film *The Wizard of Oz* show up over and over again in the writings of Robert Anton Wilson.

A few other potentially Ozian references: "Tintin tintin," pg. 235; "scarecrown," pg. 237; "oelkenner," pg. 321, which could suggest "oil can" as well future Joyce scholar Hugh Kenner whom Joyce never met nor heard of (the Scarecrow has a Joycean response in the film, "Oil can what?"); "Kansas," pg.

509 (pretty weak, I'll admit, but Joyce may have had Dorothy's Kansas in mind); "hurrigan gales," pg. 589, etc.

This whole process reminds me of the Law of Fives in *Illuminatus!* The more one looks for Oz references in *Finnegans Wake*, the more one finds them; the more one looks for the number five, the more one finds it. The same seems true of bigfoot, President Obama's socialist tendencies, etc. I've often thought of *Finnegans Wake* as a giant Rorschach test. One can find a variety of processes there, including many that Joyce likely didn't intend. ("Lots of fun at Finnegan's Wake.") This also reminds me of Crowley and/or Nietzsche's concept(s) of the Abyss.

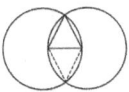

8) Page 109, Etc.

On page 90 of *Email to the Universe*, Bob notes that "riverrun," the first word in *Finnegans Wake* functions neither as a noun nor a verb but as both. I suspect Bob's fascination with Pound facilitated Wilson's understanding of this aspect of the *Wake*. Reading Pound encouraged Bob to learn about Chinese poetry, philosophy and religion, as well as the Chinese language, where the same character can represent different parts of speech. (Note that the first word of the *Wake* doesn't use a capital letter, just as the title to the first edition of Bob's last book has no capital letters.)

On page 91 Bob writes of the "superhuman effort required for an occidental" to transcend dualisms. A more Daoist response might suggest "effort" has little to do with it, superhuman or otherwise. A passage in *Schrödinger's Cat* suggests evolutionary agents like Beethoven, Joyce, Pound and Wilson often see human evolution as a Promethean struggle requiring hard work, whereas one only need to cooperate with the DNA code. In *Quantum Psychology* Bob suggests Rupert Sheldrake's model of morphogenetic fields seems a more accurate model than DNA for understanding what Tim Leary called the neuroelectric circuit. Bob used to call this circuit the neurogenetic circuit, but following Sheldrake he called it the Morphogenetic System in *Quantum Psychology*, so one could translate that line from *Schrödinger's Cat* to "cooperate with the morphogenetic fields." (Note: Bob usually referred to the levels of the nervous system as "circuits," but sometimes had called them "systems" and sometimes "dimensions.") Bob relates this in *email to the universe* with Poe's hero who "saved himself by 'studying the action of the whirlpool and co-operating with it'" (pg. 96). I guess one could see the dichotomy between "work" and "co-operating with the Morphogenetic Fields" as another false dichotomy.

    Joyce famously suggested readers devote their entire lives to studying his books. Bob doesn't go this far, but interestingly in *email to the universe* he suggests that readers "try the following simple experiment: try to say 'all' about the page (or computer screen) on which you see these words" on page 109 of the original New Falcon edition, page 111 of the Hilaritas edition. He suggests the reader spends at least two years on this "simple experiment." Well, I haven't spent two years exclusively on this page, but I've contemplated it since 2004. Bob suggests a chemical analysis of the page, so I had the chemistry teacher at my school come into my science fiction class to discuss the chemical nature of paper a few years ago. He even did an experiment, burning a page to determine the trace metals in the paper by the color of the flames. At some point in the future I hope to devote two years to this page, an experiment from Bob's final book. The idea of a huge amount of information coming from a single page seems to fit with Bob's idea of what *Finnegans Wake* does. In *The Intelligence Agents* Tim Leary recommends to "constantly revise your reality maps" (pg. 78). I think Bob intends this exercise to facilitate this sort of revision, and I think he saw studying Joyce as another tool in reality map revision. Of course, Leary said reading Joyce helped prepare him to enter psychedelic space.

    On reading page 109/111 yet again, I noticed the references to "nanosecond" both near the beginning and the end of the page: "nanosecond" appears on the second line and "nanoseconds" appears on the third line from the end. That suggests a 23 which I don't think Dr. Wilson planned, but I suspect it would make him smile.

I find it interesting that two of Beethoven's final three piano sonatas have the opus numbers 109 and 111 which correspond with these alternative page numbers as well as suggesting the 111's that haunt *Finnegans Wake* and the writings of Aleister Crowley.

In the Shem chapter of *Finnegans Wake* Joyce incorporated negative reviews of his own work into the novel. Bob did the same sort of thing when he incorporated reviews of his work into the comments about Sigismundo's concert in *The Earth Will Shake*. He also incorporated this Robert Shaffer comment on page 147 of *email to the universe*:

> Wilson describes himself as a "guerilla ontologist," signifying his intent to ATTACK language and knowledge the way terrorists ATTACK their targets: to jump out from the shadows for an unprovoked ATTACK, then slink back and hide behind a hearty belly-laugh.
> – The Skeptical Inquirer, Summer 1990

Bob has Prof. Sheissenhosen say the following about the mysterious Timothy F.X. Finnegan:

> Sheissenhosen evidently believed that "parapsychology" represented an unprovoked attack on his language and thought, and that Finnegan often leaped from shadows; he even suspected the Dalkey sage of slinking and of hiding behind a belly laugh, although the latter seems physiologically impossible. (I tried it once and found it made me more visible, not less.)

Rereading *Masks of the Illuminati*, the comment about the 114 sonnets in Crowley's *Clouds Without Water* on page 137[19] made me think of Joyce hearing the story from Sir John. This reminded me that the prose narrative at this place in the novel suggests the narrative Sir John tells Joyce and Einstein in Zürich. One interpretation of the title *Masks of the*

Illuminati would look at the many possible approaches to the novel or "masks" of the novel. One could read it focusing on its relationship to horror fiction, such as that of Arthur Machen and H. P. Lovecraft; one could focus on the occult notions; one could focus on the physics or the literary milieu of London before World War I, etc.

~•~

19) Astronomer Arthur Eddington commented on the importance of the number 137, which approximates the reciprocal of the fine structure constant in physics, according to Wikipedia. I remember Bob commenting on this years ago. I don't think he deliberately put this bit of information about *Clouds Without Water* on page 137, but this sort of coincidence did play a role in Bob Wilson's work (and in a different way in Phil Dick's work.)

~•~

When I first read the novel in August 1982, I knew next to nothing about Aleister Crowley or James Joyce, having just started reading Wilson a few months before, but I did know a little about Einstein, having taken a few physics classes in college. My friend the novelist Paul Chuey read the novel shortly after I did. At the time he knew very little about Joyce or Einstein, but he had read Crowley's *Magick in Theory and Practice*. His future wife Kathy Kelley then read the book. She knew little of Crowley or Einstein, but she had read Joyce's *Ulysses*. The novel revealed very different things to each of us at the time, based on our previous knowledge. It introduced me to Crowley and Joyce, and it presented me with new perspectives on Einstein. Paul and Kathy had similar but parallel experiences.[20] Each time I read the novel (or any novel) I come to it with a slightly different perspective. I've forgotten much of the math and physics I knew in 1982, alas, but other areas of my understanding have grown over the years.

~•~

20) One might say "complementary" experiences. Niels Bohr's theory of complementarity suggests that one can

use the wave model of light in some circumstances and the particle model of light in other instances, even though those two models seem to contradict each other. I don't think the Joycean, Crowleyan and Einsteinian glosses of *Masks of the Illuminati* contradict each other, but they provide wildly differing models of the novel's events.

~•~

Bob frequently used devices learned from a lifetime of reading Joyce when presenting altered states of consciousness in his novels, such as dreams, the transition from waking to dreams, and drug scenes. In *Illuminatus!* when Saul Goodman enters the "Playboy Club" under the influence of some drug (pg. 173), his mind starts playing Joycean tricks, changing "odd directions" to "Odd erections," and "Medium well" to "medium wall."

Wilson frequently said Joyce taught him the art of saying multiple things at once in his work. One can see this in page 177 of *Illuminatus!* during Saul's initiation. The screen asks him a series of questions ending, "HOW MUCH IS REALITY?" The next paragraph begins, "Suddenly, Saul was in Copenhagen." In Joycean fashion, Wilson and/or Shea suggests the Copenhagen Interpretation of quantum mechanics. The uncertainty at the heart of the Copenhagen Interpretation fits well with Saul's uncertainty in this scene. (Bohr suggested the idea of complementarity in the Copenhagen interpretation. One could model the electron as a wave or as a particle without attributing objective truth to either model. Similarly, one can ascribe the Joycean juxtaposition of ideas here to Wilson, Shea, random chance or some combination thereof.)

A few pages later when George Dorn smokes a joint, a style reminiscent of *Finnegans Wake* suggests the change in George's consciousness: "What son? What the son done cannot be undone but is well dun" (pg. 195).

On November 25, 2010, Tom Jackson posted a 1979 letter from Robert Anton Wilson to the fanzine *Diagonal*

Relationship to his invaluable blog *RAW Illumination*. In the letter Bob says, "Joyce *eliminated* obscenity from his world view, as he eliminated anger, pity, sentimentality, and all other subjectivities; he simply observes, with Zenlike detachment, and reports what he sees." This seems to get at the heart of one of the aspects of Joyce's writing Bob found so fascinating and useful.

When I asked Bob what aspect of his writing he would like me to focus on in writing about his work, he said most critics had not commented of the deep influence Joyce had had on his writing. I wrote my first book while earning my Master's degree, so those two projects overlapped in my mind, and I wrote my thesis on Joyce's influence on Bob. That thesis began as a paper for my Literary Theory class, and I asked Bob which of his books I should study to illuminate Joyce's influence on him. He replied *Masks of the Illuminati*. When I noticed that *Masks* had five sections, I asked if he had based that on the five section structure of *Portrait of the Artist as a Young Man*. He said, no, he'd based it on the Law of Fives. In *Illuminatus!* Simon Moon suggests that the Law of Fives influenced Joyce in the construction of *Portrait*. (Incidentally, Wilson and Shea incorporated a negative review of *Illuminatus!* into *Illuminatus!*[21])

> For instance, in 1914, when the fifth and final stage of Western Civilization was dawning, James Joyce published *A Portrait of the Artist as a Young Man*. The five chapters of that novel not only suggested five stages in the hero's growth, but by the alternation of styles from chapter to chapter suggested analogies with other five-stage processes. This was too much for the Illuminati Primi of the time, who warned Joyce to be more careful in the future. A battle of wills ensued, and all through the writing of *Ulysses* Joyce was still considering a novel built entirely around the Law of Fives. When

the Illuminati gave him what they call "the Tiresias treatment" – blindness – he finally compromised. *Finnegans Wake*, when it appeared, broke with the Joachim-Hegel-Marx three-step but did not include the *funfwissenschaft*. Instead, the Viconian four-stage theory was resurrected, a middle path that appealed to Joyce's sense of synchronicity, since he had once taught at a school on Vico Road in Dublin and later also lived in a house on Via Giambattista Vico in Rome.

(*Illuminatus!*, pg. 745)

~•~

21) The review comments, "The time sequence is all out of order in a very pretentious imitation of Faulkner and Joyce" (pg. 238).

~•~

I don't think Joyce had ever heard of the "Law of Fives," and I don't think Wilson and Shea thought he had either. By the way, T. S. Eliot called Tiresias "the most important personage" in *The Waste Land* (Eliot's own note 218 to that poem which Joyce considered a rip-off of *Ulysses*). Tiresias also plays a central role in Pound's Canto I.

Joyce loved to celebrate various days such as Easter and St. Patrick's Day, and he arranged for the publication of *Ulysses* and *Finnegans Wake* on his birthday. Bob Wilson similarly uses dates as markers in his novels, with lots of 23's of course. He and Shea have a significant event occur to Adam Weishaupt on February 2, 1776, on page 262 of *Illuminatus!*

Simon Moon, a huge Joyce fan, says "That same mix of revelation and put-on is always the language of the supra-conscious, whenever you contact it, whether through magic, religion, psychedelics, yoga, or a spontaneous brain nova" on page 271 of *Illuminatus!* The next page mentions

"Joyce's drunken claims to be a prophet." This suggests the language of *Finnegans Wake* as well as a reason why Wilson and Shea suggest the Law of Fives influenced Joyce.

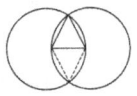

Synthesis

This machine for splitting butter and cheese out of a single emulsion, milk, represents allegorically the world process itself, which bring thesis and antithesis out of synthesis.
— *A Skeleton Key to* Finnegans Wake by Joseph Campbell and H. M. Robinson, pg. 117

Maybe Shem is Bruno's thesis, Shaun his antithesis, and godlike H.C.E. in whom these contraries coincide, their synthesis.
— *A Reader's Guide to* Finnegans Wake by William York Tindall, pg. 11

We're in science fiction now.
— Allen Ginsberg, "In History"

Eight hundred years is more than enough on a losing project.
— Cardinal Luigi Mozzarella

James Joyce is more important than Jesus, Buddha and Shakespeare put together.
— Robert Anton Wilson, *New Libertarian Notes/Weekly* 39, September 5, 1976
(Thanks to rawillumination.net for this quote.)

He learned by heart the fantastic legends of the crumbling book, the synthesis of the studies of Hermann the Cripple, the notes on the science of demonology, the keys of the philosopher's stone, the *Centuries* of Nostradamus and his research concerning the plague, so that he reached adolescence without knowing a thing about his own time but with the basic knowledge of a medieval man.

– Gabriel García Márquez,
One Hundred Years of Solitude, pg. 383

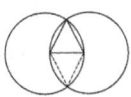

9) Psychedelic Howth Castle Music

Just as Joyce liked to commemorate his birthday, Bob celebrates his birthday and birth year in "The Horror on Howth Hill," in which he discusses the importance of 1932 and even slips in his birthday, January 18 (*email to the universe*, pg. 185-187). In that piece (essay? short story?) Timothy Finnegan serves as an alter ego for Wilson much as Stephen Dedalus does for Joyce and Lewis Carroll does for Charles Dodgson.

The third section of *Masks of the Illuminati* has Joyce contemplating his composition of the sermon on Hell from the third section of *Portrait of the Artist* (Wilson, *Masks*, pg. 226-227). That sermon on Hell provided the basis for the sermon on Hell Wilson composed for *The Earth Will Shake*. (One could see *The Earth Will Shake* as *A Portrait of the Magus as a Young Man*.)

Responding to a blog post by Tom Jackson on the influence of Joyce's *Portrait of the Artist as a Young Man* on Wilson's *The Earth Will Shake*, Bobby Campbell responded:

> Re: "The Earth Will Shake" & "Portrait of the Artist as a Young Man" connection. I noticed this when I happened to be reading "Earth" at the same time as listening to "Portrait" on tape. I hit the 'hell sermons' of each book on the same day and asked RAW about it and he responded:

"No writer ever knows consciously all the influences on his work but I did know the influence of Portrait of the Artist on Earth Will Shake & two others you didn't mention: Huckleberry Finn by Twain and Intruder in the Dust by Faulkner. Replace religious bigotry with racism and you'll see the Mississippi/ Napoli parallels."

– Campbell

Of course, *The Adventures of Huckleberry Finn* shows up over and over again in *Finnegans Wake*. Bob included Faulkner's *Go Down, Moses* on his Recommended Book List on his website (http://www.rawilson.com/bookstore.html). When I finished reading *Go Down Moses,* I asked Wilson which Faulkner book to read next, and he recommended *Intruder in the Dust.*

Joyce and Wilson shared a Catholic upbringing and education. Wilson attended a Catholic elementary school, although he attended a secular high school. Sigismundo Celine's thoughts during the opening mass reveal Wilson's knowledge and understanding of Catholicism. (Sitting here reading *The Earth Will Shake*, I find it illuminating to google images of the Cathedral of San Francesco di Paola in Naples, pg. 3, and frescos by Filippo Lippi pg. 4, work by Fra Angelico, pg. 5, the Bay of Naples, pg. 11, and the Teatro San Carlo, pg. 17. Perhaps one day we'll have hypertext for all of Wilson's novels or perhaps beautiful illustrated hardcovers like those available for *The Da Vinci Code.* I just finished reading the text of *The Adventures of Huckleberry Finn* in *The Annotated Huck Finn*, and I found the presence of the illustrations, maps, and copious notes a great aid in understanding the novel. I hope someday editions like that of Bob's novels exist.)

(I put on a CD of Horowitz playing Domenico Scarlatti to read this section of *The Earth Will Shake* because I knew Sigismundo loves Scarlatti's music, preferring him to Vivaldi, whom his uncle Pietro much prefers. I find it interesting that the first two musical references in the book refer to Vivaldi, pg. 5 and pg. 8. Perhaps Wilson did this to establish the accepted music of 1764 Naples [Vivaldi] as opposed to Sigismundo's more adventuresome tastes [Scarlatti and Telemann, pg. 11]. The first reference to Scarlatti appears on page 11.)

The boys clamoring for details of Sigismundo's fight with Cagliostro echoes the reenacting of the shooting of Boggs in *Huckleberry Finn*. The feud in *The Earth Will Shake* between the Celines and the Maldonados parallels that between the Grangerfords and Shepherdsons.

Faulkner? Um. I will have to reread *Intruder in the Dust*. [22]. I read it when Wilson recommended it to me, and I read it again when I taught it and *Go Down, Moses* a few years later, but I don't immediately see the parallels with *The Earth Will Shake*.

~•~

22) Well, upon rereading *Intruder in the Dust*, I can see what Bob meant. Both it and *The Earth Will Shake* deal with a young man dealing with a murder and having their view of the world radically alter. Both the men have uncles who seem to play a bigger role in their lives than their fathers. This seems true of Sigismundo at the beginning of the novel until he learns the identity of his genetic father. Certainly his Uncle Pietro plays a larger role in his life and in the novel than the man he had thought of as his father.

~•~

On page 21 of *The Earth Will Shake* the phrase "down, down, down" occurs. I used to think this referred to the Dylan Thomas poem "The Ballad of the Long Legged Bait," but Bob told me he meant it to refer to the descent into Dante's *Inferno* as referred to on this page.[23] When Sigismundo descends into the Naples market intent on killing a member of the Maldonado family, he encounters young Carlo. This again echoes the feud in *Huckleberry Finn* where Twain emphasizes the tragedy of the young men becoming victims of the feud. Twain once

Straight Outta Dublin

said he intended Huck's age as fourteen, the same age as Sigismundo at this point in the novel. Of course, Sigismundo's forbidden love of Maria Maldonado echoes *Romeo and Juliet* as well as the lovers from the feuding families in *The Adventures of Huckleberry Finn*.

~•~

23) The phrase "down, down, down" appears again on page 46, again linked with Dante's *Inferno*. According to Richard Ellmann, Joyce considered Dante his favorite author. Robert Anton Wilson's comments on Dante on *Robert Anton Wilson Explains Everything* seem less fully enthusiastic about the Italian poet. Dante shows up again in *The Earth Will Shake* with the place name Osteria Dante on page 90 and in Sigismundo's drug induced vision that "Dante was being eaten alive" on page 99. The Dominican at Sigismundo's retreat calls Dante "the greatest poet the world has ever known" (pg. 134). Einstein quotes Dante from the conclusion of the *Paradiso* on page 229 of *Masks of the Illuminati*.

~•~

Bob Wilson loved the films of Akira Kurosawa. On page 39 he wrote, "Sigismundo hated guns. The sword was a weapon of elegance, of art, of honor; guns simply killed people, even at a distance, without giving them a chance to fight back. They were ugly, and he had refused to learn anything about them." This foreshadows the duel later in the book, and it also makes an interesting comparison with Kurosawa's *Seven Samurai*, where all four samurai who die, die by gunfire. On could see the film as a McLuhan-esque critique of how the new medium of guns changed the culture of elegance and honor exemplified by the samurai. Welles' *The Chimes at Midnight*, another Wilson favorite, deals with a similar crux in history.

Opera seems central to life in Naples in *The Earth Will Shake*. (See for example the reference to women fainting when hearing popular tenors on page 72.) Opera plays a similar role in Joyce's Dublin. Characters in Joyce's novels and short stories frequently discuss opera. Of course, Joyce considered a career as a singer.

When Pietro and Sigismundo travel to Rimini to visit the Tempio Malatesta, Ezra Pound's influence becomes evident. The temple fascinated Pound, as did Sigismondo Malatesta (1417-1468), who commissioned its reconstruction. Malatesta worked as a general for hire and poured the money he earned as a general into the Tempio. Pound saw Malatesta as a test case for his way of writing about history in *The Cantos*. The primary sources for Malatesta's life utterly contradict each other. Some call him a murderer and a rapist. (His enemy Pope Pius had Sigismundo's effigy burnt in Rome, and he canonized Sigismundo as a saint of hell, the only time that has happened.) Others saw Sigismundo as a great patron of the arts and an opponent of papal excesses. Pound wanted to get his readers to think for themselves, so he devoted Cantos VIII – XI to Sigismundo, and Sigismundo and his Tempio show up repeatedly in the rest of *The Cantos*. On page 85 of *The Earth Will Shake* Uncle Pietro says of Sigismundo Malatesta, "He died nearly bankrupt, a considerable feat for a man born so rich." Bob Wilson may well have had the parallel case of Aleister Crowley in mind when he wrote this.

(The discussion of historical horrors between Sigismundo and Father Ratti on page 87-89 echoes Joyce's/Stephen Dedalus's theme that "History is a nightmare from which I am trying to awake," as well as in the comments after Sigismundo's capture on page 95 or the discussion of Peppino Balsamo on pages 107-109. In fact that idea of history as a nightmare permeates the novel and Wilson's view of history in general.)

And then the retreat. Sigismundo attends a Dominican retreat clearly patterned on the Jesuit retreat in honor of Francis Xavier Stephen Dedalus attends in *A Portrait of the Artist as a Young Man*. The Dominican speaker in Wilson's book makes many negative and sarcastic comments about the Jesuits.

On page 114 of *Portrait* just before attending the retreat, Stephen asks himself, "Does a tiny particle of the consecrated bread contain all the body and blood of Jesus Christ or a part only of the body and blood?" Basically Stephen asks if one can model the consecrated bread as a hologram. Bob Wilson has called the text of *Finnegans Wake* hologramatic prose: each part of it contains the whole.

Both retreats begin on a Wednesday. Both retreats begin by dealing with the final things: "death, judgment, Hell, and Heaven" (*Earth*, 133) and this quote from Ecclesiastes in *Portrait*, "Remember only thy last things and thou shalt not sin for ever" (*Portrait*, 116). Joyce also lists the final things, but he does not capitalize hell or heaven (pg. 117). Wilson's Dominican uses the line "We must die" (pg. 133), an idea Bob himself did not believe, since he believed in the possibility of human immortality, at least in the 21st century and thereafter.

Sigismundo's retreat includes this passage:

> This is only one day in all the history of the world. And yet this day has been full already. You can remember waking, and washing, and eating breakfast, and walking to this chapel. You may remember those you spoke to before coming in. Every hour is full of incidents and events.
>
> (134)

One could see this as a description of the day June 16, 1904, in *Ulysses*.

In *Portrait* the speaker at the retreat becomes the narrator in pages 119 – 122. In *The Earth Will Shake* Wilson always puts the speaker's words in quotation marks, marking a clear separation between the speaker's words and Sigismundo's thoughts. Both Sigismundo and Stephen Dedalus think the retreat intended just for them. "For that matter, was the retreat especially for him, because he was so far gone in heresy?" (*Earth*, pg. 137). "Every word of it was for him. Against his sin, foul and secret, the whole wrath of God was aimed" (*Portrait*, pg. 122). Wilson's retreat contains a discussion of secret societies, which fits in with the themes of the novel. Also, Wilson's retreat contains more negative references to women than does Joyce's: "'*occasions of sin*,' as the great San Tomasso called them, these '*sacks of dung,*' in Origen's words…" (*Earth*, pg. 138). Wilson's retreat also has more references to censorship and book burning. Wilson's retreat takes place over a hundred years before Joyce's, which could account for these differences. Also, the book burning theme ties in with the secret society theme, and it also ties in with Sigismundo's encounters with forbidden books.

(This also makes me think of my experiences conducting a high school *Finnegans Wake* Club. One mother, a former English teacher, forbade her daughter from participating in the club. When two members went to a Barnes and Noble bookstore to buy a copy, an employee tried to talk them out of it. Two other members have told me about step-parents trying to talk them out of studying *Finnegans Wake*. One step-mother said, "You should read Virginia Woolf instead.")

Sigismundo also has a conflict about betraying his Uncle Pietro, an admitted Mason. Stephen mostly fears his own damnation. (He does have a vision of the Virgin Mary comforting him and Emma [*Portrait*, pg. 126]). Sigismundo's retreat instructs the boys to turn in their relatives. This echoes the Nazi's encouraging children to betray their parents if their parents harbored Jews and contemporary American schools encouraging children to turn in their parents if their parents smoke pot. (William S. Burroughs has written about this parallel between Nazi Germany and contemporary America.) An echo of this retreat and its theme of betrayal appears later in the novel when John Babcock's school tries to get him to betray his lover.

Both sermons contain anti-Semitic passages: "A religion without Christ in the center of Catholicism" (*Earth*, pg. 139) and "hustled through the streets by the jewish rabble" (*Portrait*, 126). Both retreats focus on the darkness of hell (*Earth,* pg. 134-135, and *Portrait*, pg. 127). Joyce's sermon has many echoes of Dante's *Inferno* with its discussion of the damned in Hell. Wilson quotes Dante's phrase from Canto I of the *Inferno* "*selva oscura*" ("dark forest") on pg. 143. That phrase recurs many times in the novel.

    Sigismundo's decision not to turn in his uncle and to risk hellfire parallels Huck's decision not to turn Jim in in *The Adventures of Huckleberry Finn.* Huck decides, "All right, then, I'll go to hell" (Twain, pg. 344). He decides to choose his friend Jim over the morality he has learned. Sigismundo decides, "I cannot betray my friends, and that is all there is to it. To hell with mathematics, to hell with probability, to hell with logic, to hell with theology, to hell with all the philosophical spaghetti" (*Earth*, pg. 144). Consequently, Sigismundo decides not to give a full confession, thinking of Sigismundo Malatesta's motto "*Tempus loquendi, tempus tacendi*" (pg. 145). ("There is a time to talk; there is a time to keep quiet.") Pound quotes this line many times in *The Cantos*. On the other hand Stephen Dedalus gives a full confession (*Portrait*, pg. 149 – 152), including confession of his sexual sins, his visits to prostitutes which virgin Sigismundo has only dreamt of at this point in his life. When Stephen receives communion at the end of chapter three of *Portrait*, he thinks, "Another life! A life of grace and virtue and happiness" (pg. 152), echoing Dante's *Vita Nuova* (*The New Life*).

    In *Masks of the Illuminati* Wilson has the character James Joyce comment to Einstein about writing the retreat sermon in *Portrait of the Artist as a Young Man*:

> By God, Einstein, I spent several months, last year, writing the most gruesome and fetid sermon on Hell ever composed. I took bits from every theology class and religious retreat of my youth, and from Jesuit textbooks, and organized it into what I hope is a

truly blood-freezing, stomach turning, hair-raising harangue which will give the non-Catholic reader some sense of the cheerful hours which my hero had to endure in the course of a pious Irish Catholic education. But, to be honest, I was having a wonderful and glorious time all the while I was writing this bloody horror, because such things no longer have the power to frighten me and I could write it all down with cold clinical documentary detachment.

(pg. 226 – 227)

I wonder if Bob had "a wonderful and glorious time all the while" writing his sermon in *The Earth Will Shake*. Of course, the retreats occurs in chapter three of *Portrait* and part three of *The Earth Will Shake*, although *Portrait* has five chapters and *The Earth Will Shake* has seven parts.

On pages 150 of *The Earth Will Shake* Uncle Pietro says, "There is a legend that once there was only one 'club' and all those with the fourth soul were members." The ending of Wilson's *The Walls Came Tumbling Down* has a communion of saints of this sort, and Robert Shea's novels *Shike* and *All Things Are Lights* posit an alliance of international mystics hundreds of years before the events of *The Earth Will Shake*.

On page 155 people hurl "bricks and rocks at the police." This echoes Bob's essay "An Incident on Cumberland Avenue" in *Illuminati Papers*.

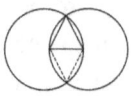

Parenthesis and/or Paralysis

I can easily look at my own prose and see whose voices are represented. There's a great deal of Ezra Pound, a great deal of James Joyce, a great deal of Raymond Chandler, a touch of William Faulkner, and a *soupcon* of H. L. Mencken.
– Robert Anton Wilson (*email*, pg. 214)

Joyce taught me a great deal about how to vary the tone of a paragraph and create emotional processes.
– ibid.

I admire Thomas Harris [author of *Silence of the Lambs*] more than any novelist since James Joyce.
– ibid., pg. 240

Like just about every other aspect of *Ulysses*, paradox is both a method and theme, contributing to stasis and motion. Seen as negation, that is as a cancelling out of one item by its contrary, it is equivalent to paralysis, another of Joyce's favorite themes and a term applied to the Dublin of *Dubliners*.
– David Hayman (pg. 75)

The novel is called *Ulysses*, and is impregnated on every page with coded mystical revelations.
– Mama Sutra in *Illuminatus!* by Shea and Wilson, pg. 521 – 522

You see, Joyce knew he was a genius, but he never understood the nature of genius, which is to be in better touch with the universal consciousness than the average man is.
– James Cash Cartwright
in *Illuminatus!*, pg. 581 - 582

(So, at last, I learn my identity in parentheses, as George lost his in parentheses. It all balances.)
– FUCK-UP in *Illuminatus!*, pg. 722

My intention was to write a chapter of the moral history of my country and I chose Dublin for the scene because the city seemed to me the centre of paralysis.
– James Joyce, from Gorman's *James Joyce*

Pynchon would obviously like to imagine some way out of the paralysis toward which his comedy is always pointing.
– Richard Poirier on Pynchon's *V*
in *The New York Review of Books,* June 1, 1963

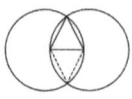

10) The Sisters[24] and/or Ode to Joy

For Robert Anton Wilson, written when he died in 2007

~•~

24) "Every night as I gazed up at the window I said softly to myself the word *paralysis*. It had always sounded strangely in my ears, like the word *gnomon* in the Euclid and the word *simony* in the Catechism. But now it sounded to me like the name of some maleficent and sinful being. It filled me with fear, and yet I longed to be nearer to it and to look upon its deadly work." (Joyce, "The Sisters," *Portable*, pg. 19)

~•~

When I take out the trash at night and see Sirius, I think about Bob and wonder about the world he left.[25] I imagine speaking at his centennial in 2032, perhaps on a space colony in Earth orbit, about how he proved so accurate about so much. I suspect the next 25 years will show the human race choosing Utopia over Oblivion. We will see.

~•~

25) "In the dark of my room I imagined that I saw again the heavy face of the paralytic. I drew the blankets over my head and tried to think of Christmas. But the gray face still followed me. It murmured; and I understood that it desired to confess something. I felt my soul receding into some pleasant and vicious region; and there again I found it waiting for me. It began to confess to me in a murmuring voice and I wondered why it smiled continually and why the lips were so moist with spittle. But then I remembered that it had died of paralysis and

I felt that I too was smiling feebly as if to absolve the simoniac of his sin." (Joyce, "The Sisters," *Portable*, pg. 21)

~•~

I first met Bob in Dallas in 1987. We had begun corresponding the previous year, and he had sent me his itinerary for his American speaking tour. (He and Arlen lived in Howth, Ireland, at the time.) Dallas seemed the closest stop to my then Arizona home. Plus, my friend Jai had moved to Fort Worth the previous year, and this would give me an excuse to visit him. Bob gave a terrific talk on Friday night and an all day seminar on Saturday. Rev. Ivan Stang of the Church of the SubGenius attended, and I had a great talk with him about Claude Rains' performance in *The Invisible Man*. You see, Rev. Buck Naked had an Anti-Stang Devival scheduled that Saturday night, and Stang contemplated attending wrapped up like the Invisible Man.

The next year in Phoenix David Mayne decided he wanted to bring Bob to Phoenix, so he got a bunch of Wilson fans together to make it happen, including Mark Johnston, publisher of *The Mindblaster,* and the egregious Frank Dracman. Bob stayed for a week at the home of Steve and Vicki Snow, and that week my friendship with Bob really blossomed. I remember the first night we sat in Steve and Vicki's apartment while Mark interviewed Bob for *The Mindblaster*. Bob had brought an Endomax brain machine with him, and I got to try it first. Steve and Vicki had stocked Guinness Stout, knowing Bob liked it, although they chilled it and he preferred it at room temperature the way they drink it in Ireland. (My grandmother once asked my Dad how he could drink warm beer in England. My dad replied, "Nothing is warm in England.") Folks in the room enjoyed beer and other intoxicants as Mark and Bob rapped about distimming the framigoshes. Bob noticed that Steve had a copy of *Insatiable*, which he had never seen, so Steve popped it in the VCR with the sound off and put Beethoven's Eighth on the CD player. I thought I felt the Endomax working as I got off on the music and the friends and the wise banter, but it turns out I had the Endomax set on fast forward by mistake. At one point Bob looked at the TV and commented, "This must be the famous pool table scene."

In 1988 I had an obsession with basketball and I had the idea of publishing a poetry zine which would include basketball commentary.[26] (The NBA had 23 teams at that time.) I thought I would call it either *noon blue apples* or *Gide's Telegram*. (My favorite story: On February 19, 1951, "André Gide, 81, dies in Paris. A few days later a telegram with Gide's signature appears on a bulletin board in a hall of the Sorbonne: 'Hell doesn't exist. Better notify Claudel.' Paul Claudel, the Catholic mystic poet, had once tried - unsuccessfully – to convert Gide." From *A Book of Days for the Literary Year*.) I asked Bob which name he liked better. He said *noon blue apples*. (I also liked that name for the NBA acronym.)

~•~

26) "That's what I'm always saying to that Rosicrucian there: take exercise" (Joyce, "The Sisters," *Portable*, pg. 20).

~•~

I began publishing *nba* in October of 1988, and Bob wrote back after just about every issue, with wonderful wacky letterheads and a few short contributions. When I got my first email account in 1996, most of our interactions switched to the electronic realm. Now I will have to rely on dreammail.

> The great learning [adult study, grinding the corn in the head's mortar to fit it for use] takes root in clarifying the way wherein the intelligence increases through the process of looking straight into one's own heart and acting on the results; it is rooted in watching with affection the way people grow . . .
> – Confucius, *Ta Hsio*, trans. Ezra Pound

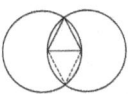

11) An Encounter and/or On Robert Anton Wilson and Misunderstanding *Finnegans Wake*

a chapter written in 2012

I started reading Bob Wilson in 1982, which led me to check *Finnegans Wake* out of the library in 1983. I had little success with the book, but after reading more of Bob's writing I decided to buy a copy of *Finnegans Wake* on February 2, 1984, Joyce's birthday. I still couldn't make much sense out of the book. In 1985 I read *Prometheus Rising* in which Bob mentioned a *Finnegans Wake* study group. Aha, I thought, I could do that, patterning it on Bible study groups I'd attended – a group of people studying a book few if any of whom had read all the way through and likely none of them really understood. I invited everyone I knew to come over one Thursday, and only one other person showed up along with one of my roommates, but we kept Finning on Thursdays for the next twelve years at least semi-regularly, joined by various other pilgrims, until I moved from Arizona back to California.

In 1988 a group of us brought Bob Wilson to Arizona to give a talk and a workshop. I wanted to make Thursday a Finn day, so we took him to see the new film of *The Dead*, which he loved because it reminded him so much of Dublin. We went to a vegetarian restaurant that night which one of our group recommended, but afterwards Bob asked me to take him back to the hamburger joint we had enjoyed the day before. That night Bob came over to my house and we had a raucous Finn session enhanced by Guinness Stout.

My Finn group meets on Wednesdays now, so it fell on the anniversary of Bob's death last week and it fell on his birthday this week. We've almost reached the song at the end of chapter two, which makes me think of the performance of that song at Bob's Memorial BB-Q five years ago. I still have trouble understanding *Finnegans Wake*, but it always makes me think of Bob, and I feel grateful for the ongoing confusion.

2017 Update: The students in my high school Finn group asked to move our meetings to Fridays because they liked the alliteration of Finn Fridays. We have just started the twentieth year of our *Finnegans Wake* club at the high school. Conrad Holt, Robert Rabinowitz, and I had our first *Finnegans Wake* study group in March of 1985, thirty two years ago.

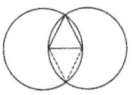

Paralysis and/or Paresis
August in Paris

For all the potential selves we can imagine stop short of what we are, and this is true however little we may be satisfied with what we are. Dubliner after Dubliner suffers panic, thinks to escape, and accepts paralysis.
— Hugh Kenner,
"Joyce's *Portrait* – A Reconsideration"

"Parysis . . . belongs to him who parises himself" (155.16-17) confirms the presence of Yeats's Joyce. The paresis of his exile in Paris is Dublin's paralysis, which, celebrated in *Dubliners*, belongs to him as Ireland belongs to Stephen Dedalus.
— William York Tindall,
A Reader's Guide to Finnegans Wake, pg. 120

The curiosity of Joyce's mature technique is that while on first reading *Ulysses* seems only intermittently funny and consistently "naturalistic" (realistic), on successive re-readings it becomes progressively funnier and spookier.
— Robert Anton Wilson, *Coincidance*, pg. 94

. . . in 1904 the term *paralysis* was frequently used in medical parlance (and by Joyce to mean "general paralysis of the insane," i.e., paresis, syphilis of the central nervous system).
— Don Gifford, *Joyce Annotated*, pg. 29

Sir Vaseline Foppe-Wellington was acquitted of similar rape charges twice in the next ten years, but eventually acquired paresis and spent his last days convinced he was the late King James II and his house was infested with Orange agents in wooden shoes attempting to poison him.
— Robert Anton Wilson, *Nature's God,* pg. 33

"A is not A," Hagbard explained with that tiresome patience of his. "Once you accept A *is* A, you're hooked. Literally hooked, addicted to the System."

I caught the reference to Aristotle, the old man of the tribe with his unfortunate epistemological paresis, and also to that feisty little lady I always imagine is really the lost Anastasia, but I still didn't grok. "What do you mean?" I asked, grabbing a wet handkerchief as some of the teargas started to drift to our end of the park.

"Chairman Mao didn't say the half of it," Hagbard replied holding a handkerchief to his own face. His words came through muffled: "It isn't only political power that grows out of the barrel of a gun. So does a whole definition of reality. A set. And the action that has to happen on that particular set and on none other."
— Robert Shea and Robert Anton Wilson, *Illuminatus!*, pg. 149 – 150

Thus, this theory literally means that somewhere in super-space, a universe exists with an Earth just like this one, except that Adolph Hitler, over there, never went into politics and remained a painter, but Van Gogh, after his brain had collapsed from paresis, did enter politics and emerged as a Great Dictator.
— Robert Anton Wilson, *Quantum Psychology,* pg. 155

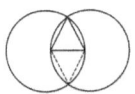

Chapter 12: Araby[27] and/or Coincidance

> Everybody in the story is involved in misunderstandings or ambiguities that become clearer and more hilarious on each re-reading[28]
> – *Coincidance.*, pg. 95

> Where *Ulysses* is an epic of the day, *Finnegans Wake* is an epic of the night; where the former dislocates our normal notions of "reality" only indirectly and on careful re-reading, the latter makes no concession to day-time "reality" at all and plunges us, from the first page to the last, in Altered States of Consciousness[29]
> – Ibid., pg. 97

~•~

27) "The other houses of the street, conscious of decent lives within them, gazed at one another with brown imperturbable faces." – "Araby" by James Joyce (*Portable* pg. 39)
28) "The implication of this color is spelled out in *Stephen Hero*: 'one of those brown brick houses which seem the very incarnation of Irish paralysis' (p. 211)." – Gifford, pg. 43
29) "My aunt was surprised and hoped it was not some Freemason's affair." – "Araby" (pg. 42)

~•~

On page 160 of *Coincidance*, Bob refers to "Hamlet's notorious puns to Ophelia on lap meaning vagina". From *Hamlet,* Act III, Scene 2:

HAMLET
> Lady, shall I lie in your lap?
>> *Lying down at OPHELIA's feet*

OPHELIA
> No, my lord.

HAMLET
> I mean, my head upon your lap?

OPHELIA
> Ay, my lord.

HAMLET
> Do you think I meant country matters?

OPHELIA
> I think nothing, my lord.

HAMLET
> That's a fair thought to lie between maids' legs.

OPHELIA
> What is, my lord?

HAMLET
> Nothing.

Removing the "o" illuminates "country matters". The Renaissance joke saw men as having a thing and women as having no-thing, and "noting" or "nothing" also referred to intercourse, giving multiple meanings to *Much Ado about Nothing*.

On page 166 of *Coincidance* Bob notes that the "Tunc" from *The Book of Kells* "makes an easily deciphered permutation of what Earwicker was evidently peeking at in the bushes of Phoenix Park." Joyce said that the intricate patterns on the Tunc page of *The Book of Kells* provided a model for *Finnegans Wake*.

On page 225 of *Coincidance* Bob describes the conversations between Major General de Lafayette and Seamus Muadhen where "each of them was convinced he was a little bit off his head." This reminds me of the conversation between Bob and Phil Dick. Bob thought Phil wanted to evaluate Bob's sanity, because if Phil considered Bob sane, with all his talk of communication with Sirius, perhaps Phil might consider himself sane with all his odd experiences from 1972 to 1974.

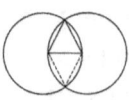

13) Eveline[30] and/or *The Earth Will Shake*

~•~

30) "I think of this story first when thinking of *Dubliners* not because it is the best story in the book but because it is the most nearly straightforward expression of paralysis and one of the most moving." – William York Tindall, *A Reader's Guide to James Joyce*, pg. 21.

~•~

On page 183 of *The Earth Will Shake* Maria Maldonado contemplates the passage "the kingdom of heaven is at hand" from Matthew, chapter 10, verse 7. She wonders, "Was it possible that the kingdom of heaven *was* at hand all the time, and we had only to open ourselves to receive it?[31] The way Mother Ursula opened herself to let God heal Hercules through her?" Bob admired a similar thought from the film *They Might Be Giants*, "You see, we were never put out of the Garden of Eden. It's still all around us. You only have to learn to look . . ." (Wilson, *Sex, Drugs & Magick*, pg. 67). Bob also said, "The joyous and hilarious *Skidoo!* and *I Love You, Alice B. Toklas* had echoed the open-ended optimism of the early 1960s" (ibid., pg. 148).

~•~

31) "But Irish paralysis frustrates her bold design." – ibid.

~•~

I find it interesting that both *Skidoo!* and the Monkees' film *Head* feature scenes of characters flipping television channels. This allowed for a new kind of montage. Tim Leary used the changing the channel image frequently, most famously in his "Turn on, tune in, drop out." One might see the writings of Joyce and Pound as anticipating the possibility of changing channels. *Ulysses* changes from one type of novel to another over and over again. *The Cantos* changes from one kind of poem to another. Bob Wilson suggested that Pound tried to create the internet on paper, with all sorts of jumps to various hyperlinks. When Pound edited Eliot's *Waste Land*, he cut out the transitions. Narrative art, in the shadow of the classical unities, had relied on transitions for millennia. Movies taught audiences to jump from one scene to another in an instantaneous cut. Joyce and Pound both learned from the movies. D. W. Griffith pioneered the importance of editing, and Eisenstein learned from him. Editing became more and more important to Orson Welles throughout his career.

Joyce influenced many figures in the 1960s. Tim Leary said Joyce's prose prepared him for psychedelic space. Joyce had a central influence on Marshall McLuhan. Joyce and Eliot influenced Grateful Dead lyricist Robert Hunter. When I attended the North American James Joyce Conference in 2011, the first paper I heard dealt with Syd Barrett of Pink Floyd and Joyce, and the second paper dealt with Van Morrison and Joyce. McLuhan's ideas shaped the Monkee's *Head*. He also had a cameo in *Annie Hall* and showed up in the lyrics to Genesis's *The Lamb Lies Down on Broadway*: "Marshall McLuhan, casual viewin', head buried in the sand." That last image suggests an ostrich, and ostriches became very important to Bob Wilson near the end of his life.

Interestingly, the passage quoted above from page 183 of *The Earth Will Shake* has a minor character named Portinari and another called Beatrice, whom Mother Ursula sends to Via Dante. This suggests the Beatrice Portinari whom Dante loved. Ezra Pound and T. S. Eliot saw Dante as a master psychologist who perceived the variety of roles people could play and put those roles in Hell, Purgatory, and Heaven. Wilson would suggest that various brain circuits make Hell and/or Heaven available to us each instant.

On page 186 Mother Ursula tells Maria to read the life of Joan of Arc and, "Tell me if you think Joan was really a witch, as the Inquisitors claimed". Leslie Fielder's *The Stranger in Shakespeare* has an interesting discussion of Shakespeare's presentation of Joan in *1 Henry VI* and the perception of Joan as a witch.

On page 205, Sigismundo and his uncle Pietro discuss Sigismundo's horoscope. Pietro says,

> I have seen only three horoscopes that compare in any way with yours, and since it is very dangerous to say even as much as I have said already, I am afraid to tell you which three men had those particular horoscopes. I will say only that everybody alive has been influenced by them.

I suspect Pietro means three of the following: Buddha, Jesus, St. Paul, and/or Mohammed. Crowley has an interesting passage discussing these four in *Book Four*, and Bob refers to this passage in *Masks of the Illuminati*. Bob echoes Crowley's discussion of these four in *Prometheus Rising*.

Sigismundo speaks many languages, as did James Joyce and Ezra Pound. Bob Wilson, like me, did not. Bob peppers his books with phrases in many languages, but I do not think he could actually converse in another language very well.

On page 209, Sigismundo writes to his uncle, "I already begin to understand your ideas about free thought and free markets." Karl Popper suggested that the greater amount of freedom of expression a country has, the greater the amount of wealth it will create. This theme recurs on page 215.

When I heard Bob speak in LA in the late 80's, he said that only twenty percent of people in the American colonies attended church regularly in 1770. Also, he said law books outsold all others in the colonies at that time. Sigismundo's comments on page 210 suggest the latter point.

On page 214 Edmund Burke says he speaks so eloquently because he "was born in Dublin, where eloquence is studied as passionately as Music is in Napoli." This foreshadows the Irish material in *The Widow's Son*. This page also includes a reference to a cow giving birth to two monkeys and an ostrich. Little did Bob know the role Olga the ostrich would play in his life in the next millennium.

On page 215 Charles Putney Drake criticizes the architectural style of Sir Christopher Wren. The architecture of Nicholas Hawksmoor, who worked alongside Wren, plays a major role in Alan Moore and Eddie Campbell's *From Hell* which also has major Masonic elements. So does *War and Peace* by the way. Those Masons just keep popping up everywhere.

On page 217 Sigismundo meets a factory worker named Joyce. Sigismundo writes, "keep thinking about the man named Joyce, and I feel there is a specter haunting Europe, but I do not know its name." The Italian film *La Terra Trema* (*The Earth Will Shake*) deals with the theme of workers' rights. This page of *The Earth Will Shake* deals with the novel's title: the earth will shake when the Finnegans awake.

Sigismundo then discusses Gibbon's *The Decline and Fall of the Roman Empire*. Joyce and Pound scholar Hugh Kenner called this work by Gibbon the great epic poem of the eighteenth century, and he called *The Oxford English Dictionary* the great epic poem of the nineteenth century. Kenner saw the role of poetry declining in the scientific age, and he saw these paradigm shifting works as playing roles similar to those played by epic poetry in the past. Pound saw the declining role of poetry in our culture over the past few hundred years, and he wanted to write poetry that would prove as useful to the culture as the novels of Stendhal, Flaubert, and Joyce.

Wilson mentions Howth Castle just north of Dublin on page 249, "where the castle door was always open at dinner time, because of some inscrutable Irish superstition". Pages 21 – 23 of *Finnegans Wake* tell the story of the English pirate Grace O'Malley (c. 1530 – c. 1603, whom Joyce calls the Prankqueen) who supposedly kidnapped the children of the Lord of Howth when denied traditional Irish hospitality. She returned the children on the promise that future visitors would receive hospitality. Hence the castle doors remained open at dinner time until the mid-twentieth century when many homeless people would come from Dublin seeking food, and it seemed likely the Prankqueen had long since died.

The references to Bishop Berkeley on pages 252-253 remind me of Yeats's lines:

> And God-appointed Berkeley that proved all things a dream,
> That this pragmatical, preposterous pig of a world,
> its farrow that so solid seem,
> Must vanish on the instant if the mind but change its theme;
>
> from "Blood and the Moon" in
> *The Winding Stair* (1929)

Maria Maldonado's dream journal beginning on pg. 276 starts on Joyce's birthday, February 2. Wilson learned a ton about dreams from Joyce's *Finnegans Wake*. On page 293 Sir John Babcock, Maria's future husband, contemplates his father's dying words, "The same bleeding nonsense all over again" and the idea of reincarnation. One might see the film *Groundhog's Day*, set on February 2, as a story of reincarnation.

On page 296, Maria refers to Sir John as "a cousin of the Greystokes". One Lord Greystoke would become Tarzan. Philip José Farmer created a family tree of literary characters including Tarzan, Doc Savage, Sherlock Holmes and Leopold

Bloom. This would make Sir John a distant relative of Joyce's Bloom.

The watery third movement of Sigismundo's Sonata 23, "Fire and Water," on pages 304-305, suggests the watery Anna Livia chapter of *Finnegans Wake,* and the way the variations become progressively more pathetic parallels the progress of the cups cards in the Crowley tarot as the watery energy descends the Tree of Life. The use of repetition in this movement might anticipate Beethoven's use of repetition in his Piano Sonata Opus 110 although Beethoven's Sonata doesn't emphasize humor the way Sigismundo's does. On pages 305-306, an audience member says of Sigismundo's Sonata 56, "The Two Nations", "He thinks the *clavicembalo* is a percussion instrument," anticipating Beethoven's Hammerklavier Sonata, Op. 106. (Note the number 56 plays an important role in Aleister Crowley's kabbalah. Sir John imagines part of this sonata as "like a mob of peasants storming the palace. No; as Sir John listened, it seemed more like goblins and clowns." This anticipates both the French Revolution and the Romantics' fascination with the supernatural. This piece's massive variations of a commonplace theme anticipate Beethoven's Diabelli Variations.

On page 309 the narrator says, "An elderly priest, who was named Ratti if Sir John had caught that correctly." Father Ratti had appeared a number of times earlier in the novel. Even though the narrative voice remains in the third person, it assumes Sir John's uncertainty about Father Ratti's identity. Hugh Kenner calls this the Uncle Charles Principal after the way the third person narrative voice in *Portrait of the Artist* mimics Uncle Charles's consciousness in a scene featuring Uncle Charles.

The novel echoes *Portrait of the Artist* after Sigismundo has success with the Middle Pillar Ritual the night before his duel:

Sigismundo was aware of himself breathing slowly and easily, in his bedroom, in the Celine villa, high on a hill in Napoli, on the continent of Europe, on the planet earth, in the system of nine planets circling the Inner Sun, in a vast turning spiral, in a womb, in the pink erotic waters, midway between existence and nonexistence.

Ah, those carefree days when we considered Pluto a planet.

Bob loved a line from the movie *They Might Be Giants*, "You see, we were never put out of the Garden of Eden. It's still all around us. You only have to learn to look . . ." The novel echoes this on page 362, "And as they walked towards the botanical garden Sigismundo looked about him with awe, as Adam must have looked at Eden on the first morning, seeing every blush, every flower, every petal with that new vision, knowing his invulnerability." In the fifth circuit chapter of *Prometheus Rising*, Wilson quotes the Gospel of Matthew, "And as ye go, preach, saying, the kingdom of heaven is at hand."

In the same chapter on the fifth circuit, Wilson writes, "Everybody 'knows' that the Sixth Symphony is 'pantheistic,' but whether Beethoven was an ideological pantheist or not, that way of responding to nature is normal and natural right-brain Circuit V functioning." Interestingly, all of Beethoven's symphonies have four movements except for the Sixth which has five movements. Also, Beethoven gave the movements of the Sixth Symphony programmatic titles as well as titling the symphony "Pastoral Symphony, or Recollections of Country Life".

I. Awakening of cheerful feelings on arrival in the countryside

II. Scene by the brook

III. Merry gathering of country folk

IV. Thunder, Storm

V. Shepherd's song. Cheerful and thankful feelings after the storm

Wilson also referred to the Sixth Symphony on my favorite page of *email to the universe*. On page 109 of the original New Falcon edition (and on page 111 of the Hilaritas edition) Wilson asks, "Does Van Gogh tell more or less about vegetation than Beethoven's Sixth, Darwin's *Origin of Species*, or the latest papers on botany?" I discussed this page in an earlier chapter. Originally I associated this page with Beethoven's Sixth Symphony and the Piano Sonata Opus 109 because of the page number, but since the Hilaritas edition came out, I also associate it with the Piano Sonata Opus 111.

The first exercise in the fifth circuit chapter of *Prometheus Rising* tells the reader to "Get the lesson book from the local Christian Science Reading Room and read the lessons for a month" (pg. 193). A friend of Arlen Wilson's, raised a Christian Scientist, said, "Christian Science only works if you are dumb enough to believe it." Bob wrote me that Aleister Crowley provides the trick for having it work but not remaining stupid. Bob said he had thought about writing *Science and Sanity with Key to Scriptures*. I joked about writing *Science and Health with Key to* Finnegans Wake. *Christian Science Quarterly* provides the daily readings from the Bible and Mary Baker Eddy's *Science and Health with Key to Scriptures.* They used to have the readings online for free. I did them for years (although I only read part of the weekly readings each day), and I found I got sick less often, fewer colds, etc. Then they started charging for the readings, so I started buying *Christian Science Quarterly* at my local Christian Science Reading Room. I did that for a few years, but then I learned I hadn't followed the Christian Science procedure correctly since I had only read part of the weekly readings each day. I remembered W. C. Fields' sage advice, "If at first you don't succeed, try, try again. Then give up. There's no use being a damned fool about it," and I stopped doing the readings.

Our local Christian Science Reading Room closed, but they have started putting the readings online for free again at quarterly.christianscience.com, so I have started doing the readings again. Perhaps my healing powers will match Maria Babcock's. Perhaps not.

I remember I tried to heal my checkbook with Christian Science in the 1980's. I enjoyed Mark Twain's book on Christian Science. At the World Science Fiction Convention in San Francisco in 1993 they had an actor playing Emperor Norton throughout the convention. A local writer channeled Mark Twain all week as Dead Guest of Honor. I had a nice conversation with him about his books on Christian Science and Mormonism.

The second exercise in the fifth circuit chapter says, "Attend a Sufi week-end seminar" (pg.194). I highly recommend the online classes at Beshara.org. During the 2020 pandemic they made their online classes free and put some of their in-person classes online and made them free as well. For a fascinating account of the Beshara School and much else, check out *I, Wabenzi* by Rafi Zabor. I used *Cosmic Trigger* and *I, Wabenzi* as textbooks for a class I taught at the Maybe Logic Academy called "Chapel Perilous" in 2009.

Exercise three says, "Acquire my book *Sex and Drugs: A Journey Beyond Limits* (New Falcon Publications) and try the tantric exercises there described" (pg. 194). When I first read *Prometheus Rising* in 1985, I could not find a copy of the original 1973 Playboy Press edition of *Sex and Drugs*. In 1987 New Falcon reprinted *Sex and Drugs* with a new introduction, so when Bob's 1997 revised *Prometheus Rising* appeared he referred to the New Falcon edition. In 2000 his revised *Sex, Drugs & Magick: A Journey Beyond Limits* appeared, and now many states have legalized marijuana. *Finnegans Wake* remains legal in all fifty states, although many educators still try to dissuade young readers from attempting to read it.

In the "Preface to the 2000 Edition", Bob writes "I can only wonder how much of the current Robert Anton Wilson literary output of palaver will embarrass me when I reach 75-80" (pg. 12). Alas, he died just before his 75th birthday.

The 2000 introduction continues,

> The major blunder I acquired from the 1960s counterculture was the notion that the Enemy (with a capital E) was ignorance and that this could be cured by education. I now feel more inclined to accept R. Buckminster Fuller's description of the four major problems confronting the world as "ignorance, fear, greed and zoning laws." Being untypically brave (like most fools), I always underestimated the role of fear in human affairs; having simple desires, I underestimated greed; and not being an architect, I never grasped the perfidious nature of zoning laws
> – pg. 12

Just before he died, Ezra Pound wrote in a brief preface to his *Selected Prose,* "re: usury – I was out of focus. The problem is avarice." Pound also wrote, "The enemy is ignorance, our own."

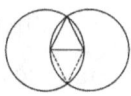

14) After the Race and/or *Prometheus Rising,* Chapter 1

Prometheus Rising holds a unique place in Robert Anton Wilson's output. He points back to it over and over again in his later books, essays, and introductions. Over and over again he said that if you want to make positive changes in your mind-body system, do the exercises in *Prometheus Rising.* On page 7 of the Hilaritas edition, it says,

> Sad as it is to say, you never understand anything merely by reading a book about it. That's why every science course includes laboratory experiments, and why every consciousness-liberation movement demands practice of yogas, meditations, confrontation techniques, etc. in which the ideas are tested in the laboratory of your own nervous system.
>
> The reader will absolutely *not* understand this book unless he or she does the exercises given at the end of each chapter.

Tom Jackson had the idea to host a "Do the Exercises" action and discussion group for *Prometheus Rising* at rawillumination.net facilitated by Tom, Apuleius Charlton, and myself, beginning on Crowleymas, October 12, 2020. We planned for the group to last at least 23 months. In preparation I reread the opening pages up until the first exercise in chapter one. I finished reading that at 2:18 PM on August 31, 2020, and I began visualizing a quarter.

The first edition of *Prometheus Rising* came out in 1983, and I first saw it and immediately bought a copy in March 1985. I have spent a lot of time doing the exercises over the last 35 years. In the early 90's Bob wrote a lot about E-Prime, and I learned to write, speak and think in E-Prime. In 1997 I decided to translate *Prometheus Rising* into E-Prime. Shortly after I started I ran across the Revised Second Edition of *Prometheus Rising* at Borders. To my mind, Bob radically improved the book. He did not put it entirely into E-Prime, but he brought to bear on the text all he learned in the thirteen years since the book had first come out. I highly recommend you get either the Hilaritas edition (based on the Revised Second Edition) or the New Falcon Revised Second Edition.

Bob designed the exercises in *Prometheus Rising* to weaken the existing imprints and to help the experimenter become a self-metaprogrammer, reimprinting the nervous system as each individual sees fit. Originally when I bought the book in 1985 I read up to the end of Chapter 1. I decided to stop until I had done the Chapter 1 exercises for six months. Yeah, right. After some brief attempts to find a quarter, I broke down and read the rest of the book. I couldn't bear to let an unread Wilson book sit on my shelf. I felt like Snoopy in an old Peanuts cartoon where Charlie Brown left Snoopy two bowls of food. Charlie Brown told Snoopy his family planned to take a trip so he brought Snoopy food for tomorrow. After Charlie Brown left Snoopy struggled with himself and finally snarfed down both bowls thinking, "I'd hate myself if tomorrow never came."

Well, I gluttonously devoured the rest of *Prometheus Rising*. Incidentally, this led to the formation of my first *Finnegans Wake* study group. I had purchased a copy of the *Wake* on Joyce's birthday the previous year (2/2/1984), but I had had very little success reading it. Reading Bob mention his own *Finnegans Wake* study group in *Prometheus Rising* led me to start my own.

I graduated from ASU June 1985 and then flew to the Ezra Pound Centennial at the University of Maine, Orono, meeting Allen Ginsberg, Robert Creeley, Hugh Kenner, etc. Next I flew to Europe, visiting Ingolstadt, Bavaria, on July 23. I had kept up my half-hearted search for quarters, but I put it on hiatus while away from the USA. (It seems reasonable for those not living in the USA to look for a local coin instead, as Damian Lee suggested.)

I did many of the exercises in PR over the next three years. Then in the summer of 1988 I decided to try to finish sombunall the exercises I hadn't done yet. Around that time I also began to associate the days of the month with the chapters of *Prometheus Rising*. On the first of the month I'd try to do some exercises from Chapter 1, on the second Chapter 2, etc., up until the 19th. On the first of the next month I'd start again. I even wrote a long poem as a sequel to *Prometheus Rising* called *Big Trouble in Little Blandings (Reggie Theus Rising)* with sections numbered 20 to 31. The poem dealt with a poetry contest held on a space colony. (Obsessed with basketball at the time, I published a poetry/basketball zine called *noon blue apples*. Reggie Theus played for the Atlanta Hawks, conjuring images of Horus. I also found it significant that the NBA had 23 teams at the time.)

October 18, 2020

I sometimes feel a little like Kinbote in Vladimir Nabokov's *Pale Fire*. I spent decades obsessed with the writings of Robert Anton Wilson, and even after Wilson's death I keep writing myself into his story.

I wonder why Bob told us to look for quarters. Perhaps he wanted us to notice how much trouble we had sticking to the exercise. This month I've noticed that I know that I only look for quarters intermittently when I go to the store. I think about it from time to time, but shopping, woolgathering, and social distancing often dominate my thoughts. I wonder how many quarters on the ground I have missed over the last month. Over the last 35 years?

Prometheus Rising begins with

> DEDICATED
> To
> Timothy Leary
> &
> William S. Burroughs
> dove sta memoria

The last three words come from Guido Cavalcanti's Canzone "*Donna Mi Priegha*". "*Dove sta memoria*" means "where memory liveth". In the poem a lady asks Cavalcanti about the nature of love. In his discussion Cavalacanti says, in Ezra Pound's translation:

> Where memory liveth,
> it takes its state

We often think of love as residing in the heart, but Cavalcanti sees love taking its state in the memory. This makes me think of Marcel Proust and his ideas about memory.

FNORD

October 24, 2020

I still haven't found a quarter. At the end of the Preface to the Second Edition Bob asks, "Who was that Prometheus guy and why did he give us fire in the first place?" (v). I looked up Prometheus in Wikipedia, and the article reminded me of the subtitle of Mary Shelley's *Frankenstein; or, The Modern Prometheus*. I remember Bob telling me around 1989 that he had learned that Percy Shelley admired Adam Weishaupt and that Percy had encouraged his wife to have Dr. Frankenstein go to college in Ingolstadt because of the Weishaupt connection.

During Bob's participation in the Maybe Logic Academy from 2004 to 2006 he began choosing a Movie of the Week each week. The first three weeks he choose the 1931 *Frankenstein, S1MONE,* and *Educating Rita.* Afterwards he commented that one might see the latter two films as retellings of the *Frankenstein* story. *Educating Rita* profoundly affected me when I first saw it around 1983 or 1984 with its story of a student transforming herself while earning an English degree. Around that time I changed my major from math to English, and I really related with the main character with her interest in Yeats, Blake and Mahler.

FNORD

On the morning of October 31, 2020, I found a quarter in the drive-through of a Sonic Drive-In before they opened. Later that day I had to take my beloved dog Pookie to an emergency center, and we had to put him to sleep. He would have turned fifteen on November 26. On November 1, I found two quarters at a Taco Bell drive-through. An hour and a half later I found my final quarter in that same drive through. I find it an interesting coincidence that I found these quarters in rapid succession after two months of unsuccessful searching at the same time I lost Pookie. In terms of the Thinker and the Prover, before Pookie started throwing up and I took him to the emergency vet, I thought that his health seemed OK. I considered spending a lot of time with him this year a great blessing, a positive side effect of working from home. When people talked about wanting to jump forward in time to the end of the pandemic, I thought that I wanted to treasure each day, because I feared Pookie would not outlive the pandemic. (What the Thinker thinks....) After talking with the vet, I could see how much Pookie was struggling. Before that night I modeled his behavior as normal for an aging dog. Holding him that night I could see his labored breathing and feel how slender he had become, and I could feel his suffering.

After having found the quarters the next day, I decided to continue with creating my own similar experiments. I decided to see if I could flip a coin three times in a row and get heads each time. It took me 19 flips to get three heads in a row. I explained that by selective attention and tried to get three heads in a row again. This time it took ten flips. I explained that by mind over matter and tried again. This time it took 29 flips to get three in a row.

Next I decided to lose a pound. It took me one day. I explained that to myself as selective attention. I tried to lose another pound. Once again it took a day. This time I explained it as mind over matter, and I decided to lose another pound. This time it took me two days. I do not draw any strong conclusions from the quarter or weight loss exercises. My data sets seem too small.

After rereading the chapter, I confronted the party exercises. Well, during this pandemic I don't plan to attend any parties, so I decided to use Zoom meetings. At the first one I considered myself ugly, unattractive and boring. I thought of the exercise a number of times during the meeting. I held myself back from making jokes. I did make one joke, and it got a good laugh. Perhaps I usually share weak jokes, but because I thought of myself as boring during this exercise, I held my tongue until I had a strong joke to share.

> "Life is just a party, and parties weren't meant to last."
> – Prince, "1999"

This morning I tried the next party exercise. I didn't have a particularly strong experience. I will try the exercise again, perhaps at an actual party.

I have observed the Thinker and the Prover in two close friends. I hope to get into discussions with some relative strangers in the near future and observe their Thinkers and

Provers. I don't talk much with relative strangers during the pandemic.

Well, thanks to Zoom I got to talk with a few relative strangers and observe their Thinkers and Provers as well as to observe my own Thinker and Prover. I contemplated my expectations of this *Prometheus Rising* group. I think I've given these exercises a pretty good try over the past 35 years, and I think I've gleaned the main lessons from them, but I also think I may have missed the point sometimes, and these exercises may have a lot more to teach me. My Prover sort of has the next 22 months planned out, but it also may prove that I have missed the point and that I can reach new perceptions. Hopefully I will have an even more positive experience with these exercises than I anticipate. We will see. I found the moments when I found those quarters after months of unsuccessful searching very charged.

FNORD

On Monday, November 23, 2020, birthday of both Harpo Marx and Boris Karloff, I went to the emergency room. I had had sharp pains in my lower left side two days before and again that morning. I suspected that I had had an attack of diverticulitis. I had one once before over ten years ago. (Bob Campbell told me at the time that Bucky Fuller also suffered from diverticulitis.) On my way to the hospital listening to Elliott Carter (my favorite music for the chaos of 2020), it struck me that this might prove a good chance to try an exercise from *Prometheus Rising*. I would view this visit to the ER as a party, and I would imagine myself as handsome, irresistible, and witty. I figured this would at least get some endorphins flowing to help with my healing. I did in fact talk with more people in person that day than I had since the pandemic shut-down started in March.

I had on a t-shirt with a bunch of DC characters on it. While in the waiting room the security guard commented on my cool t-shirt. I mentioned that my wife had gotten it for me at Target and that it came from a 1980's TV show. An older couple came over to take a look at the t-shirt (maintaining social distance, of course). They also liked the shirt. The man, leaning over his walker, said, "Yup, that's from the 80's. I'm an expert on cartoons from the 50's and 60's." I had only ever gotten one comment on the shirt before (from a security guard at Walmart – I haven't talked with many people this year). I don't know if this interest in the shirt came from my metaprogramming exercise, but I've never talked so much with strangers at the emergency room (and I have spent a lot of time in ER's with my family).

Update as of December 5, 2020: yes, I had diverticulitis, and all goes well.

FNORD

I have found it sobering to examine my own Thinker and Prover. Despite decades of work on the exercises in *Prometheus Rising* and in using E-Prime, I still have a lot of negative self-talk. My Thinker tells me negative things about myself, often using the verb "to be", and my Prover methodically sets about proving them. Hopefully I can alleviate this situation over the next 21 months by doing the exercises in *Prometheus Rising*.

I notice that stress makes the situation worse. My physical health seems OK, but I allowed myself to get behind in my grading while I felt under the weather. It has proved a challenge to get all my grading done over the past two weeks. Plus, the holidays provide some stress as well. At least my Thinker thinks so, and my Prover complies, perceiving stress and castigating me for getting behind.

My Thinker also thinks *Prometheus Rising* has a lot to offer, especially if one does the exercises. My Thinker has pointed out my ongoing struggles with self-fulfilling prophecies. At times in the past I have had a Kinbote-like zeal for proselytizing for Dr. Wilson's ideas and especially for the value of doing the exercises in *Prometheus Rising*. My Thinker wants these exercises to prove beneficial for me and anyone else who does them, but my Thinker also has lingering doubts about their efficacy. We will see how my Thinker and Prover respond to the experiences of the next 21 months.

I have found the exercises in *Prometheus Rising* useful, and some of their effects have lasted a long time. However I do not think I have completely resolved my issues with circuits one through four. In fact, I don't accept the eight circuit model as much as I used to. I have struggled with my weight for almost fifty years. My weight has yo-yoed during the 35 years during which I have (off and on) worked with the exercises in *Prometheus Rising* and other Wilson materials. In chapter three he says you will get to a healthy weight when your brain begins operating properly. Well, I spent a little time at a healthy weight in the early 90's after having done a ton of the exercises in PR, but my old programs reasserted themselves. I would like to have my brain operating properly (b.o.p. - perhaps Charlie Parker and Thelonius Monk's music can help me).

FNORD

Bob Wilson died on January 11, 2007. January 18 marks the 89th anniversary of Robert Anton Wilson's birth. Deadheads call the period between August 1, Jerry Garcia's birthday, and August 9, the anniversary of his death, "The Days Between" after one of the final songs he wrote with Robert Hunter. I've taken to calling the week between January 11 and January 18 "The Days Between" as well. The date 1/11 relates to the number 111 which plays an important role in *Finnegans Wake* as well as in the Kabbalah of Aleister Crowley. Beethoven's final piano sonata has the opus number 111 as well.

Chapter 1, exercise 5, says, "With your own ingenuity, invent similar experiments and each time compare the two theories – 'selective attention' (coincidence) vs. 'mind controls everything' (psychokinesis)." On January 7 I decided to start with the hypothesis that James Joyce's work has something to offer me right now. I will spend 23 days beginning using a "selective attention" model and then 23 days using a "mind controls everything" model. During the first few days of using the selective attention model I read Joyce's short story "After the Race" with some commentary, read a chunk of *Ulysses* and a bit of *Finnegans Wake,* and finished rereading a book on Joyce by Sheldon Brivic.

My *Finnegans Wake* Club at the high school started its 23rd year last August, and we began again at the beginning of the book. We finished chapter three on January 6, the Feast of the Epiphany and the date of Joyce's story "The Dead", and we started chapter four on January 13. I watched a nice Anthony Burgess video on the *Wake* on YouTube and started listening to a Bob Wilson interview on Joyce and Joseph Campbell. I didn't realize Bob had met Joseph Campbell.

For the 23 days of "selective attention" I just read Joyce (and his commentators) and tried to understand Joyce and his works. I focused on what I thought would help me with my *Finnegans Wake* Club as well as with future exercises in *Prometheus Rising*. Chapter 5 will ask for a character analysis of Leopold Bloom, and chapter seven asks about the reception of Ulysses. Other chapters have Joycean aspects as well. For the "mind controls everything" 23 days I have begun to look at Joyce's works as magickal texts. I plan to approach them less rationally.

FNORD

Well, I have begun to look at Joyce's works with a "mind controls everything" model as previously described. I came across this sentence on pg. 97 of the paperback *Finnegans Wake*: "Preservative perseverance in the reeducation of his intestines was the rebuttal by whilk he sort of git the big bulge on the whole bunch of spasoakers, dieting against glues and gravies, in that sometime prestreet protown." (A hardcover edition of *Finnegans Wake* has a different pagination. I have seen multiple books on the *Wake* which say that all editions of *Finnegans Wake* have the same pagination. As Tim Leary used to say "T.F.Y./Q.A. – Think For Yourself and Question Authority.")

The expression "reeducation of his intestines" struck me. In an earlier entry I mentioned that in November I went to the emergency room for diverticulitis, a disorder of the intestines.

Well, over the past thirty years I've tried to use *Finnegans Wake* for healing in much the same way Christian Scientists uses the Bible, but I have not had a ton of success. Due to Bob's influence I read *Science and Health with Key to Scriptures,* and I used its methods back in the 1990's to try to heal my checkbook without much success.

At the present moment I feel tired and overwhelmed by the world of 2021. I just read the final pages of the fourth chapter of *Finnegans Wake* three times. Over the past ten years I have started *Finnegans Wake* four different times with groups of high school students. The first three times we only got about as far as page 80. (One of those groups had a large membership, but most of them started as juniors, and we usually only met for fifteen minutes a week, making it hard to make it through much of the book.) This year's *Finnegans Wake* Club started once again at the beginning, and we've already reached page 95. We have all freshmen in the club this year, and they seem like they may want to carry on over their high school careers and read the whole book. Our pace seems good. I've decided to read the book three more times along with them, finishing the three previous starts I've made over the past decade. About ten years ago I had a large *Finnegans Wake* Club that read the whole book over three years. I remember the joyous day when we reached the final sentence and returned to the beginning of the book, "riverrun, past Eve and Adam's...." A number of students who hadn't participated for a while joined us for that final meeting just before they graduated.

One can't step in the same river twice, and one can't read the same book twice. Studying the *Wake* over Zoom in 2021 differs from any other reading of the book I have done. I will continue to use Joyce's work to reeducate my intestines.

FNORD

Well my Joyce experiment for the chapter one exercise in *Prometheus Rising* went OK. Reading the list of alternative names of *Finnegans Wake* on pages 104 through 107, I recalled the first time I met Robert Anton Wilson. I had written to him in 1986, and we began corresponding. In 1987 he planned to fly from his home in Ireland to do a speaking tour of the United States, and he sent me his itinerary, which included Dallas. My friend Jai Jeffryes had moved to Fort Worth the previous year, so I decided I would kill two birds with one stone. I would visit Jai and meet Dr. Wilson. Bob gave a talk on Friday night and then he had a seminar on Saturday. At one point during the seminar he passed a copy of *Finnegans Wake* around, and he had each of us read one of the alternative names for the *Wake* on pages 104 through 107. In the book a hen picks a letter out of a dump. The letter corresponds with the *Wake*. Joyce calls the hen Belinda after the Belinda in Alexander Pope's "The Rape of the Lock".

This week I noticed that a few pages later on page 112 Joyce gives a nice introduction to *Finnegans Wake* in this short paragraph:

> You is feeling like you was lost in the bush, boy? You says: It is a puling sample jungle of woods. You most shouts out: Bethicket me for a stump of a beech if I have the poultriest notions what the farest he all means. Gee up, girly! The quad gospellers may own the targum but any of the Zingari shoolerim may pick a peck of kindlings yet from the sack of auld hensyne.

Typing this out I notice that Word only underlines nine words in this paragraph with red indicating a misspelling or a "word" unknown to the program. Joyce mostly uses short, ordinary English words in this paragraph. I have certainly felt "lost in the bush" trying to understand *Finnegans Wake*. It does seem like a simple jungle of words at times. I almost shout out: Bethinket me for a son of a bitch if I have the paltriest notion of what the heck he means. The quad gospellers refers to the authors of the four Gospels in the Bible, who in the *Wake* correspond to the four old men, the four animals in the Book of Ezekiel, the four bedposts of the sleeper's bed, the four divisions of Ireland, etc. In this paragraph I see the quad gospellers as referring to the professional Joyceans who write learned books and articles on the *Wake*. I think Joyce means here that anyone (the Zingari schoolerim) can find meaning (pick a peck of kindlings) in the book (the sack of auld hensyne, which combines "Auld Lang Syne" with the letter the hen pulls from the dump). Of course Joyce wanted his readers to devote their whole lives to his works, but as critic Harold Bloom noted, the more one puts into one's study of Joyce, the more one tends to get out of it.

Note: Shortly after writing the above I unexpectedly got my first dose of the Covid-19 vaccine. I don't say that studying Joyce got me the vaccine magickally; I just note the coincidence.

FNORD

Why did Bob ask the reader of *Prometheus Rising* to spend at least six months on the first nine exercises of chapter one? He says on page 8, "With real work, in six months you should be just beginning to realize how little you know about everything." Well, I can see that. Some have complained that spending six months on these exercises seems painfully slow and boring. Chogyam Trungpa observed that dealing with boredom seems part of the process of meditating. In *The*

Karate Kid, Daniel thinks at first that Mr. Miyagi has exploited him in getting him to wax all the old cars.

I have spent six months on these exercises a few times over the past 36 years. I don't know the specific point of looking for quarters, etc., but I think I have slowly begun to realize how little I know about everything.

Chapter 1, exercise 10, asks the reader to "Believe it possible that you can float off the ground and fly by merely willing it. See what happens." I have never had much success with this exercise. In 1984 Rafi Zabor reviewed a record of Kiri Te Kanawa singing *Chants D'Auvergne* by Canteloube. He called it "music to levitate to". I had never heard of Te Kanawa or Canteloube, but I went out and bought the album. When I first read this exercise in *Prometheus Rising* in 1985, I immediately thought of that review and put on that LP. I had no luck with levitation, but I have associated that music with this exercise ever since.

I got my first CD player for Christmas in 1986, and Te Kanawa became my go-to soprano. In 1987 I also got CD's of her singing Mahler's Fourth Symphony and Mozart *The Marriage of Figaro*. Lots of great music, very little levitation.

A creepy coincidence: on Sunday I finished watching the Netflix documentary on the Night Stalker. One of the cops who first interviewed Richard Ramirez in custody said that at the time he was thinking that if Ramirez started levitating, the cop would walk right out of the interrogation.

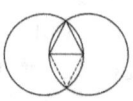

15) Two Gallants and/or *Prometheus Rising*, Chapter 2

Gallant 1:

The role of computers has radically transformed and expanded since *Prometheus Rising*'s publication in 1983. Coincidentally, I first heard Timothy Leary speak in 1983, and he talked a lot about the importance of computers that night. I first heard of Steve Wozniak and Steve Jobs when Tim talked about them that night. Of course, John Lilly had paved the way with his 1968 book *Programming and Metaprogramming in the Human Biocomputer.* I remember once in the mid-1980's attending the Visiting Nurses Book Sale in Phoenix. The one book I wanted to find in those pre-internet days: Lilly's *Programming and Metaprogramming in the Human Biocomputer.* I did find a copy that day. I think it cost ten cents.

In *Schrödinger's Cat* a character refers to T. S. Eliot's *Four Quartets* as "the gospel of my youth." Books like *Prometheus Rising,* especially the sections dealing with the semantic dangers of the verb "to be," seem like the gospel of my youth. Of course, I don't think Bob wanted his books to serve as anyone's gospel. I have tread a Kinbote-like path too close to that of a disciple of Dr. Wilson's for decades. Nonetheless, the discussion of the verb "to be" seems very useful in chapter two. Bob doesn't mention E-Prime, but he outlines its importance.

Wilson's idea that our brain software exists "anywhere and everywhere" (*Prometheus Rising,* pg. 17) parallels Proust's notion that our memory exists outside of us in the world around us. Anything in the exterior world can act as a trigger to stimulate the release of non-voluntary memories, memories we could not consciously recall. The madeleine famously acts as such a trigger in Proust's novel. The narrator dips a madeleine in tea where it partially dissolves. When he tastes a teaspoon of the mixture, it brings back a flood of memories.

On page 20 Bob says of the eight circuit model of the brain, "I assume it will be replaced by a better map within 10 or fifteen years." The revised second edition of *Prometheus Rising* appeared in 1997. It seems time for a new model.

Exercise 1 for chapter two says, "If you don't already have a computer, run out and buy one." Well, in 2021 most of us have multiple computers. I did the chapter two exercises in March, and I didn't intend to buy a new computer, but my cell phone died that month, and I got a new iPhone. As I write this in April, I once again didn't intend to buy a new computer, but my wife decided to get a new computer last week. The rhythms of this book and its exercises seem to play a synchronistic role in my life.

Gallant 2:

I hope all goes well. On February 2, 1984, I went into Books, Etc. in Tempe, Arizona, thinking of James Joyce's birthday. I picked up a copy of *Finnegans Wake* and opened it at random. I saw the line "Please stop if you're a B.C. minding missy, please do. But should you prefer A.D. stepplease" on page 272. The side notes had a musical staff with the notes B, C, A, and D. I thought, "Hey, I can do this," and I bought my first copy of *Finnegans Wake*. At the time I interpreted it as meaning "Please stop if you have a past oriented B. C. mind, please do. But should you prefer the future, A. D., step right up."

At the beginning of May 1982 I bought my first Robert Anton Wilson book. The cover of *Schrödinger's Cat: The*

Universe Next Door had caught my eye repeatedly at Changing Hands Bookstore in Tempe, Arizona. It had a woman's face superimposed on a cat's face. I had read a positive review of Wilson's *The Illuminati Papers* by Spider Robinson in *Analog Science Fiction Magazine*, and I really valued Spider's opinion. He argued that we really needed optimism like Bob Wilson's in the wake of John Lennon's murder. I had also read the Neal Wilgus interview with Wilson in *Science Fiction Review*. I read *The Universe Next Door* and enjoyed it. I lived in Tucson for the summer, but my family visited my grandfather in Scottsdale in June. I stopped by the One Book Shop in Tempe and bought *Schrödinger's Cat: The Trick Top Hat*. I loved that book, and I became obsessed with Wilson's writing for the next 23 years (and then some).

I had forgotten that chapter two of *Prometheus Rising* mentions Radio Shack. *Tempus fugit*, time flies. As a kid I remember building a rudimentary robot with a kit from Radio Shack. Now I sit here typing this on my MacBook Pro with two iPads and an iPhone on the table next to it. And I don't even particularly like Apple products. My dad worked for IBM for over thirty years. I worked at IBM three summers during college. I fought kicking and screaming against switching to Apple products ten years ago at my high school, but now I've gotten used to them. As Bob said, "The brain is an organ of adaptability."

I just got done doing my daily tai chi. I've done it most days during the past year of lockdown. It has made me aware of the changing relationship of the earth and the sun as I do tai chi at different times due to the changing weather. I try to orient myself to avoid the sun getting into my eyes. I like to practice at about 63 degrees Fahrenheit. Living in Corona, California, that means going out early in the morning in May. It meant going out at the warmest part of the day during winter. (I realize our winter doesn't seem cold compared to much of the world's.)

Martial arts takes us into chapter three of *Prometheus Rising*. I took a little bit of karate and judo back in the 1970's. In the fall of 1985, after reading *Prometheus Rising*, I thought about taking kung fu to do the exercise from chapter three of taking a three month course of martial arts. However, I felt like a bit of a pacifist at the time, so I took yoga instead. I didn't get serious about martial arts until the year 2000.

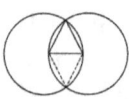

16) The Boarding House and/or *Prometheus Rising*, Chapter 3

An exercise in chapter 3 of *Prometheus Rising* calls on the reader to take a martial arts course for at least three months. I have had the great good fortune to study kenpo and tai chi with Mr. Gary Toppins and karate do with Dr. Craig Hargis. Dr. Hargis kindly consented to the following interview.

1. How did you get involved in the martial arts?

My dad was stationed in Japan after the war and was impressed by Japanese martial arts. He put me in Judo at ten years old and karate a couple of years later. Back then the words judo and karate were almost always used together and few people really knew the difference. There was always some karate included in judo self-defense practice.

2. Why did you choose to focus on karate do?

I did not really mean to leave judo, I was actually kind of talented in it. It was just that karate increasingly absorbed my practice time. I practiced judo even out here until 1974 at LACC with Hayward Nishioka. Judo is really a sport, and real karate decidedly is not. That was the gravity of karate for me.

3. Whom do you consider some of your significant teachers?

I define a teacher as being someone you directly ranked with. Mine would be Yoshio Kimura, Kiyoshi Yamazaki, and Ed Hamile and Ken Funakoshi. I was very lucky to find myself in Southern California where most of the important instructors visited frequently, so I at least met them.

4. Has practicing karate do affected other areas of your life?

Mr. Egami, a great Shotokan master, said that, put simply, karate do is life and life is karate do. A karate man is always a karate man, though good ones hide that from others. What that means is that when you think of yourself, you think of karate first and most often. It is more than anything else your identity. Karate is all consuming or should be. People around you may (or should) have no idea how much karate influences everything you think and do. I once heard karate defined as observing economically. You let life wash over you.

5. Texts like *Karate-Do Kyohan* by Gichin Funakoshi and *Dynamic Karate* by Masatoshi Nakayama seem very important to you. What do those books mean to you?

Books are so much better than video. These books are symbols of continuity. They are things to which you return for a lifetime. A book can be held and carried. In many ways, the key books are karate itself. The young men in the pictures grew old and died but they have never changed in the book. The pictures and text combine to make an indelible imprint in the mind of what good form looks and feels like. The imagination can easily link still pictures in motion but can never extract terminal positions from video. Because you have met and known many of the authors the books keep karate forever young.

6. What other martial arts books do you recommend?

Shigeru Egami: *Karate Do Beyond Technique*. This is the best book on the emotional, spiritual, and mental reality of karate ever written.

7. You recently posted on Facebook, "To my Karate friends. Of all the Japanese instructors, who did you find the most approachable, open, friendly and likable?" What provoked you to ask this question?

Curiosity. I meant to say "not the best instructor but simply the nicest and most approachable famous teacher." Most are really quite friendly. CW Nicole writes in *Moving Zen* of a Japanese rough who tried to pick a fight with Nakayama Sensei on a subway. Nakayama got off at the next stop and Nicole wrote, "So Sensei left and the fool never knew how close he was to death." I always loved that simple idea.

8. You spent decades as a college and high school teacher. How did your martial arts practice influence your teaching?

Just to be myself, be confident, and know that most of the students would like me. Also to try and get odd angles on a subject. You try to be open, and personable like a good karate instructor. Teaching a physical art is different than teaching a text – though arguably kata is a text.

9. How has martial arts training helped you deal with life challenges?

Life is a challenge, and you can't deal with it really. To try and defeat it is your death. The down side of karate is living too much in the past and relying too much on memory. It is lonely. The old *Kung Fu* series did a great job of demonstrating this. Back to life: You have to somewhat ignore it, let it go. You are immersed in water but you are not the water. Though of course you ultimately are water but not manifested as so. Life is standing in a stream of running water--sometimes deep, sometimes slow, and sometimes fast. But it always flows around you, over you but not through you. If the water flows through you it means you have drowned, died. But karate is in the end a perfection in waiting or even in loneliness in that it cannot be shared, and very few know who you are.

10. Thank you very much.

I realized I had forgotten to ask Dr. Hargis about his rank, so I sent him a follow up query. He responded, "My permanent rank is godan (5th degree black belt, highest technical rank in traditional Shotokan). Instructor title is Hanshi, International master instructor."

Rereading *Prometheus Rising* in 2000, I signed up for Chinese kenpo classes at Mr. Toppins's East Wind Martial Arts in Riverside, California, and studied with a few interruptions for ten years. During that time I also had the opportunity to study karate do with Dr. Hargis. In 2010 I had some knee trouble so I stopped martial arts for a while. In 2016, once again working on *Prometheus Rising,* I decided to study Yang long form tai chi (108 movements) with Mr. Toppins. That worked out much better for my knees, and I hope to continue practicing tai chi for the rest of my life. I finished learning the form in 2019, and I continued studying with Mr. Toppins until the beginning of the pandemic in 2020. I hope to continue my lessons soon.

For this run through of *Prometheus Rising* I decided to focus on tai chi for three months starting March 6, 2021. Fortunately I remember the form well enough to practice by myself without a teacher.

Well, today June 6 has arrived. I have practiced tai chi most days for the last three months. Reading this chapter of *Prometheus Rising,* I note on page 28 Bob suggests that "opium and its derivatives return us to the 'safe space' on the biosurvival circuit." I suspect that binge eating also returns us to a similar "safe space".

By the way, I got another new computer this week. My high school decided to replace all of our iPads with new ones. I find this an interesting synchronicity. When Tom, Gregory, and I decided to start this *Prometheus Rising* study group, I had no intention of getting a new computer to go along with the exercise in chapter two. Instead I have gotten three. I wonder what other surprises we will encounter over the next sixteen months (and beyond).

I was born prematurely and spent some time in an incubator. I suspect this led to my taking my strongest imprint on the first circuit and has contributed to my lifelong weight issues. The description on page 35 of "persons who take their *heaviest* imprint on the first (oral) circuit" fits me to a T. Interestingly, when I first read this book in 1985, I didn't see this. I thought I had taken my strongest imprint on the third circuit. My friend Jai Jeffryes told me that he thought I had taken my strongest imprint on the first circuit, but I refused to see it at the time. I felt very proud of my powerful third circuit intelligence, but I lacked self-insight.

> "God wishes for you ease and does not wish for you difficulty."
>
> *– Quran* 4:28

The recursive calls at the end of some exercises to "reread this chapter" like in exercises 4 and 7 in this chapter, could go on infinitely. One might take a three month course in kung fu, reread the chapter, reach the exercises and take a three month course in karate and read the chapter, etc. ad infinitum. This leads us to the metaprogramming circuit, what Bob calls the seventh circuit in this book.

I would like to visit the Long Beach Aquarium or Sea World after the pandemic and do exercise 6. I have visited some doctor's offices lately that have fish tanks, and I have observed them very closely.

I got a chance to see my baby great-granddaughter on Mother's Day 2021, but I didn't think of exercise 7 from this chapter at the time. This reminds of the time in 1985 when my roommate Robert Rabinowitz left quarters on our driveway after I had left to go on a walk looking for quarters. By the time I had returned to the house my mind had wandered so much that I didn't glance down and notice the quarters. Fortunately, I got to see another baby granddaughter on Memorial Day and I did remember to keep the exercise in mind this time.

The opening quote in this chapter from *Sociobiology* by Edward Wilson points forward to the collective neurogenetic (morphogenetic) circuit, what Wilson calls the sixth circuit in this book.

I find it interesting that Bob mentions UFOs on page 28. As the pandemic enters its endgame, UFOs have entered the news. I wonder how they will emerge as we continue working through the book.

The reference to how one can find people with negative first circuit imprints in fringe groups of the extreme Left and extreme Right on page 36 makes me think of the political world of the U.S.A. in 2021, January 6, in particular. Coincidentally, James Joyce's great story "The Dead" takes place on January 6, 1904. I took Bob to see the John Huston film of that story in 1988.

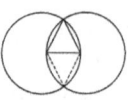

17) A Little Cloud and/or *Prometheus Rising*, Chapter 4

"Hey, hey, we're the Monkees!"

The discussion of the second circuit, walking, and "learning to manipulate others politically" reminded me of a story a ballet teacher told of her ex-husband as a teenager walking across his room listening to Beethoven's Coriolan Overture imagining himself as a prince. In a few years he would get cast as a prince in traditional ballets.

Mike Gathers has observed the deep impact Freud made on Bob's interpretation of the eight circuit model. I just reread *Portnoy's Complaint* by Philip Roth getting ready for chapter five of *Prometheus Rising*. Freud's impact on Portnoy intrigued me.

Bob Wilson imagines the imprints landing in quadrants of Leary's Interpersonal Grid (or "cover two or more quadrants partly"). Mike Gathers has observed that Leary did not intend for this use of the Grid. Leary outlined a more complex system in *The Interpersonal Diagnosis of Personality* using a sliding scale for various areas of the Grid for clinicians and others to utilize.

I fear I usually fall in the hostile weakness quadrant. I hope my imprints become "a little less rigid, a little more flexible" as we proceed.

FNORD

Well, I've struggled to practice two fifteen minutes meditation sessions every day. I have meditated most days, but have missed a few sessions. I do plan to get up to a month in a row. We will see. I have allowed life's chaos to interfere with this exercise. I did find it interesting to return to Christopher Hyatt's *Undoing Yourself with Energized Meditation*. I have the third edition. I remember haunting bookstores in the 1980s searching for Wilson and related books in those pre-Amazon days, especially Alpha Book Center in Phoenix which got most of the Falcon titles.

I remember in 1986 feeling delighted when I found a copy of the second edition of *Undoing Yourself* at Alpha Book Center. I started reading it at my job at Hunter's Books, and around pg. 36 I came across "The oral-anal pit can be referred to as 333. If you don't know what that number means please look it up." (I don't know the page number in the second edition. I may still have a copy in a box in the garage. If it turns up, I will look it up. I don't think any of my local libraries have a copy of any of Hyatt's books.)

Well, back in 1986 I didn't know about 333 and Choronzon, and Hunter's Books didn't have any Crowley. We did have *Cosmic Trigger*, though, the only Robert Anton Wilson book I could order through our distributor at the time. I didn't recall any reference to 333, but I looked it up in the index. Lo and behold, it did have an entry for 333. Wilson discusses 333's appearance in a UFO story in *Fortean News* and he adds, "333 is the Cabalistic number of 'that mighty devil, Choronzon,' who once afflicted Dr. Dee in the 17th Century and gave Aleister himself a rough time in Bou Saada, North Africa, 1909, as recounted in *The Vision and the Voice* by Aleister Crowley."

Rereading *Undoing Yourself* in 2021, it struck me that Hyatt pulls the reader's leg at times, playing the trickster. On page 19 he tells the reader, "Now stand on your head and reread *Info-Psychology*." Bob Wilson pulls the reader's leg at

Straight Outta Dublin

times, and I wondered if he really wanted the reader to do all of the exercises in *Prometheus Rising*, or at least to do them in the way he described them. Some people have complained about taking six months or more for the chapter one exercises, for example.

Upon reflection, I think Bob really did want us to do these exercises pretty much the way he wrote them in the book, especially in the revised second edition. He pointed to *Prometheus Rising* over and over again in his writings after 1983, saying basically that "if you want to improve your life, try the exercises I put in this book." I may seem gullible in this conclusion.

Last century I attended three encounter groups: Omega Vector, Omega II, and Delta Vector. I found them interesting, and I appreciated that they didn't charge any money. I have some friends who paid for the EST Training. I love the send-up of EST in the film *The Spirit of '76*.

I look forward to visiting the Lion House again. Nora Joyce liked the fact that one could hear the roaring of the lions in the Zurich zoo from James Joyce's grave in Zurich. Since I first bought *Prometheus Rising* in 1985, I have visited lion houses in zoos in Dublin, London, Tucson, Phoenix, Los Angeles, San Diego, and Honolulu.

In 1988 I attended *Who Framed Roger Rabbit?* with a friend and his two kids to fulfill the exercise to watch a film "that small children like". I wonder if the screenwriters named Roger and Jessica after the characters in *Gravity's Rainbow*? A few months later I saw a theater marquee with a missing letter: *Who Framed Roger Rabbi ?*

In 2021 I watched a few Three Stooges short films and Abbott and Costello's *Buck Privates* (1941). I had recently watched *Full Metal Jacket* (1987) for the first time in over twenty years, and I found it interesting to see the similarities between *Buck Privates* and *Full Metal Jacket*. They both deal with an overweight private going through basic training.

Of course, *Buck Privates* functions primarily as a comedy. Watching both films, one can see the radical changes in society and cinema from 1941 to 1987. The world of *Buck Privates* has no sense of the Holocaust or the atomic bomb or of anything going on in Europe at the time. In *Full Metal Jacket,* the drill sergeant seems at all times aware of the possibility of death awaiting his Marines in Vietnam. I also just rewatched the film *Conspiracy* (2001), a chilling film which deals with the January 20, 1942, Wannsee Conference, a meeting held by Reinhard Heydrich where he coordinated the bureaucracy of the Holocaust. *Conspiracy* deals with the horror of men outlining mass murder in relative calm that reminds me far too much of many work meetings I have attended over the years.

 I spent over three hours last Sunday watching animal shows on TV. I went to work Monday and observed "the primate pack hierarchy." One of the TV shows on monkeys opened with the theme from *The Monkees* which I coincidentally quoted to open this chapter. The last animal show I watched dealt with relocating a lab chimp to a refuge in Louisiana. Before going to work on Monday, I saw this on Facebook: "You're now cursed with the job the main character has in the last movie/TV show you watched. What's your new profession?"

 I answered, "Lab chimp." At work I found myself wondering in a Phildickian mood, "Perhaps I am a lab chimp. My last 23 years teaching high school might have been part of an experiment that has gotten cancelled due to new legislation, and my keepers have decided to relocate me to a teacher refuge in Louisiana. That would explain a lot." On the show the keepers put bananas in the trees in the refuge and poured apple sauce into artificial termite mounds. Coincidentally, I had brought two bananas and some apple sauce in my lunch that day, as I did most days. I wonder what my keepers think of this blog? Does it make them smile and think, "He's adapting nicely."

I have meditated a half hour a day for the past 21 days. I hope to meditate for the next ten days. The two days after that I have a teacher training scheduled where I well may run into "someone who always manages to upset you or make you defensive." Lucky me. I have never established a steady meditation practice, but I have done one month blocks a number of times when working through *Prometheus Rising*. I never had as much trouble keeping a month-long streak going as I have this year. I guess my life has become more distracted.

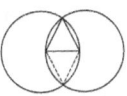

18) Counterparts and/or Did Pink Floyd Play Woodstock Europa?

Yes, but in the world of *Illuminatus!*, they played as a five piece. Doc Sportello somehow convinced Syd Barrett's parents to let Syd come with him to Germany to attend the concert. On April 30, 1976, Syd stood in the crowd in Ingolstadt, Bavaria, not too far from the stage, while his former band performed their whole album *Wish You Were Here* which dealt in part with the band's guilt and regret over kicking Syd out of the band due to his mental illness and drug challenges. Syd had on a "Life Is Better on the Lake" t-shirt he had just bought from a vendor. He had put it on over his white button-down shirt.

As the band began their final song "Shine On You Crazy Diamond (Pts. 6-9)", Syd approached the right side of the stage. He got to within ten feet of the musicians, standing directly behind keyboardist Richard Wright. The crowd had begun to get a little restless. Odd things had begun to happen in Ingolstadt and in the nearby lake.

Syd climbed up on stage and sat cross-legged right behind Wright. The band didn't seem to notice him, and they continued playing. Near the end of Part 9, Wright played a bit of the melody of Syd's song "See Emily Play". When he heard this, Syd stood up and stepped to the front of the stage and stood still, staring at the audience.

Unlike the previous year when Syd had wandered into

their recording studio and no one in the band had recognized him at first, all four of the musicians looked at each other as they realized who had shown up this Walpurgisnacht. They thought about extending the song, but Roger Waters and Nick Mason looked at each other and gently shook their heads no.

As the song ended, Syd started gently hopping up and down. The audience cheered the set, a little confused at this bald, slightly overweight man jumping up and down in front of the band. As the applause died down, Syd stopped jumping. He looked at his friend David Gilmour and walked over to Gilmour's mic.

"Like Puck in *A Midsummer's Night Dream,* Oberon, Admired Miranda, my Miranda, complex Titania, and...." He paused and stared blankly out at the audience again.

"Stairway. Astrally projecting to Venus. No, Neptune. Frequent, flyer. Miles to go. Cor nullum et anima nulla."

Syd looked at the ground for a few moments. He looked back up at the crowd and extended his arms to his sides. "Underground."

Syd walked off stage and back into the crowd.

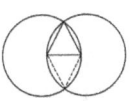

Chapter 19: Clay and/or *Prometheus Rising*, Chapter 5

1. Looking at the Leary Interpersonal Grid on page 55 of *Prometheus Rising,* Scarlett O'Hara seems most often to fall in the IMPATIENT WITH OTHERS, SELF-SEEKING, SARCASTIC box on the far left of the diagram. Over the course of the novel (and the film) she shows a lot of different aspects of her personality. Turner Classic Movies created a nice introduction for *Gone With The Wind* where Black scholar Jacqueline Stewart puts the film in historical perspective. Bill Maher complained that we don't need introductions like these because "We know the history," but I liked the introduction, and if I teach this film again, I would like to show this introduction to the class. When I taught this novel to a tenth-grade English class, a student called Scarlett "a twentieth century woman stuck in the nincteenth century." I like that analysis.

2. King Kong seems SELF-RELIANT AND ASSERTIVE, SELF-CONFIDENT, INDEPENDENT, especially before he encounters Fay Wray,[32] Kong seems to function as a solitary peak predator during the early part of the film.

~•~

32) Whatever happened to Fay Wray?

~•~

3. Odysseus seems to function mostly in the HOSTILE STRENGTH quadrant. My friend Dr. Craig Hargis suggests

that Odysseus, as the complete human, functions in all areas of the grid, but to me he rarely seems SPINELESS or a CLINGING VINE.

4. Dr. Hargis made the same observation about Hamlet, seeing him acting in all areas of the grid. It seems to me Hamlet spends a lot of time SKEPTICAL, OFTEN GLOOMY, RESENTS BEING BOSSED. Having watched and read this play repeatedly over the past half century, I do not claim to know what Shakespeare really had in mind. Harold Bloom called *Hamlet* the *"Poem Unlimited"*.

5. Like Scarlett O'Hara, Bugs Bunny frequently falls in the IMPATIENT WITH OTHERS, SELF-SEEKING, SARCASTIC box, but he acts in a trickster, ludic fashion. He can certainly COMPLAIN IF NECESSARY, and he sometimes acts FRIENDLY and CONSIDERATE

6. I read *Portnoy's Complaint* (1969) by Phillip Roth back in the late 1980's when working through *Prometheus Rising*. I found it interesting to reread the novel in 2021. It certainly demonstrates the quantum leap in allowable depictions of sexuality since the publication of *Ulysses* in 1922. Also, in the decades since I had first read *Portnoy's Complaint,* I read a number of other narratives about growing up as a Jewish male in the United States which had made me think of *Portnoy's Complaint* such as *I, Wabenzi* by Rafi Zabor, *The Miranda Complex* by Barry Smolin, and various writings by Louis Zukofsky. Portnoy seems to spend a lot of time in the BITTER, RESENTFUL, COMPLAINING box.

7. In *Ishtar Rising* Bob Wilson calls Leopold Bloom "a completely oral personality." Bloom seems FRIENDLY, CONSIDERATE, and HELPFUL. He certainly has a different personality than his model Odysseus. Where Portnoy certainly considers himself Jewish, Bloom usually does not except when

confronted by the anti-Semitic Citizen. However, the other characters in the novel overwhelmingly perceive Bloom as a Jew.

8. Nixon seems a challenge; he often falls in the SHREWD AND CALCULATING, ONLY THINKS OF HIMSELF, SELFISH box, but I suspect that he usually perceived himself as acting in the national interest. Preparing to write on this chapter I rewatched *Frost/Nixon* which gives an interesting McLuhanesque picture of the role of television in the creation of the national image of Richard Nixon.

9. Thomas Jefferson: a great writer, a slave owner, and a rapist. I remember talking with Bob Wilson about Thomas Jefferson the last time I saw Bob in 2000 at a Richard Bandler Neuro-Linguistic Programming workshop in Anaheim. We talked about how people in the future might judge us for actions which many accept today. I think of how some Americans consider abortion murder and some Americans consider eating meat murder. Jefferson's public image has declined in the decades since Bob and I had that conversation. Bob used to watch the musical *1776* every year on the Fourth of July. I just finished rewatching it on July 4, 2021. That film certainly whitewashes the troublesome aspects of Jefferson's life. On the Interpersonal Grid Jefferson seems to often fall into the MAKES A GOOD IMPRESSION, OFTEN ADMIRED, RESPECTED BY OTHERS box.

10. Karen Armstrong suggests that St. Paul didn't actually write some of the letters attributed to him in the New Testament. She sees him as a much more revolutionary figure than many of his critics do. She sees what some see as Paul's misogyny as the contribution of later writers, and she sees Paul's attitudes as closer to those of the historical Jesus. He might fall in the LOVES EVERYONE and TRIES TO

COMFORT EVERYONE boxes. I know this differs from the Nietzschean perception of Paul.

11. Donald Duck seems a great example of hostile weakness. Interestingly, in the Disney cartoons Mickey Mouse seems an example of friendly strength and Goofy of friendly weakness. Pete seems an example of hostile strength, and Minnie has a touch of hostile strength with her cutting sense of humor. Donald's behavior often falls in the BITTER, RESENTFUL, COMPLAINING box.

12. Iago seems to fall in the CRUEL AND UNKIND box. Orson Welles saw impotence as the heart of Iago's problem. Hate seems to fuel a lot of Iago's behavior. Leslie Fiedler wrote a terrific book called *The Stranger in Shakespeare*. It focuses on the outsiders in Shakespeare's plays: the Woman Joan of Arc in *1 Henry VI*, the Moor Othello in *Othello*, the Jew Shylock in *The Merchant of Venice*, and the Native Caliban in *The Tempest*. Fiedler saw Iago as motivated by homosexual jealousy.

13. Jane Eyre seems one of the most centered characters Wilson asks the reader to analyze. She seems SELF-RESPECTING, HELPFUL, CONSIDERATE, FRIENDLY, COOPERATIVE, and APPRECIATIVE. She CAN BE OBEDIENT, CAN COMPLAIN IF NECESSARY, CAN BE FRANK AND HONEST, and CAN BE STRICT IF NECESSARY. She seems ABLE TO CRITICIZE SELF, ABLE TO DOUBT OTHERS, and ABLE TO TAKE CARE OF SELF. She often has behaviors in all of the boxes in the inner circle of the Interpersonal Grid except for WELL THOUGHT OF, but that changes by the end of the novel. I love film historian David Thomson, and he loved the 2011 film version of *Jane Eyre* and wrote disparagingly of the 1943 version starring Orson Welles. I loved the 2011 film as well, but when I reread the novel I kept hearing Rochester speaking in Orson Welles' voice.

14. Joseph Stalin seems to fall into the DICTATORIAL box. Stalin's alcoholic father beat him as a child. I find the mix of fictional and historical characters on this list interesting. Of course, fictional accounts have shaped my perceptions of many of the historical figures, especially Joan of Arc and Thomas Jefferson.

15. Films have really shaped my perceptions of Joan of Arc, especially Rivette's two-part film *Joan the Maiden* (1994) and Dreyer's *The Passion of Joan of Arc* (1928). As a visionary, her behavior doesn't fit in the Interpersonal Grid as easily as does that of most others on this list. She CAN BE OBEDIENT, she seems ABLE TO GIVE ORDERS, and sometimes her behavior falls in the MANAGES OTHERS, DOMINATING, BOSSY box.

16. Dr. Tim seems like a somewhat centered person who could move into all four quadrants when necessary. He seems ABLE TO DOUBT OTHERS and ABLE TO CRITICIZE SELF. He often seemed SELF-RELIANT AND ASSERTIVE, SELF-CONFIDENT, INDEPENDENT.

17. Uncle Al also often falls in the SELF-RELIANT AND ASSERTIVE, SELF-CONFIDENT, INDEPENDENT box. Crowley also seems ABLE TO CRITICIZE SELF and at times seems IMPATIENT WITH OTHERS' MISTAKES, SELF-SEEKING, SARCASTIC.

18. Dr Wilson, like Dr. Tim, seems a rather centered person. He seems HELPFUL, CONSIDERATE, and FRIENDLY, but he could COMPLAIN IF NECESSARY. He rarely seemed OBEDIENT.

19. Mao once again seems DICTATORIAL. As with Stalin, Mao's father beat him as a child.

20. Carl Jung seems rather centered. His autobiography *Memories, Dreams, Reflections* gives an interesting view of his world.

21. The Wikipedia page on the Secret Chiefs talks about the Sufi "cosmic spiritual hierarchy". As with Joan of Arc, these sorts of visionary personalities don't behave in the same way as ordinary people, and their behavior doesn't fall as simply into the Interpersonal Grid.

22. Hannibal Lecter terrifies me. Bob Wilson said he would have liked to have dinner with Dr. Lecter. I would want to stay very far away from him. Lecter tends to kill most people who perceive his murderous nature. He doesn't choose to kill Clarice Starling, however, since he finds a world with Starling alive a more interesting world. Perhaps he would have found a world with Bob Wilson alive a more interesting world as well. Lecter's behavior often falls in the CRUEL AND UNKIND box.

23. I seem somewhat centered, but all too often I fall in the SKEPTICAL, OFTEN GLOOMY, RESENTS BEING BOSSED box.

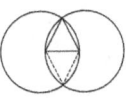

20) A Painful Case and/or *Prometheus Rising*, Chapter 6

Well, I finished my month of meditating "for two fifteen-minute sessions a day for a month." I saw two people who "always manage to upset you or make you defensive." They could still press my "territorial retreat buttons." I guess one month didn't do it, at least for me. Bob said that he intended the exercises in *Prometheus Rising* to loosen the imprints. I think they do that, but more profound change may call for something more. In *The Illuminati Papers* Bob says, "Want to contact Higher Intelligence? It's easy, really" (pg. 3). I misremembered that as saying, "Brain change is easy." I think about how *asana* means "easy pose". Many yoga asanas do not seem easy. When brain change goes well, it often seems easy. I know that when I lose weight steadily, it seems easy. I find myself in that "zone" where I lose weight without much apparent struggle. I have trouble reentering that zone though. I think of Catullus's poem "Odi et Amo" which Pound translates:

I hate and love. Why? You may ask but

It beats me. I feel it done to me, and ache.

Bob says something similar about bravery and cowardice. The brain-body system as a whole acts without the conscious mind's control. In *Schrödinger's Cat* he talks about quantum causality, how the whole system causes changes in the whole system, and domesticated primates tend to take too much credit and too much blame.

After decades of martial arts, Weight Watchers, ballet, yoga, therapy, etc., I still struggle with the first circuit. During the first eight months of lockdown last year I lost 78 pounds. Then during the holidays I fell off the wagon, and I have struggled to get back on. I feel like Gene Kelly in *Brigadoon*. I found this magic place where I lost weight in an easy fashion without much struggle. Now I don't know how to find my way back. Hopefully it will not take me a hundred years.

Speaking of immortality, if I do live another hundred years or more, I want to do a lot of reading. For chapter six of *Prometheus Rising* Bob tells the reader to subscribe to some magazines. In the 1980's I didn't consider myself a liberal or a conservative, so I didn't subscribe to the first two magazines at that time. I did subscribe to *Fate* and *The Skeptical Inquirer*. In 2021, I find myself much more of a liberal politically. Some people might consider me conservative in some areas: I prefer books made of paper to ebooks, I prefer jazz and classical music, etc. In any event, I have subscribed to all four periodicals in the first four exercises of chapter six this year. I find it interesting that in the age of next day deliveries, magazine subscriptions still sometimes take months to process. I have one issue of *National Review,* two issues of *The New York Review of Books,* and three issues of *Fate* sitting here to read right now. *The Skeptical Inquirer* has not started to arrive yet. I suspect these four exercises will take up a big chunk of my reading time for the next year or so.

I have read two issues of *National Review* so far. They have a variety of authors but the writing tends towards conservative, Catholic viewpoints. Most writers seem anti-Trump and anti-Democrat. I find it interesting that many people today know Robin Williams's impression of William F. Buckley from *Aladdin,* but they have never heard of Buckley, the founder of *National Review.*

I have started reading an issue of *The New York Review of Books.* I remember in 1999 they still allowed free access to their archives online. I read all of the available articles there by musicologists Joseph Kerman and Charles Rosen that summer.

FNORD

I had forgotten the vicissitudes of getting magazines by snail mail. The cover of the new issue of *National Review* arrived with nothing inside. Either intentionally or accidentally most of the magazine did not arrive in my mailbox. Oh well. I must admit it pleased me to have such an easy excuse not to read the new issue. *The Skeptical Inquirer* still hasn't arrived.

I enjoyed reading *Fate* magazine. I read a nice article on pets on the Titanic, and it pleased me that one author still believes in the Priory of Sion. I wonder what Bob Wilson would have made of the debunking of that conspiracy.

About fifteen years ago, doing the exercises in this chapter, I bought a copy of *Scientific American*. It had an article on how researchers had burn victims play a skiing video game, and playing the game lessened the patients' perceived pain as they vividly imagined the intense cold of the world of the game. This pleased me because some of my fellow teachers at the time perceived videogames as worthless.

I have had a number of discussions with intelligent Muslims recently. I forwarded Bob Wilson's interview with David Bohm to some Muslim friends, and they really liked it. This year I heard more references to Ramadan than ever before. Even Weight Watchers had an article on how to follow the WW plan during Ramadan this year. I don't remember Weight Watchers ever mentioning Ramadan before (and I first joined Weight Watchers back in 1978).

I have little desire to "find a victim and explain the universe to him or her, until they are able to escape you" at this time. I may not repeat this exercise this time around. I fear I have done too much of this over the years. In high school I defined my life mission as love, learn, create. About twenty years ago I revised that to love, listen, learn, create. I would like to learn to listen better.

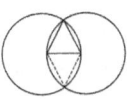

21) Ivy Day in the Committee Room and/or *Prometheus Rising,* Chapter 7

Exercise one asks the reader to "Compare Greece in the 4th Century BC, Rome in the First Century AD, Southern Europe at the beginning of the Renaissance, England c.1600-1900, New York c. 1900-1950, and California today." I find it interesting that the first four categories parallel the structure of *Asimov's Guide to Shakespeare.* Asimov divides the poems and plays into four categories. He begins with works set in Greece, then in Rome, then in Italy and southern Europe, and then in England. Now the dates don't exactly parallel those Wilson gives, but Shakespeare seems fascinated by those times and places teeming with new ideas: Classical Greece and Rome, Renaissance Italy and his own England. He also had a fascination with the deep background for the England he lived in. Ezra Pound's *Cantos* also focus a great deal on the focal points of Ancient Greece, Ancient Rome, southern Europe in the late Middle Ages and the early Renaissance, and Early Modern England.

I love Robert Graves's *I, Claudius* and *Claudius the God* and the BBC television series based on them. I have had the pleasure of showing the TV series to a number of high school classes, often after teaching Shakespeare's *Julius Caesar* and *Antony and Cleopatra.* I found it interesting to teach these works during the last three presidential administrations. I found it interesting to see the parallels between Ancient Rome and contemporary America.

Contemplating New York from 1900 to 1950, I think of Henry James's visit to New York in 1904. He seemed deeply aware of the cultures of both London and New York at the time of this transition of world power and wealth. Louis Zukofsky found it significant that James visited New York in the year of Zukofsky's birth. Zukofsky lived mostly in New York, and Pound had a huge influence on him. Zukofsky's *"A"* seems to me a valuable work for examining the shifting strands of world culture and history during this period. Contemplating this period I also think of the evolution of jazz, from the music of Louis Armstrong to that of Duke Ellington to the new bebop of the 1940's developed by Thelonious Monk, Dizzy Gillespie, Charlie Parker, and others.

"California today" has at least three meanings: the California of 1983, the original publication date; the California of 1997, the revised second edition's publication date, and the California of 2021. I first read *Prometheus Rising* in Arizona in 1985, and I looked towards California as sort of a promised land where Leary lived and Bob had lived (and would live again). I reread the book many times in Arizona and did most of the exercises there. I moved back to California in 1997. (My family had moved from San Jose to Tucson in 1978). It seems less of a promised land to me today, but it also seems as though we find the fastest growing economies today in Asia. In the future I suspect that a lot of future wealth will come from space as we have completed our circumnavigation of the globe over the past few thousand years.

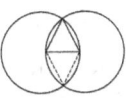

22) A Mother and/or *Prometheus Rising* Chapter 8

Bob alters Crowley's attributions of the Tarot, attributing the Knights to earth and the Princesses to fire where Crowley attributes the Knights to fire and the Princesses to earth. Many people have tinkered with the attributions of the Tarot for various reasons. Bob also consistently reversed the order of the High Priestess and Empress trumps. He and Leary did that in *The Game of Life*, and Bob also used that ordering in a *Finnegans Wake* workshop I attended in Dallas in 1987.

It seems clear that my two strongest imprints fall on the first and third circuits. I have wondered whether I fall more in the Prince of Discs category or in the Knight of Swords category as described in this chapter. I always wanted to fall in the Knight of Swords category ("sometimes the artist"), but I suspect I fall in the Prince of Discs category (if not the Knight of Discs category). My wife has frequently told me I should have become a lawyer.

I find it humbling that I had forgotten that Bob mentions Scarlett O'Hara on page 117. I spent a lot over the last year thinking about Scarlett for the exercises for chapter five of *Prometheus Rising*, and I totally forgot that Bob mentions her in chapter 8. I sometimes arrogantly think I know this book backwards and forwards, but the space-time event of the actual book contains more than my memory of the book. (Part of me could become lost just rereading Proust's *In Search of Lost Time* over and over again, since the actual novel contains so much more than my memory of that novel about memory.)

I love Johann Sebastian Bach's music, but I do not think he wrote "the sexiest music in history." Bob Wilson radically affected my taste in music, but I think the thirty years that separate our births led me to my having a very different musical fourth circuit imprint than he did.

FNORD

On page 125 Wilson writes, "A mass made of people who have intense curiosity about why Beethoven went in for string quartets after the Ninth Symphony . . . is not a mass that will be easily led into dull, dehumanizing labor at traditional jobs." I asked on Facebook, "Why do you think Beethoven focused on string quartets after the Ninth Symphony?" Novelist Rafi Zabor answered,

> Turn it down! It's so loud can't hear a fuchen thing! Okay, a bit more seriously: at least since the Razumovskys and probably before, he had brought his most uncompromising summings-up and steps-ahead before the demanding bar of the quartet form, its inherent possibilities and limitations. And there he was, either at an end or a new beginning, or both. So he wrote quartets. Sounds like a good answer, and though it likely won't last it's good enough for now.

He added, "Compare/contrast, say, with the primary inwardness of the last three piano sonatas, which must have been a relief to compose during the monstrous work of getting the Missa and the Ninth done."

Composer Robert Rabinowitz responded,

> Rafi Zabor I was thinking that as well. For my own compositions I find it particularly daunting to tackle more than about 8 instruments. Sometimes it's just the massive amount of notes on a single page that

can just become stressful to look at. Even though the reality is there is a lot of section playing going on so, of course, it isn't as if there are 70 or more instruments playing different lines. Hmmm - wonder if that's been done, I may have to do it.

At Rawillumination.net, Tom Jackson asked, "Is it just a coincidence that the Beethoven-obsessed Wilson brings up string quartets in a chapter about the four circuits? And if not, what instruments relate to which circuit? I would say the cello is Circuit One, viola Circuit Two and the two violins circuits Three and Four." The cello seems very erotic to me, so I would associate it with the fourth circuit. At first I thought to assign the two violins to the first two circuits. The top dog – bottom dog dynamic works well for the second circuit, but I don't think the viola fits in well with the third circuit. The viola seems the least egotistical part of the string quartet. It rarely gets the solo voice or the strong bass line of the cello. ("It's all about the bass.") When following a score for a string quartet, I find it easiest to follow the first violin part or the cello part. I have to strain to follow the viola part which tends to play a largely supportive role in Beethoven's quartets. I would associate the viola with the first circuit and the violins with circuits two and three. The verbal chatter of the third circuit fits in well with the first violin, and the second violin fits in well with the second circuit. I find it interesting that a string quartet has four members, and most of Beethoven's quartets had four movements. Four times four equals sixteen, the Tower in the Tarot, and Beethoven wrote 16 string quartets. The Tarot has sixteen court cards as well. Sixteen flowerpots play a pivotal role in P. G. Wodehouse's *Leave It to Psmith*, one of my favorite books.

Amazon informed me that they cannot fulfill my order for *The Skeptical Inquirer* and refunded my money. I do find myself enjoying reading *The New York Review of Books*. The October 7, 2021, issue includes a review of a biography of

Portuguese writer Fernando Pessoa. The review says Aleister Crowley "had plans to tap Pessoa to lead a Lisbon brand of his Ordo Templi Orientis" (pg. 19). Bob Wilson wrote that some intrepid soul sent out cards making over 1000 people Outer Heads of the O.T.O. As an Outer Head of the O.T.O. myself, I declare all of you reading this Outer Heads of the O.T.O. as well.

I have deliberately stayed away from Crowley's books over the past sixteen years, but they have definitely shaped the way I see the world.

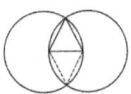

23) Grace and/or *Prometheus Rising* Chapter 9

The discussion of Patty Hearst's "responsibility" for her actions as Tania make think of comparing the novel *The Shining* by Stephen King with the film *The Shining* directed by Stanley Kubrick. King has complained that in the film Jack seems firmly responsible for his actions, whereas in the novel the hotel seems at least in part responsible for his actions. One might model the Overlook Hotel as a model of Chapel Perilous, especially at the end of the film. In fact, various models of Chapel Perilous appear in Kubrick's films, from the ending of *2001: A Space Odyssey* to the brainwashing scenes in *A Clockwork Orange* to basic training in *Full Metal Jacket* to Tom Cruise's New York City wasteland quest in *Eyes Wide Shut*.

Apuleius Charlton pointed out that many of Jim Jones's victims did not commit suicide; armed followers of Jones forced many of them to drink the poison. I remember seeing part of a TV movie about Jim Jones starring Powers Boothe. I thought of that film when I saw Oliver Stone's *Nixon* where Powers Boothe played Alexander Haig and Bob Wilson's beloved Anthony Hopkins played Nixon. I contemplated writing a book on the magic of casting called *Casting Spells*. The movie *Nixon* seemed rather sympathetic to the character Richard Nixon, but I kept thinking of Hannibal Lecter in the back of my mind.

Bob writes of immortalism in this chapter. Someone once asked the physicist R. C. W. Ettinger why, if cryogenics provided the chance of immortality, more people didn't take advantage of it. Ettinger said, "Many are cold, but few are frozen."

Exercise 6 in this chapter says to become a Nazi for 33 minutes. I did this; I began by studying a bit of German on Duolingo. I had intended to watch a bit of Wagner's *Der fliegende Holländer* I had DVR'd next, but my wife asked me to run an errand. I had a Sonny Rollins CD on in the car, and I found it distasteful in my Nazi head-space. I switched to the classical radio station and felt grateful that they had some German music playing (Mozart's Thirtieth Symphony). I found it sobering how quickly this exercise affected my judgment.

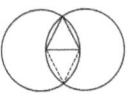

24) The Dead and/or *Prometheus Rising* Chapter 10

Exercise 1: "Become a pious Roman Catholic. Explain in three pages why the Church is still infallible and holy despite Popes like Alexander VI (the Borgia Pope), Pius XII (ally of Hitler), etc."

Brothers and sisters in Christ, thank you for spending this time with me to contemplate the role of Church in God's plan. First of all, the Church is not infallible nor has it claimed to be infallible. However, we do believe the Pope is infallible in matters of faith and morals when speaking *ex cathedra*. Please note that this belief was not canon law at the time of Alexander VI. Also, please note that the Venerable Pope Pius XII was certainly not Hitler's ally. He did all he could to protect many Jews. He had very little power at the time of the Fascist take-over of Italy, and he did all he could to protect Jews from the Nazis.

Putting all that aside, God sent his only Son to give each and every one of us the opportunity for life everlasting. This is the real life extension Doctors Leary and Wilson searched in vain for. God established the Church to guide us to everlasting life. The Church exists by the will of God. All humans except for Jesus and Mary commit sins. Popes are included in this. They may be imperfect, but that is part of God's miraculous plan.

In *Faust* Goethe has Satan say, "I am part of that power which eternally wills evil and eternally works good." In a small way we each play a role in God's miraculous plan, despite all we squander of our divine entitlements. In general, the popes have been good men, often great men, who shoulder a tremendous burden. Each priest, in fact, shoulders a tremendous burden, helping to guide the members of his flock in the right direction, dealing with all the privations of life and the hostility of so many people, especially in our modern, all too secular, world.

The Church is certainly holy. *Oxford Languages* defines holy as "dedicated or consecrated to God or a religious purpose; sacred." The Church is certainly "dedicated or consecrated to God". It always has been, and it always will be. (I find myself slipping out of E-Prime, but some things are just self-evident.) I can only feel sorry for Dr. Wilson. He was a very good man, but, alas, he was led away from the one true Church by evil companions, I fear. Perhaps the weak wording of this exercise reveals a part of him trying to remind himself of the one true Church. The sisters tried so hard to teach him about the role of the Church in history, but his human hubris led him to value his own opinions over those of the Church. He preferred to think for himself, alas, and to always question authority. Perhaps he would have had a happier life if he had just trusted God.

Exercise 5: "James Joyce said he never met a boring human being. Try to explain this. Try to get into the Joycean head space where everybody is a separate reality-island full of mystery and surprise. In other words, *learn to observe.*"

I have spent a lot of time trying to get into the Joycean head space. I wrote my master's thesis on the influence of *Finnegans Wake* on *Masks of the Illuminati*. When I interned with him, the poet B. H. Fairchild recommended the audiobook of *Dubliners* where a different Irish actor or writer read each story. I got that audiobook and listened to it over and over again in the car as I finished my master's degree and at the same time finished writing *An Insider's Guide to Robert Anton Wilson*. I also listened to a cassette of Joyce reading from *Ulysses* and *Finnegans Wake* which also included other voices reading Joyce's two books of poetry, and I listened to a cassette of Irish songs that included a short version of "Finnegan's Wake". I continued listening to this set of Joycean metaprogramming tapes after I got my master's degree as I continued working on this book on Joyce and Wilson. I would mix in some Wilson tapes as well.

During my periods of Joyce obsession I have read Joyce's books over and over again along with many books about Joyce. I had *Finnegans Wake* study groups from 1985 to 2021, and I watched a bunch of films about Joyce. I used to have a party on January 6 each year where we would watch the 1987 film *The Dead*. Joyce's story "The Dead" takes place at a party for the Feast of the Epiphany around January 6, 1904. I took Bob Wilson to see that film in 1988. My last real period of Joyce obsession came as I prepared to give a talk at the 22nd North American James Joyce Conference in 2011 on the question of whether Joyce included references to the Oz books in *Finnegans Wake*. I finished reading the *Wake* four times and *Ulysses* once that year. Of course, I think of Joyce a lot and read a bit of Joyce even when not in one of these obsessive Joyce periods. I did finish rereading *Dubliners* and two books on Joyce as I did this exercise over Christmas break 2021-2022. I also read a bit in Brenda Maddox's *Nora: A Biography of Nora Joyce*. I have tried to read that biography since it came out in the 80's. I still have about 230 pages to go. At one point she refers to some of Joyce's letters to Nora as "even worse than *Ulysses*". Now, she meant their sexual explicitness, but I kept hearing the voices of many of my professors calling *Ulysses* the greatest novel ever written, so "even worse than *Ulysses*" could refer to every novel every written. Perhaps I should have "even worse than *Ulysses*" printed on the back of all of my books. On page 296, Maddox writes of Harriet Weaver's generosity towards Joyce, "Miss Weaver's *largesse,* some have argued, also impoverished world literature by allowing James Joyce to waste his lyrical gift on the bad joke of *Finnegans Wake.*" She does not provide any citation with the identity of these "some". I know that *Finnegans Wake* frustrates many readers, including many of Joyce's admirers such as Vladimir Nabokov.

I guess this Joyce obsession has helped me to observe. It seems like looking for quarters [meaning] everywhere, in every person and every situation. Bob Wilson told me he loved Edna O'Brien's description of *Ulysses* as a day where nothing, and everything, happens. Certainly, everybody seems "a separate reality-island full of mystery and surprise". February 2, 2022, marks the centennial of the first publication of *Ulysses* as well as Joyce's 140th birthday. Small pockets of our culture will "Try to get into the Joycean head space" this year. Hopefully this will bear some positive fruit for our troubled world.

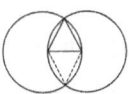

25) *Prometheus Rising,* Chapter 11

On page 166-167 of the Hilaritas edition of *Prometheus Rising* it says:

> The *avant-garde* 20% of the population, due to the Consciousness Movement (a secularization of much ancient shamanic wisdom), already understands every "wild" idea in the last few pages. They have had enough neurosomatic experience to know that they were once totally robotized (as most people still are) and are knowingly engaged in acquiring more neurosomatic know-how. *When this reaches 51% of the population, a major historical revolution will have occurred, as profound as the Life Extension Revolution.**
>
> * Please re-read this sentence, and think about it.

This passage becomes a strange loop, telling the reader to re-read "this sentence" over and over again, as well one should. Speaking of the Life Extension Revolution, I find it interesting how many people in 2022 still consider death inevitable. Also, the phrase "neurological know how" appeared earlier in Wilson's "8 Basic Winner and Loser Scripts" from *The Illuminati Papers:*

Circuit	The Eight Basic Loser Scripts	The Eight Basic Winner Scripts
1. Biosurvival	"I don't know how to defend myself."	"I will live forever, or die trying."
2. Emotional-territorial	"They all intimidate me."	"I am free; you are free; we can have our separate trips or we can have the same trip."
3. Semantic	"I can't solve my problems."	"I am learning more about everything, including how to learn more."
4. Sociosexual	"Everything I like is illegal, immoral, or fattening."	"Love and do what thou wilt "
5. Neurosomatic	"I can't help the way I feel."	"How I feel depends on my neurological know how."
6. Metaprogramming	"Why do I have such lousy luck?"	"I make my own coincidences, synchronicities, luck, and Destiny."
7. Neurogenetic	"Evolution is blind and "impersonal.""	"Future evolution depends on my decisions now."
8. Neuroatomic	"I'm not psychic, and I doubt that anyone is."	"In the province of the mind, what is believed true is true, or becomes true within limits to be learned by experience and experiment." (Dr. John Lilly)

(For circuit 6, "Luck, synchronicities, and destiny" makes a more interesting acronym.)

A couple of paragraphs later Wilson says,

> Everybody "knows" that the Sixth Symphony is "pantheistic," but whether Beethoven was an ideological pantheist or not, that way of responding to nature is normal and natural right-brain Circuit V functioning. That is, anybody on the Fifth Circuit will *"talk like a pantheist"* whether or not he has developed a "philosophy" about pantheism.
> – pg. 167

I find it interesting that many people have accused Ibn 'Arabi of pantheism. At the end of this chapter Wilson tells the reader to "Attend a Sufi week-end seminar." I have taken a few online Ibn 'Arabi classes, and last month I had a virtual "Sufi week-end seminar" which included an online Dhikr and an online Ibn 'Arabi study group as well as reading some Ibn 'Arabi on my own. Perhaps my whole life has become a virtual Sufi week-end seminar.

On page 171 Wilson quotes Scottish psychiatrist Ian Suttie, "The physician's love heals the patient." I have taught many children of doctors in high school classes. Some of these students have suggested that money means happiness. Perhaps "The physician's love of money heals the patient." (No, Eric, that sounds bitter. I have met many physicians that I like and respect.)

On page 172 Wilson quotes Ezra Pound. I started reading Pound because of Bob Wilson's writings. I bought *ABC of Reading* in either 1982 or 1983. I enjoyed the beginning of it, but I put it down when he started quoting Chaucer in Middle English which I didn't understand. In the summer of 1983 I got Pound's *Guide to Kulchur* out of the library, and reading that made me fall in love with Pound's writing. I read him voraciously, becoming horrified by his fascism. I would stop reading him for a while, but then I would return to him, learn more and become horrified again, and stop reading him for a while. In the first few years of the current century I taught the whole *Cantos* three years in a row. Each time I said I would never do it again. I found it exhausting but very rewarding. I haven't read much of him since then, although I did use the anthology he co-edited, *Confucius to Cummings,* for about twelve college courses, and I used *ABC of Reading* for a creative writing class.

Wilson discusses marijuana in this chapter. I find it interesting that California legalized recreational pot in the same November 2016 election that saw the election of Donald Trump. I have not noticed much change in California since this legalization except for the presence of pot billboards along the freeways.

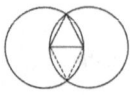

26) *Ulysses* at 100

In 2011 the North American James Joyce Conference in Pasadena, CA, had a *Ulysses* reading group and a *Finnegans Wake* reading group. I don't recall seeing anyone besides myself who attended both events. The Joyce scholars who seemed to me the "Big Guns" (Shelly Brivic, Tony Thwaites, Vincent Cheng, etc.) attended the *Wake* meeting but not the *Ulysses* event. A number of grad students from local universities attended the *Ulysses* event. They all seemed to own their own copy of the revised edition of *Ulysses*. I don't recall seeing any grad student at the *Wake* event. The *Ulysses* event took place at the Huntington Library. The *Finnegans Wake* event took place in Albert Einstein's library at Cal Tech. Ailing Joycean John Bishop attended the *Wake* event via Skype.

I just finished watched Ken Burns and Lynn Novak's documentary on Ernest Hemingway. Some people consider Hemingway the dominant author in English in the twentieth century. Others think Joyce had a bigger impact. McLuhan thought Joyce prefigured the radically changed technologies of the twentieth century and beyond. Perhaps our current world resembles the works of Robert Heinlein, Robert Anton Wilson, and Philip K. Dick more than the worlds of Hemingway and Joyce.

I write this on January 31, 2022. February 2 marks the one hundredth anniversary of the publication of *Ulysses*. The Washington Football Team plans to announce its new name on the same day. I don't see any connection between the two events, but I plan to celebrate both. I have loved Washington's NFL team since 1971, but its name has bothered me for years. I liked when it changed its name to the Washington Football Team. I have read *Ulysses* thirteen times at this point. Bob Wilson told me to read it forty times. I don't plan to do that anytime soon, but if I live beyond the age of 111, I may well read it a few more times. I may even reach forty read-throughs.

At the time Bob told me to read *Ulysses* forty times, we had just discussed Ezra Pound's suggestion to read forty Henry James novels if you want to learn how to write a novel. Bob and I commented that neither of us had ever had much success reading Henry James. I suspect that conversation influenced his *Ulysses* comment. Of course, I have a tendency to take Bob too literally, and he might have simply meant simply to read the book a lot.

In his 1996 essay "Brain Books", Bob Wilson wrote: "Nobody has really entered the 20th century if they haven't digested *Ulysses*. And if they haven't entered the 20th century, they're going to fall pretty far behind pretty soon, as we enter the 21st."

The *Christian Science Quarterly* gives the Bible readings and readings from *Science and Health with Key to the Scriptures* for each week with the intention that the reader do these readings every day. You can order the *Quarterly* here:

https://quarterly.christianscience.com/

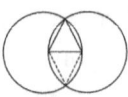

27) *Prometheus Rising* Chapter 12

The "language" of this circuit [the sixth/morphogenetic] is the multi-level language of *Finnegans Wake*, where Finnegan is Finn-again, Finn Mac Cool of Irish legend reborn and Huck Finn again also, sailing down "Missus Liffey," both the river Anna Liffey in Ireland and Huck Finn's Mississippi; where Mark the Wan is King Mark, cuckolded by Tristan, but Mark the Twy is Mark Twain, married to a wife he called "Livvy" just like the Irish river, and Mark the Tris is cuckolded Mark and cuckolding Tristan in one; while Marcus Lyons is all of them, plus Mark the apostle, his emblematic lion (always shown with him in medieval art), Leo the lion, Leo in the zodiac, and all associated fire-signs, and one of the Four Old Men (Matt Gregory, Marcus Lyons, Luke Tarpey and Johnny McDougall) who haunt the dreamer all night long, symbolizing the four evangelists, the four bedposts surrounding the sleeper, the four antique circuits, the four suits of Tarot or ordinary playing cards, the four elements of the ancients, and all the other fours that Jung has found omnipresent in the "collective unconscious."

- *Prometheus Rising*, pg. 187

Beethoven, to cite him one more time, said "Anybody who understands my music will never be unhappy again."⁽³³⁾ That is because his music is the song of the Sixth Circuit, of Gaia, the Life Spirit, becoming conscious of Herself, of Her powers, of Her own capacities for infinite progress.

– ibid., pg. 190

~•~

33) Perhaps – scholars remain unsure about whether the Big B actually said this.

~•~

In a February 15 comment on Tom Jackson's blog post about the sixth circuit chapter of *Prometheus Rising,* Spookah (BFHN) said...

> Thank you Tom Jackson for opening the discussion on chapter 12, and for providing the links. The first exercize sort of links back to the Heinlein quote, along with the picture, on page 107.
>
> I'd say that we are maybe more used to comparing big city life with ant colonies, with the type of time-lapses found in Ron Fricke's *Koyaanisqatsi* or *Baraka* now fairly common place. Ex. 5: "see how long after reading this chapter you encounter an amazing coincidence." So I read this chapter 12 on Monday afternoon. Then the same evening, I watched the last episode of the docu mini-series *Capitalism* (2014), which featured excerpts from the films *Intolerance* (the Babylonian part) and *Scarface* (the 1932 Howard Hawks version). It so happened that I had watched *Intolerance* the previous week, and *Scarface* the previous day. *Intolerance* was a favorite of RAW, it gets a haiku in *Email to the Universe*, and he asked to watch it on the first week of the MLA 8 Circuits of Mind course. As for *Scarface*, a few hours before going to see it I was

reading a few pages from Eric Wagner's *Insider's Guide to RAW*, including the lexicon entry for 23, which ends with this: "after reading sombunall of this book, you will probably notice a few more 23's than usual. Perhaps a lot more. Just a coincidence, I suspect." I did spot a 23 during the film, as a street number right above the main character's head. Ex. 6: "What messages is your right brain trying to send to your left brain?" So far I came up with three possibilities. The first is that Bob Wilson really seems up to something here, and that I should keep on studying *PR* and doing the exercizes. Another is that Eric Wagner might already be part of the Jungian collective unconscious, conspiring together with Ishtar and Al Capone in the mythical realm. The last one is wondering if I should start to worry, because it's usually not a good sign when you think the TV is talking to you.

Intolerance also has a scene in the modern section where someone finds a quarter. I wonder if that scene inspired the quarter finding exercises in *Prometheus Rising*. For a few years a mall in Hollywood had an elephant design motif inspired by *Intolerance*, but they removed the elephants because the film Griffith directed before *Intolerance*, *Birth of a Nation*, contained so much egregious racism. Thinking of elephants makes me think of Heinlein's "The Man Who Traveled in Elephants."

The coin flipping character George Raft played in the original *Scarface* became a cinematic archetype, showing up in the final dance sequence in *Singin' in the Rain* and most interestingly in *Some Like It Hot* where an older George Raft responds to the trope.

I like the film *Ishtar*, and I enjoyed the condescending responses I got from people who had not seen the film but who "knew" how bad it "was" when I rented the video thirty odd years ago. I love how Neil Gaiman used Ishtar in *Sandman*. People have different notions about the ordering of the sixth and seventh circuits. Leary usually saw the sixth circuit as the neuroelectric circuit and the seventh circuit as the neurogenetic circuit. Bob Wilson usually reversed these. Richard Rasa addresses this in the afterword to the Hilaritas edition of *Prometheus Rising*. I love Tim Leary's comment, "This listing of possible future levels of human intelligence is necessarily tentative, suggestive, semantically fragile, and intellectually risky" (*Flashbacks,* pg. 386).

In *Quantum Psychology* Bob uses the Leary order, but he renames the neurogenetic circuit the morphogenetic circuit inspired by Rupert Sheldrake. Bob commented, "Where Leary and Grof, like Jung and Freud, assumed the non-ego information, not known to the brain, must come from the genes, Sheldrake, a biologist, knew that genes cannot carry such information. He therefore posited a non-local field, like those in quantum theory, which he named the morphogenetic field" (pg. 191).

In *Schrödinger's Cat* Bob suggests that many people like to think of evolution as a Promethean struggle, but, really, one only needs to relax and cooperate with the DNA code. Following his observation in *Quantum Psychology,* I tend to think of this as cooperating with the morphogenetic fields rather than the DNA code. Promethean struggle makes me think of Beethoven's music, and cooperating with the morphogenetic fields makes me think of Mozart's. I had planned to spend most of 2022 listening to Beethoven CDs when driving and then switch to Mozart as the year progresses, but a CD got stuck in the CD player yesterday. Perhaps I will switch to streaming Mozart piano concerti. One might see this as a synchronicity since the CD got stuck as I prepared to write this entry on this chapter which features Beethoven's music so prominently.

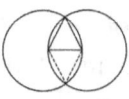

28) *Prometheus Rising* Chapter 13

In response to my last post, Tom Jackson commented on February 23, 2022,

> As I've written earlier, I have been concentrating on Bach this year, as I don't know Bach's music as well as I know Beethoven's and Mozart's. Still, as you note, Beethoven looms large in this chapter and the previous chapter. If I take time to listen to Beethoven again, should I concentrate on the later sonatas and string quartets, do you think?
> (Comment at rawillumination.net 2/20/2022 post)

Great question, Tom. From a Wilsonian perspective, the Ninth Symphony seems the cornerstone. After that, the Hammerklavier Sonata, Op. 106 shows up repeatedly in Bob's writing. He also occasionally refers to the Third, Fifth, Sixth, Seventh, and Eighth Symphonies, as well as the late string quartets.

From my perspective those all seem like important works. Rafi Zabor has really helped me gain more insight into Beethoven's music over the past 17 years. I love Solomon's recording of the Piano Sonatas Op. 106, Op. 109, and Op. 111 and Artur Schnabel's recordings of the Piano Sonatas Op. 109, 110, and 111. I love Furtwängler's 1942 recording of the Ninth Symphony. I love Horenstein's recording of the Missa Solemnis and the recordings of the late quartets by the Budapest Quartet and by the Takacs Quartet.

FNORD

Some people have suggested updating the exercises in *Prometheus Rising.* I generally prefer to do the exercises the way Bob suggested, but on June 6, 2021, I wrote the following to Robert Anton Wilson scholar Michael Johnson of overweeninggeneralist.com:

> Exercise 3 in chapter 13 of *Prometheus Rising* asks the reader to "Read Brain/Mind Bulletin for any recent year, and observe that similar healings are reported regularly and attributed to endorphins in the brain." Since this publication ceased publication years I ago, I would really appreciate it if you would create a new exercise for our *Prometheus Rising* study group at rawillumination.net. We plan to start chapter 13 in March 2022. You combine the unique combination of a deep knowledge of Wilson's work and a strong background in brain science. I suspect you could come up with a great substitution. (I think of Coltrane playing chord substitutions in 1959.)

Michael kindly wrote back:

> I suspect you assume more knowledge about neuroscience on my part than I possess. Having said that (<--- I feel a jerk typing that phrase), and not having read that chapter of PR in a long time, I suspect my response would be too demanding and long. The mystery of healing and endorphins has gone supernova since RAW wrote that (his PhD diss).
>
> Among many other things, I'd include readings from articles and books on:
>
> -How the dopamine system was linked to positive placebo effects, but dopamine is NOT as simple as most people think. There are many other

neurochemicals that make us feel good. Levodopa for Parkinson's increases dopamine in the brain, but doesn't bring on pleasure or happiness; it makes us feel lousy. Dopamine=pleasure/happiness is too widely believed and too simple. Other neurotransmitters that contribute for feeling good: endorphins, oxytocin, serotonin, glutamate, and GABA: And it's just really, really, RILLY complex.

-Current neurobiological explanations for placebo has to do with action in the dorso-lateral and medial-ventral areas of the PFC (pre-frontal cortex) overriding signals from the amygdala: I'd call on the readers to read a basic article on what the amygdala does, and then, maybe, read pp.60-62 of Robert Sapolsky's *Behave*, but preferably, pp.20- 80 of that book, which will go on to be one of the great non-fiction books of the 21st century, I predict.

-There's a lot of stuff now on oxytocin and touch and activation of the immune system, as you may know. Oxytocin is not dopamine, and carries its own social problems, mostly the down-sides of its ability to foster the in-group "us" feeling. Strong "us" feelings tend to amplify strong "them" feelings, and you can see where that goes. Just watch a goddamned Dump rally.

-Since RAW wrote, a lot (A LOT) of words have been written on the Nocebo effect: how negative emotions can affect health. This would have to dovetail with at least a soupcon of info on the dizzying complexity of the immune system. T-Cells "talk" to neurons...Bacteria in the gut probably has something to do with the emerging "Psychobiome." Etc, etc, etc, etc.

-RAWphiles really should know basic stuff about RAW's favorite drug: cannabis. I'd recommend reading chapters 6 and 7 from Julie Holland's

The Pot Book, "The Endocannabinoid System" and "Anandamide and More", pp.52-72. The endocannabinoid system predates vertebrate life and is implicated in a host of healing pathways. Anandamide is the analogue to THC, but it's endogenous.

Dinner time. I could write another 8000 words on this but I hope you get the picture. Like I said, since *PR*: supernova.

Thank you, Michael! I bought the two books Michael recommended, and I have started reading *Behave*. I did not know about Konrad Lorentz's Nazi past which I learned about from Sapolsky's book.

FNORD

The discussion on pg. 197 of whether the UFOs exist inside or outside of the observers parallels the question in the final exercise of the next chapter of whether "I AM WHO I AM" exists inside or outside of Moses.

I enjoyed doing Michael Johnson's substitute exercise for exercise #3 of chapter 13. I found Sapolsky's explanation of the placebo effect a bit glib, but who knows? One minor synchronicity: I heard "Rocky Mountain High" by John Denver at an El Pollo Loco restaurant while carrying my copy of *The Pot Book*. An early chapter of that book suggests that Jesus may have used anointing oils which contained cannabis. This provides another filter/model for exercise #4 trying to explain the miracles in the New Testament.

Years ago I had the idea to write a book on brain chemistry called *Why Do You Think They Call It Dopamine?* Of course, I know very little about brain chemistry. The readings Michael suggested mapped out my ignorance a little bit. Thank you again, Dr. Johnson.

As I mentioned earlier, in the late 80s and early 90s I used to associate the chapters in *Prometheus Rising* with the days of the month. I would read chapter one and do the exercises in chapter one on the first of the month; I would read chapter two and do the exercises in chapter two on the second of the month, etc., through the 19th of the month. Then for the rest of the month I worked on a long poem called *Big Trouble in Little Blandings (Reggie Theus Rising).* The poem had twelve sections numbered 20 through 31. I worked on section 20 on the 20th of the month, section 21 on the 21st, etc., and I published them in *noon blue apples* #20 through 31.

We have 23 more weeks of this study group. Some people thought we should work through the book more quickly. I thought 23 months might prove too short. One could spend a lot more time on these exercises. I have devoted a lot of time to these exercises during this study group as well as during the previous decades, but I realize I could spend a lot more time on them. I wonder what the next 23 weeks will hold. I wonder if I will ever dive as deeply into this book in the years to come. If I live another 23 years, perhaps I will never again devote so much time to this book. If I live another 23 decades, I may well return to this book again and again. Most people in 2022 still consider death inevitable. I still suspect I may live for a very long time.

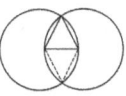

29) *Prometheus Rising* Chapter 14

Coincidentally, I had Beethoven's Hammerklavier Sonata playing this morning as I began to reread this chapter which mentions the sonata on its first page. I had not intended this connection. I had put on the sonata opus 90 earlier this morning, and the recording reached the Hammerklavier before I began to review the chapter.

Page 207 tells the reader to imagine an astral computer which "exists early in the next century". I have always read this as early in the 21st century, but I think I will start imagining it as existing early in the 22nd century from now on.

Page 209 tells the reader, "Yogis, mathematicians and musicians seem more inclined to develop metaprogramming consciousness than most of humanity." I've done a fair amount of yoga, and I started out college as math major, but my decades as a musician seem my most likely avenue for metaprogramming consciousness.

I find it interesting that *Alice's Adventures in Wonderland* and *Through the Looking Glass and What She Found There* each have twelve chapters. Leary broke down each of the eight circuits into three components for 24 divisions. One might see the 24 Alice chapters as corresponding to Leary's 24 caliber brain.

Exercise 2 on page 212 tells the reader to "Consider the belief system or reality tunnel of an educated reader 1200 years ago." I looked up the year 822 A.D. just after Russia invaded Ukraine in 2022. 822 A.D. seemed filled with territorial wars, and it seemed less foreign to me than the last time I did this experiment, alas.

Exercise 3 tells the reader to "Consider the reality-tunnel of an educated person 1200 years from now." As a teenager I read a lot of science fiction and watched a lot of science fiction movies and TV shows. I don't do that as much in recent years, and most science fiction doesn't look that far ahead. I did recently watch the second episode of the 2005 relaunch of *Doctor Who* which takes place much further in the future where the Doctor and his companion watch the death of our sun.

I do notice that since Donald Trump's election in 2016 I feel far less confident about making predictions about the future. Tim Leary's SMI²LE model still seems useful to me, but in our current information explosion, I feel much more uncertain than I did in the relatively carefree world of 2015 and before. I just read the wonderful new Hilaritas Press edition of Wilson's *Natural Law: Or Don't Put a Rubber on Your Willy and Other Writings from a Natural Outlaw.* There as elsewhere Bob Wilson predicted a world of radically unpredictable new technology and information overload. He sure seemed to have hit the nail on the head.

Robert Heinlein noted that people rarely foresaw the behavioral changes provoked by new technology. When people invented the automobile, they didn't foresee how this technology would affect courtship behavior, etc. Heinlein wrote an essay "Spinoff" (included in *Expanded Universe*) about how spinoff technology from the space program in weather prediction and medical technology, etc., more than paid for the costs of the space program. Bob Wilson once told me he considered Bob Heinlein as the first writer to include sociology in science fiction.

Exercise 4 tells the reader, "Re-read Moses' encounter

with I AM WHO I AM in Deuteronomy. Try the theory that Moses was talking to his own metaprogramming circuit." Well, I have contemplated that theory over the past 37 years, and I reread the opening chapters of Exodus recently. (Did Bob mean Exodus and not Deuteronomy? I don't know. I've read both books repeatedly over the past 37 years.) At least in 2022, the model of Moses talking to his own metaprogramming circuit doesn't work too well for me.

I just reread the first chapter of Deuteronomy. This does remind me of some of Wilson's experiences as related in *Cosmic Trigger*. I find it humbling and disturbing that I remembered this exercise as "Re-read Moses' encounter with I AM WHO I AM in Exodus," not the way Bob actually wrote it. Too often I confuse my faulty memory of the text with the text itself.

I wrote to Richard Rasa, the formidable editor of Hilaritas Press, wondering if Bob had intended Exodus rather than Deuteronomy in *Prometheus Rising*. Richard posted the following on Facebook:

> I just got an email from Eric Wagner, author of *An Insider's Guide to Robert Anton Wilson*. Eric has been really helpful in finding typos in RAW's books. Hilaritas Press has a number of people who do proofreading, but I've never met a proofreader who was able to find every typo or error.
>
> In this case, Eric wrote, "On pg. 212 of Prometheus Rising, I wonder if Bob meant Exodus and not Deuteronomy."
>
> I'm now wondering if that was an error from Bob, or some obscure joke on Bob's part. I suspect a mistake, but I'm thinking about it.
>
> Deuteronomy is where Moses waxes on about recent history, although I think he doesn't sufficiently explain why it took 40 years to travel less than 500

miles. If the phrase was from Deuteronomy, then the phrase would be "I was that I was." (That's me being a wise ass, but it may make some sense).

In the Queen James version of the Bible, the phrase is translated as, "I am that I am." My German sweetheart, Marlis (author of the new Hilaritas Press publication, *From Now To Now*), was surprised at that because in German, the phrase is the same as the current accepted Hebrew in translation, "Ich werde sein, der ich sein werde" ("I will be what I will be").

Wikipedia notes ...

אֶֽהְיֶה אֲשֶׁר אֶֽהְיֶה

"The traditional English translation within Judaism favors "I will be what I will be" because there is no present tense of the verb "to be" in the Hebrew language."

No verb to be!!

I just sent a message to Mimi (Hill) Peleg, co-author of RAW's *Everything Is Under Control*. She speaks Hebrew, and she confirms that, yes, that's true about Hebrew. I told her, "Korzybski would be delighted!" She wrote back, "Yes, Bob loved that too about Hebrew."

I just got off the phone with Marlis, and when I told her what Eric had found, she reiterated the German translation, "I will be what I will be," and she added, "It's all about evolution!" That was a thought I had not considered.

Interestingly, "I will be what I will be" seems like an appropriate mantra for the metaprogrammer.

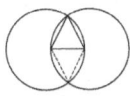

30) Neo-Decembrist Ramblings

(This chapter originally published in the Hilaritas newsletter.)

In August of 2004 Bob Wilson began to teach four online classes at the Maybe Logic Academy. I took two of those classes, but I didn't take his *Illuminatus!* class. In the *Illuminatus!* class he told the students:

> Read the neo-Decembrist agitprop in gunsanddopeparty.net
>
> Program your search engine for Decembrist + Illuminati See what you find

I think he repeated similar instructions in an interview, and I googled "Decembrist + Illuminati". I didn't see much interesting. I've repeated that search a number of times in the last 18 years, but I still haven't found much. I tended to take Bob's suggestions seriously, but I thought I had come up dry on this one.

After my first book came out in December of 2004, I decided to expand my master's thesis on *Finnegans Wake* and *Masks of the Illuminati* into a book mostly on Joyce and Wilson. I tended to feel guilty for any reading I did that didn't relate to this topic, but in 2006 I decided to finally read *War and Peace*. Around this time Bob Wilson tended to sign his emails "The Last Decembrist". Only after I finished reading *War and Peace* did I learn that Tolstoy had started writing the novel trying to explain the origins of the Decembrist Revolt of 1825.

April 7, 2022: Mike Gathers invites me to talk with him about Beethoven and Wilson on the Hilaritas podcast.

April 12: I accept.

April 13: Mike suggests the date of April 23

Easter Sunday, April 17: Early in the morning *Saturday Night Live* has a sketch about Beethoven's Ninth Symphony. Lizzo plays the "Ode to Joy" on the flute.

That evening *Fear the Walking Dead* features the "Ode to Joy" and a character plays it on the bagpipes.

April 18: Mike suggests delaying the interview.

April 25: *Better Call Saul* uses music from Beethoven's Emperor Concerto.

    On Easter Sunday 2010 I had just reread *The Earth Will Shake* to get ready to write an intro to a new edition of the third book in the *Historical Illuminatus* Series, and my family went to see the Johnny Depp version of *Alice in Wonderland.* An earthquake made most of our group leave the theater before the end of the movie. Of course, *The Earth Will Shake* begins with a murder in church on Easter morning.

    Man, I haven't heard much about Johnny Depp lately. I wonder how life treats him these days?

    Beethoven died in 1827. I find it interesting how echoes from two hundred years ago keep popping up in these days of vanishing reproductive rights.

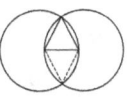

31) *Prometheus Rising* Chapter 15

This chapter opens with a quote from *Finnegans Wake:* "It* is not just a riot of blots and blurs and dislocated jottings linked by spurts of speed…it only looks as like it as damn it." Bob adds this note: "* Presumably the input (software) or the brain (hardware). Or both" (pg. 215). Part of me says, no, Joyce would likely not use this vocabulary. On the other hand, Joyce might like the way Bob uses the material from *Finnegans Wake*. Part of me enters the orthodox Joycean headspace and pooh-poohs Bob's creative use of Joyce material. Another part of me recalls that a lot of contemporary Joyce criticism echoes ideas that Bob published before anyone else. Of course, orthodox Joyceans rarely give Bob any credit.

Someone said of Alexander Pope's Homer translations, "It's a very pretty poem, Mr. Pope, but you must not call it Homer." (Ezra Pound shorted this to "Very pretty, not Homer.") Rereading *Masks of the Illuminati* over the past forty years, I have sometimes thought of this when considering Wilson's treatment of figures like Joyce and Pound and their works. The first time I read *Masks* in 1982 I knew very little about Joyce and Pound and had never read either of them. Then my Wilson obsession led me to read Pound and Joyce (and develop Joyce and Pound obsessions as well), and rereading *Masks* I sometimes found myself thinking, "Very pretty, not Joyce" and/or "Very pretty, not Pound." Then I lived a bit more as a Cosmic Schmuck, and I read a lot more, and then rereading

Masks I found myself thinking, "Well, maybe. These seem like valid insights into these two mysterious men and their works."

(It looks like the fellow in the picture on page 216 found a quarter or two.)

On pages 219-220 Bob says, "Assuming you are reading this in your own home, look around the room. Note that everything in your field of vision – furniture, paintings or posters on the walls, stereo set or absence of same, rugs, TV or not TV [34], etc. – is, in a sense, your *creation* or *co-creation*." I find myself reading this in a community college classroom surrounded by my computer, books, papers, and the James Joyce tote I got at the 2011 North American James Joyce Conference. I also have a 1988 ticket designed by Steve and Vicky Snow to a Robert Anton Wilson talk which I use as a bookmark.

~•~

34) That "is" the question.

~•~

I find it interesting that Bob mentions only dead white male (DWM) painters on page 220, and he only names dead white male composers by name (except for John Cage who died in 1992 between the two editions of *Prometheus Rising*). He does mention "Rock", "Disco", and "African chants", collective nouns that include people of color. Both Dr. Wilson and I had very Eurocentric educations, although we have both tried to overcome them. Also, since I write this in a community college classroom, I find it interesting that Bob generally doesn't use the Oxford comma, the comma in a list of three or more items before "and". Bob and I grew up in eras which considered the Oxford comma optional. Most of the grammar and writing books I have taught from in the past twenty-three years consider the Oxford comma mandatory.

Bob asks the reader to "guess which specific imprints created" Kurt Saxon and John White's reality-tunnels. I find it interesting that Kurt Saxon and Robert Anton Wilson share the same birth year, 1932. (Kurt Saxon has outlived Dr. Wilson.) I wondered if John White shared that birth year as well. I found multiple authors named John White, but the author of *Pole Shift* about whom Bob writes in this chapter seems to have the birthdate August 16, 1939. Interestingly, when I heard Bob talk in 1987 he commented on the synchronicity that the upcoming Energetic Harmonic Convergence would take place on August 16, 1987, the tenth anniversary of Elvis Presley's death. The initials E. H. C. made me think of all the H. C. E.'s in *Finnegans Wake*.

My friend and fellow Joycean Conrad Holt and I visited the energy vortices in Sedona, Arizona, on August 16, 1987. That night I went to see the film *Back to the Beach* which included appearances by two of the cast members of *Gilligan's Island*. That night I realized the isomorphism between the seven dancing girls in *Finnegans Wake* and the seven castaways on *Gilligan's Island,* and Conrad and I renamed our *Finnegans Wake Decoding Society* to *Finnegans Isle*. Of course, 1939 marked the first publication of *Finnegans Wake* as well as the birth of John White.

The Clement Attlee quote on pg. 225, "The people of the earth are islands shouting at each other over oceans of misunderstanding" seems even more relevant in 2022, alas.

Exercise 4 for this chapter says, "Write a criticism of this chapter from the viewpoint of Christian Fundamentalism."

> Brothers and sisters in Christ. I think we all know in our hearts the deep flaws in this chapter. Dr. Wilson mocks the inaccurate prophecies by Saxon and White but does not include any of his own failed prophecies from before the publication of this misguided book. He does make some ridiculous prophecies about the years after 1998, the year of the publication of the second edition of *Prometheus Rising*. We all know that God is the only source of true prophecy. Brothers and sisters, the Bible provides all we can know of universe and all we need to know of universe.

Mr. Wilson liked to mock Holy Scripture. He preferred the obscene gibberish of *Finnegans Wake*. Have you tried to use that worthless cesspool of an impractical joke to run your life? I, alas, have. Here before you sits a reformed Joycean. Oh, I want to spare you the years of degradation that that evil book has led me down. Repent, repent and turn back to God. We sit in the hands of an angry God, whom our sins offend. Pull down thy vanity, as Ezra Pound said in one of his few moments of clarity.

Like Patty Hearst, we have gotten kidnapped by Dr. Wilson's brilliant rhetoric and locked in the closet with his unfortunate heroes, the Satanist Aleister Crowley, the fascist Ezra Pound, the drug-crazed Timothy Leary, the sex-mad lunatic Wilhelm Reich, and the Anti-Christ himself, Friedrich Nietzsche. We read these dangerous authors with misgivings, but, not wanting to seem uncool, we came to understand them, even to agree with them. Before long we too disrespect our parents and storm the institutions which maintain law and order and civilization, with the machine guns of E-Prime, mocking satire, and other tools of Satan. Repent, repent, before we all stand in judgement before our Maker. We know in our hearts what we need to do get right with our Lord. Do not follow the instructions in the insidious chapter which calls for *neurological relativism*. This evil moral relativism has destroyed modern education and modern civilization.

Repent, repent, before your time runs out. Burn your Robert Anton Wilson books and read the Bible. In Mark chapter 6 the Pharisees tried to convince Jesus the disciples should wash their hands before eating. Jesus condemned the Pharisees for their narrow mindedness, just as he would condemn Robert Anton Wilson. Repent, repent!

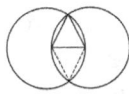

32) *Prometheus Rising,* Chapter 16

On page 232 Bob writes of FBI agents who didn't see godless communists everywhere, "To talk about such perceptions at all would be to invite suspicions of eccentricity, intellectual wiseacreing or of being oneself a godless communist." I have spent too much of my life afraid of inviting suspicions of eccentricity or intellectual wiseacreing, alas.

On page 238 Bob writes that "'Good Americans' believed Dr. Leary was a half-crazed dope-fiend." I recall in the 1980's I heard multiple people who didn't like Dr. Leary refer to him as "Mr. O'Leary", both taking away his doctorate and emphasizing his Irishness.

I find Bob's discussion of "the Mind War symphony" on page 241 very interesting. Of course, I think of Beethoven's Ninth Symphony. Bob writes about the fourth movement of that symphony in the upcoming chapter on the eighth circuit. In this chapter Bob writes:

> The *first movement* was the primitive neuroscience of ancient and medieval tyrants who acquired a great deal of pragmatic know-how about the effects of isolation, terror and intimidation; and of shamans and occultists who learned how neuro-chemicals can alter perceived reality-tunnels. The *second movement* began with modern psychology, with Freud, Pavlov, Jung, Skinner, etc., climaxing with

the LSD revolution and the discovery by millions that reality-tunnels could be radically mutated – temporarily and sometimes permanently – by neurochemistry.

The *third movement* is the growingly obvious warfare between those who would program all of us, and those of us who wish to become our own Metaprogrammers.

If one sees Beethoven's Ninth as somewhat isomorphic to this model, Bob's words on the fourth movement seem apropos:

> Mystics stammer, gibber and rave incoherently in trying to discuss this. Beethoven says it for all of them, without words, in the fourth movement of the Ninth Symphony. The words of Schiller's "Ode to Joy," which Beethoven set to this virtually superhuman music, are a linear third-circuit map conveying only a skeleton key to the multi-level meanings of the 8-circuit "language" of the melodic construction itself, which spans all consciousness from primitive bio-survival to meta-physiological cosmic fusion. (pg. 261)

The phrase "skeleton key" makes me think of Joseph Campbell and Henry Morton Robinson's *A Skeleton Key to Finnegans Wake*. (David Shenk and Steve Silberman wrote *Skeleton Key: A Dictionary for Deadheads,* inspired in part I suspect by the Campbell and Robinson title. One finds a number of Deadheads among Bob's readers, myself included.)

The phrase "spans all consciousness from primitive bio-survival to meta-physiological cosmic fusion" makes me think of Stanley Kubrick's *2001: A Space Odyssey.* Kubrick's *A Clockwork Orange* use of Beethoven's Ninth seems to fit perfectly with Bob's notion of a Mind War symphony with its brain washing theme, especially Kubrick's use of the second movement. James Joyce greatly influenced Anthony Burgess, who wrote the novel *A Clockwork Orange,* and Bob Wilson loved Burgess's novel about Shakespeare *Nothing Like the Sun.*

(Hopefully my co-workers and neighbors won't have me committed to a mental hospital before I finish writing this book.)

I found it interesting to live a whole week with the program, "Everybody likes me and tries to help me achieve all of my goals." I did encounter a number of people whom I think do not like me that week. This makes me think of the radical changes that took place in Elwood P. Dowd before the start of the play *Harvey.* He previously strode to act "oh so smart," but then he began to act "oh so kind." I fear that believing everyone likes me might make me become gullible and get taken advantage of (this sort of happens to Elwood), but that sort of reprogramming might work out well. The bunnies in the backyard have not started talking to me yet, or at least I don't think so. I have begun metaprogramming that "Everything works out more perfectly than I plan it." We will see.

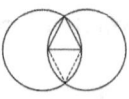

33) *Wilhelm Reich in Hell*
Questions from Tom Jackson

1. There are still a few RAW books I have not read – I read *Wilhelm Reich in Hell* for the first time last week – but I'm guessing you've read all of his works. How do you think this newly-republished title fits into the RAW canon?

    ERW: This play represents Bob's look at how our society responds to scientists outside the norms of our scientific community. Dr. Leary and Dr. Reich seem prime examples of this. Also the questions of censorship seem important to Bob. The U.S. government burned Dr. Reich's books. In the 1980s some feminists burned works they considered pornographic. When I visited the concentration camp at Dachau, I saw this Heinrich Heine quote on display, "First they burn books, then they burn people."

2. The book is essentially in two parts -- an essay and a play. I thought the essay was RAW on the top of his game; I liked the play, but my feelings were a bit more mixed. How do you think the play works as a play? Have you seen it performed?

    ERW: I love the play. I enjoyed the DVD of the play directed by Lance Bauscher. As I commented in one of my introductions, Bob ends his two screenplays with Beethoven's "Ode to Joy". This play doesn't end that way. Bob had strong utopian notions, but he realized the darker possibilities. I find this play very funny, very disturbing, and very worthwhile.

3. You wrote a new introduction for the new edition. Did Rasa give you any direction on what he wanted? What were you trying to do with the new introduction?

> ERW: No, Rasa just kindly asked me if I would like to do a new introduction. I find myself fascinated by Bob's interest in the Decembrists in the last three years of his life. I had this in my mind as I reread the book in December of 2021. As I commented in my intro, the character of Dr. Reich seemed fundamentally sane to me as I read the play. Ironically, I had forgotten that at the end of the play Reich admits to his insanity.
>
> Bob Wilson seems like one of the sanest people I have ever met. Reich in this play differs from Bob Wilson, particularly in his attitudes towards drugs. John Keats suggested that Shakespeare had the ability to negate his own personality in creating new characters, and Keats called this ability "negative capability". Wilson's portrayal of Reich in this play seems like a wonderful example of negative capability to me.

4. Do you think the book will work for RAW fans who aren't particularly interested in Wilhelm Reich?

> ERW: Absolutely. This book seems like a meditation on the outsider, and Wilson shows how Reich's case parallels those of Timothy Leary, Giordano Bruno, Ezra Pound, and others. It also deals with the theme of how we become what we pretend. Kurt Vonnegut did a terrific job with this theme in his novel *Mother Night* where an American pretended to support Naziism during World War II while acting as secret agent. However, he did such a good job pretending to support Nazism that he encouraged others to become Nazis. He wonders whether he did more harm or good by his actions.

In the play the actor playing Reich enters an odd altered state of consciousness by entering into Reich's headspace. The reader and/or viewer may enter odd altered states of consciousness while encountering and enduring the play.

5. Hilaritas Press is republishing 19 RAW titles and also brought out *The Starseed Signals* from an unpublished manuscript, with 16 books published so far. Do you have a favorite among the remaining titles? Do you have a favorite "unsung" RAW title?

> ERW: Well, I love *TSOG: The Thing That Ate the Constitution,* especially the final section on *The Tale of the Tribe.* For years I felt disappointed that Bob never wrote *The Tale of the Tribe*, but now I simply treasure the fragment in *TSOG.* In *The Romantic Generation* Charles Rosen discussed the fragment as a Romantic form. I now see *The Tale of the Tribe* as an evanescent fragment, a pointer to other universes where it sits beside an unedited version of Orson Welles' *The Magnificent Ambersons,* Joyce's novels after *Finnegans Wake* and Proust's final version of *Time Regained.* Plus I have become fascinated by Bob's interest in the Decembrists, and this book provides a number of clues to Bob's resistance to Tsarism in the United States.
>
> I love the two screenplays, *The Walls Came Tumbling Down* and *Reality Is What You Can Get Away With.* I used to have a "Reality Is What You Can Get Away With" bumper sticker which I got from Bob's newsletter *Trajectories.* These days so many streaming services search for content, so it would not surprise me if someone produces these two films sometime soon, perhaps in a language other than English.
>
> Speaking of *Trajectories,* I love both of the

Trajectories anthologies, *Chaos and Beyond* and *Beyond Chaos and Beyond*. I remember getting *Chaos and Beyond* in the mail just before I left for Egypt in 1994. In the introduction Bob talked about reading Korzybski's *Science and Sanity* over and over again, so I went to the Arizona State University Library and checked out a copy and decided to finally read it cover to cover. I took that bulky book along with me to Egypt. I didn't read much of it that trip as I visited the Stele of Revealing, King Tut's tomb and the Abu Simbel Temples, etc., but I did eventually finish it.

In terms of "unsung" Wilson titles, I would like to see everything back in print. I particularly love the original three volume edition of *Schrödinger's Cat*. They seem like great books to me. I love the condensed one volume edition, but I prefer the original version. I would like both versions to remain in print. I first bought volume one in May 1982, and I really liked it. I bought volume two the following month, and my life changed forever.

I love that you can read *The Sex Magicians*, in the form of a new edition from Hilaritas Press. Numerous studies have shown that comprehension and recall improve when reading a book made of paper rather than one on a screen. Plus, I used to teach at a high school which forbade the use of books made of paper, allowing only electronic texts. That has made me love books made of paper even more.

I would also love to see *Playboy's Book of Forbidden Words* come back into print. When I lived in Arizona, I read the copy the Scottsdale Public Library had in their reference section. One couldn't check it out, so I read it during my lunch hour each day for a few weeks when I worked at a bookstore nearby. I know the editors changed Bob's original text, but I would still like to see it in print.

I would like to see *Right Where You Are Sitting Now* come back into print. (From an E-Prime perspective I find it interesting that this book, *Reality Is What You Can Get Away With*, and *Everything Is Under Control* all have forms of the verb "to be" in their titles.) I think Michael Johnson read this book before he read any other Wilson book. I would love to see a new edition with an introduction by Michael Johnson. I remember novelist Paul Chuey and I went to see the Who in 1982, and we each brought a Robert Anton Wilson book to read. I think I brought *Right Where You Are Sitting Now.* If not, Paul brought it. We sat with our backs to the stage and read during the opening acts Loverboy and John Cougar Mellencamp. Ah youth. Someone threw a bottle that hit John Cougar in the head during his set. I don't remember if we saw the throw or not.

I used to love the Viking Portable Library paperbacks. Most bookstores used to have a number of them. I remember reading *The Portable Nietzsche* the week before I turned thirty. I own two very different editions of *The Portable Dante,* and I used the newer edition for my high school Dante Society for more than a decade. I think a lot of Joyce scholars still use *The Portable James Joyce*, which contains the complete texts of *Dubliners*, *A Portrait of the Artist as a Young Man*, *Chamber Music, Poems Penyeach*, and *Exiles*, as a well as excerpts from *Ulysses* and *Finnegans Wake.*

In the 1980's I used to fantasize that Viking would publish *The Portable Robert Anton Wilson.* I would wonder what such a volume should include. I had to keep the length under a thousand pages. I wanted to include a complete stand alone novel, so I thought

Masks of the Illuminati would work well. I loved *Natural Law, Or Don't Put a Rubber on Your Willy*, and its short length made it a good selection. Of course now Hilaritas Press has given us a longer book which includes the original essay with some other terrific selections. I also thought *The Illuminati Papers* would make a nice addition. (I liked that many of the Viking Portable books contained so many complete works.) I would also include the essay "Brain Books", and a few other essays. You can find "Brain Books" in *Beyond Chaos and Beyond*.

And, oh yes, I love *The Illuminati Papers*. I consider "Ten Reasons to Get Up in the Morning" one of my very favorite Wilson essays, and *The Illuminati Papers* also includes great essays on *Finnegans Wake*, Ezra Pound and Beethoven. Man, I pored over that book and all my Wilson books so much in the 1980's. I treasured each bit of Bob's writing back in those pre-internet days, following up leads. Of course, as with *Science and Sanity*, it took me a lot of tries to get into many of Bob's favorite books. I would get books Bob had recommended from out of the library or as gifts, and I would give them a shot. If I couldn't get into them, I would go back and reread a bit of Wilson, and then I would try another one of his recommendations.

I remember haunting the bookstores, checking various sections. I first found Bob's books in the science fiction section: *Schrödinger's Cat, Illuminatus!,* and *Mask of the Illuminati*. Then I found some in the New Age sections: *The Illuminati Papers* and *Right Where You Are Sitting Now*. In 1983 I found the new hardcover edition of *The Earth Will Shake* in the general fiction section. I don't think I've seen a Wilson book in the general fiction section since then. Then I started visiting occult book stores, especially the Alpha Book Center in Phoenix. After I checked for a new Wilson book like *Prometheus Rising,* I would scour the shelves for the Falcon Press logo, buying most of their early titles. Later in the eighties Bob started having articles in magazines like *Magical Blend* and *Gnosis.* Books, Etc. in Tempe carried both of those magazines, so I would check the magazine racks each time I visited the store.

Occasionally I would order Wilson books like *Natural Law, Or Never Put a Rubber on Your Willy* by mail. Back then delivery would take weeks, if not months. Once my friends Steve and Vicky Snow got a copy of *Cosmic Trigger II* (I think – maybe *Cosmic Trigger III,* my memory fades) from Bob himself. I didn't even know it had come out yet, so I ordered a copy. I remember feeling so jealous they got to read it first.

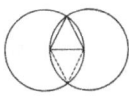

34) *Prometheus Rising*, Chapter 17

Exercise one for this chapter reads, "Make a list of ten areas where your thinking-feeling is conservative. Guess how soon the world will change so totally that those ideas will seem not merely conservative but *irrelevant* (as the theological debates of 300 AD now seem irrelevant)" (pg. 255).

1. I prefer books made of paper to books on a computer screen.

2. Well, now I started googling "conservative ideas", and I have started going down the rabbit hole of what "conservative" means. I consider learning languages valuable. Graduate schools seem to have deemphasized languages in the last seventy years, and other levels of U.S. education have as well.

3. As U2 said, I believe in love.

4. Russell Kirk says, "Conservatives are guided by their principle of prudence." This reminded me of the following passage from Wilson's *The Widow's Son:*

> The "fourth soul," or emerging brain, perceives the invisible web of connections between all things; *but it is no more infallible than the rest of the brain, or the gut, or the liver, or the gonads.* It merely works without effort, unlike the more primitive parts of

the brain, which is why *meanings seem to flow into us,* when this is activated, and we forget that we are still creating the meanings. We imagine we are "receiving revelations," and hence we do not *take responsibility* or exercise any prudence or common sense. This is why there are so many "holy fools" and so few holy wise men. (pg. 339)

This passage surprised me when I first read it. I didn't think too much of prudence at the time, but prudence and common sense do seem valuable to me today. Crowley calls the Eight of Disks Prudence, and that card tends to make me think of this Wilson passage.

5. Saving money seems like a good idea to me.

6. I love my grandkids.

7. 1939 seems like the greatest year in film history.

8. I think movies have gone downhill since 1974, the year of *Celine and Julie Go Boating.*

9. I love the music of Mozart, Bach, and Beethoven.

10. I love acoustic jazz.

So, how long until these ideas "seem not merely conservative but *irrelevant*"?

1. Marshall McLuhan saw a similarity between the invention of movable type by Gutenberg in 1450 with the invention of the computer. Few people today prefer to read handwritten books rather than printed books, although we may prefer them as art objects and look at Medieval texts in glass cases in museums. In one or two hundred years paper books may become rare, especially after a climate change apocalypse.

2. Perhaps we will learn more about language acquisition in five hundred years, or perhaps we will have telepathy (or extinction).

3. Human sexuality and marriage customs will certainly change. We see love differently in 2022 than Dante did seven hundred years ago or Ovid did two thousand years ago, but their ideas of love still resonate with current beliefs. Perhaps in 2300 years "love" will have lost its meaning, or it may become something very new I can't begin to understand.

4. Prudence may seem irrelevant in a Bucky Fuller-like utopia where no one worries about eviction or getting their next meal or getting their kids' teeth fixed. Maybe in 1500 years.

5. See number 4.

6. Like number 3, ideas about love will change, and perhaps they will change utterly. As Billie Holiday sang, "You don't know what love is".

7. Films like *Gone with the Wind* have troubling racism. *The Wizard of Oz* seems unkind to little people. Animals get shot in *The Rules of the Game*. The women in *The Women* seem too concerned about men. *Gunga Din* supports colonialism. *Mr. Smith Goes to Washington* neglects political realities. *Silk Stockings* improved *Ninotchka*. William Goldman wrote movingly about 1939 as the greatest year in film history in *Adventures in the Screen Trade,* but Mr. Goldman, alas, has died. For decades I have asked my film history students what they consider the greatest era of film history. I don't think any of them suggested any time before 1970. Of course with new technology movies don't seem nearly so important to our culture, so these discussions might seem irrelevant in sixty years.

8. See number 7. Most of my students hated *Celine and Julie Go Boating* the one time I showed it to a class. I didn't even plan to show it, but I had a copy of it on my laptop and no other technology worked that week.

9. Well, I have Beethoven playing right now. Bach, Mozart and the Big B seem irrelevant to most people today, and perhaps in 250 years they will seem as irrelevant to almost everybody as Thomas Tallis and William Byrd do today.

10. As with number 9, most people don't listen to jazz in 2022, and even fewer listen to acoustic jazz. In one hundred and fifty years this may seem irrelevant. We will see.

Exercise 2 in *Prometheus Rising,* chapter 17, asks the reader to "Make a list of ten areas in which your conceptualizing is radical. Guess how soon the world will change so totally that you will seem conservative in those areas" (pg. 255).

1. I have mixed feelings about hard work. I recognize the value of hard work, and I know that it can accomplish a lot, but I also value going with the flow. When I first visited Europe in 1985, I arranged my trip to visit Ingolstadt, Bavaria, the birthplace of the Bavarian Illuminati, on July 23, the anniversary of the beginning of Robert Anton Wilson's Sirius experience. The train from Munich to Ingolstadt passed Dachau, and on the next day I visited the concentration camp at Dachau. Over the gate of the concentration camp hung a sign reading "Arbeit Macht Frei," work will set you free. I had a sense that I had a life purpose to unlearn that sentiment.

When I returned that afternoon to Munich I had a deep sense of despair about the human condition after visiting the camp and contemplating the Holocaust. I wandered Munich, listening to oom-pah-pah bands in the park and eating a giant soft pretzel, observing naked frisbee players. I visited Munich's rich English language bookstores and even looked at copies of Robert Anton Wilson's books, trying to find some way of dealing with the nightmare of history. I later walked past a theater showing Ingmar Bergman's film of Mozart's *Magic Flute.* I saw I had just enough time to watch the film and run to the train station to catch my midnight train to Vienna. (I just wanted to get out of Germany.)

With my limited understanding of German, I could barely follow the German subtitles for the Swedish language film, but the film restored my hope in humanity. The story of a secret society of Masonic adepts trying to aid the world set to Mozart's music gave me hope. Plus I thought the singer playing Sarastro looked like I might look in the future. (Now I don't think so.)

In the uncut version of *The Trick Top Hat,* Wilson writes

> Those who had particularly keen *memories of the future* – those who could see the transformation into Immortality and Higher Intelligence that was before them – imagined that this could only be accomplished through what these primates called Promethean Struggle. They loved to dramatize themselves as heroic contestants "fighting" every step of the way from the primeval ooze to the first upright ape, "battling" mightily toward the steam engine and the Age of Abundance, etc. That all this was programmed into the DNA on every planet, and that all they had to do was cooperate with it, was a concept too humiliating to their primate egos.
>
> "It steam-engines when it comes steam-engine time," wrote one of their cleverest primate philosophers; but they did not dare to believe him. They were sure that if they stopped struggling, they would slip back into amoebahood again, or something worse. (pg. 247)

Dr. Wilson here refers to Charles Fort as "one of their cleverest primate philosophers." In *Quantum Psychology* Wilson renamed the neurogenetic circuit the "morphogenetic system": "Sheldrake, a biologist, knew that genes cannot carry such information. He therefore posited a non-local field, like those in quantum theory, which he named the morphogenetic field" (pg.191).

As I wrote earlier, I reframe the passage from *The Trick Top Hat* as that we just need to cooperate with the morphogenetic fields.

2. I do not consider death inevitable.

3. I think space industrialization can help humanity.

4. I consider the music of the Art Ensemble of Chicago very important.

5. I consider the writing of Rafi Zabor very important.

6. I consider the writing of Robert Anton Wilson very important.

7. I suspect the writing of Ibn 'Arabi has great value.

8. Paying attention to dreams seems valuable to me.

9. I like E-Prime.

10. The writing of Robert Heinlein seems important to me.

Bob asks the reader to, "Guess how soon the world will change so totally that you will seem conservative in those areas."

1. Bob Wilson and Bucky Fuller thought we might have a post-work economy by the 1990s. I suspect it will take at least a few hundred years to move to a world where hard work no longer seems so central. We may never get there.

2. Perhaps we will all die. Perhaps medicine will radically improve in the next century.

3. Perhaps we will reap the benefits of space industrialization in the next sixty years.

4. Most years I look at the voting for the *DownBeat* Hall of Fame. Of the members of the Art Ensemble, only Lester Bowie has gotten voted into the Hall of Fame. I think much of Art Ensemble's music seems less radical today than it did fifty years ago.

5. Hopefully more people will recognize the value of Rafi's work during his lifetime.

6. Perhaps Bob Wilson's work will have a Renaissance in the next few decades.

7. Many people value Ibn 'Arabi's work already. Much more of it has gotten translated into English in the last forty years. Perhaps he will become as popular as Rumi in the next fifty years, or least have a significantly greater profile in the West.

8. People have paid attention to dreams throughout history (and probably before it). With Freud people started looking at dreams in some new ways. I suspect we will learn more and more about dreams in the coming century, just as we have learned more and more about the brain in the last thirty years. Perhaps people will learn new things from *Finnegans Wake*, Joyce's prophetic vision of the world of the night.

9. I've written, talked, and thought mostly in E-Prime for about thirty years. I no longer have the evangelical zeal for it that I once did, but I still find it a valuable tool. Perhaps it will seem a conservative practice in eighty years, or it may take centuries.

10. Many science fiction fans grew up on Heinlein, especially people my age and older. I have encountered some younger Heinlein fans. His vision of a world impacted by changing technologies and the changes in people's behavior affected by these technological changes seems relevant in 2022. However, some of his ideas about men and woman seem very outdated to some readers. He gets ignored by academic writers on American literature, but he seems central to writers like Bob Wilson and Phil Dick. Perhaps my ideas about Heinlein's importance already seem conservative to some.

Exercise three says,

> Accept the longevity hypothesis. Imagine you are going to live at least 300 years. How much of that time do you want to spend loafing? How many different jobs would you like to work at? How many sports, arts or sciences you never had time for, would you then find the time to enjoy? (pg. 255)

Well, I just turned sixty. Thinking of Tim McGraw's song "My Next Thirty Years", I think about "My Next 240 Years". I would like to spend a fair amount of time loafing which will also involve watching the world change. I have grown tired of most of my jobs, although I still love teaching my college classes, especially when I returned to the classroom after over a year on Zoom due to the pandemic. I suspect I will have to work for a good part of the next 240 years. I do enjoy working a lot of the time. Perhaps I will work 42 jobs; perhaps retirement, writing and teaching will take up a good share of my time.

    I suspect I will continue to practice tai chi, and I suspect I will explore other martial arts and complementary practices like kettlebells in the future. My wife suggested I buy a basketball for when the grandkids come over, so their taste in sports will likely affect my taste and practice of sports. I suspect I will keep writing and trying to improve my writing. Ezra Pound emphasized how language study can help one's writing, and I suspect I will keep learning languages for the rest of my life. I find it interesting how some skills erode over time if one doesn't nurture them. I look forward to experimenting with various learning processes over the coming centuries. These days I study Arabic a little bit every day. Perhaps I will eventually become fluent and will nurture my Arabic skills as well as my skills in other languages, and I will see how that affects my writing.

    I also suspect I will play music, and perhaps I will practice more regularly at various times in the coming years. Perhaps I will go back to ballet, or I might work on drawing. Who knows? It would not surprise me if I die before I turn ninety. If I keep on living, various passions and curiosities will likely emerge. Of course, I may spend my time foraging for water and food in a climate change nightmare with little time for poetry or architecture.

    I haven't taken a science class since 1980. I started school as a math major, but I have neglected math and sciences over the past forty years. Bob Wilson got me to read about quantum mechanics, but I have not done much of that this century. I remember reading that in the fifties Isaac Asimov found himself on a panel with Philip José Farmer. Someone asked how they stayed current with science. Asimov thought to himself, well, I have a Ph.D. in chemistry, this question doesn't apply to me, but he liked Farmer's response. Phil said that he read *Scientific American* every month. Asimov realized that a lot had happened in science since he got his degree, and more and more would continue to happen, so he decided to follow Phil's example and he subscribed to *Scientific American*. Perhaps in a few years I will subscribe to *Scientific American* (if they even continue to publish a paper magazine). Of course, passions have tended to drive my education. Sometime in the coming centuries I may develop a passion for some science that will get me to study a lot.

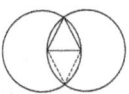

35) *Prometheus Rising,* Chapter 18

Dude, we've made it to the eighth circuit! Bob starts this chapter with a quote from *Ulysses.* Joyce provided both Leary and Wilson with many maps to the higher circuits.

About thirty years ago I repeatedly read the final novels of Philip K. Dick. While reading *The Divine Invasion* I had the idea of setting up a team of astral projectors who would try to restore the ancient library at Alexandria. About eleven years ago I got a group together, and we made the attempt without any apparent success. We also investigated the Kennedy assassination. I associated Bach's Cello Suites with the Alexandria attempts and Beethoven's late String Quartets with the Dallas 1963 attempts.

Tim Leary divided each of the eight circuits into three phases, making the eighth circuit stages 22, 23, and 24. Both Leary and Wilson relate the eighth circuit to quantum mechanics. Leary mentions quarks in his discussion of Stage 22 in *Musings on Human Metamorphoses* (pg. 109) and in his discussion of Stage 23 in *The Game of Life* (pg. 278-279). Physicist Murray Gell-Mann, of course, got the name quark from *Finnegans Wake.* In *The Game of Life* Leary mentions Robert Anton Wilson in his discussion of Stage 23.

For the past few days I have wondered how many times the movement Stroke the Peacock's Tail (right) appears in the 108 Movement Yang Long Form of Tai Chi. I finally figured it out this morning: eight times. (I don't think the tai chi peacock has anything to do with the streaming service.) This mild coincidence of eights fits in with this mild chapter. I have far less visceral experience of the eighth circuit than I do of the other seven circuits.

> THE VOYAGE DEPENDS UPON STEP-BY-STEP,
> MOMENT-TO-MOMENT
> ACTIONS BY INDIVIDUAL SINGULARITIES.
> – Timothy Leary, *The Game of Life* (pg. 281)

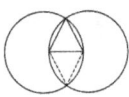

36) *Prometheus Rising*, Chapter 19

I guess I would consider myself an Evolutionary Agent using the criteria on page 274 of *Prometheus Rising*. I don't think I've mastered the metaprogramming circuit yet, although I think I've experienced it over the past 39 years. In 1983 my roommates and I decided to have a 123rd birthday party for Gustav Mahler on July 7. I spent the month before the party metaprogramming Mahler, reading about him, listening to his music, studying his scores. One time I woke up in the middle of the night hearing Mahler music in my head, but not music Mahler had actually composed. My mind had started creating pseudo-Mahler music for my first experience of metaprogramming.

I also don't consider myself a "neuro-quantum" adept yet. In fact, I don't connect with the eight circuit model as much as I used to. I find it a very useful model, but I look forward to even better models. On pg. 20 of *Prometheus Rising* Bob wrote:

> Following Dr. Timothy Leary (with a few modifications) we shall divide this brain hardware into eight circuits *for convenience.* ("For convenience" means that this is the best map I know at present. I assume it will be replaced by a better map within 10 or 15 years; and in any case, the map is not the territory.)

Bob wrote *Prometheus Rising* in 1983, and he revised the text for the 1997 Second Revised Edition. Twenty-five years have passed since then.

Perhaps "more of Beethoven's intelligence" (pg. 271) will help us find and/or create even better maps. Tim Leary had more interest than Bob did in contemporary music like rap and rock. I love how Tim wrote about Stevie Nicks and David Bowie in the seventies, for instance. On page 275 Bob wrote:

> By the time the Consciousness Revolution peaks, the Longevity Pill is widely available, cloning is normal and all the ideas in this book, including the most wild and radical ones, seem quaint and old-fashioned – i.e., about 2005 – we will probably be growing accustomed to thinking in terms of revolutions-per-year.
>
> There is no reason to accept the tunnel-reality of this book as final. If you really understand the message, you will invent a bigger and better Future than I have suggested. As Barbara Marx Hubbard says:
>
> THE FUTURE EXISTS
> FIRST IN IMAGINATION,
> THEN IN WILL,
> THEN IN REALITY.

I don't think that happened by 2005, but perhaps it will happen in the next 23 years, or by next Tuesday after lunch.

In the mid-80's I used to revel in reading Tim Leary while listening to Fleetwood Mac. I wonder how the synergy of texts and music will help us navigate the next few years. I thank you for joining us on this voyage.

I wonder what "Meta-physiological cosmic vision" pre-capitulates in the book's final line.

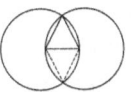

Coda

In his Afterword to the Hilaritas edition of *Prometheus Rising,* Richard Rasa relates how Bob Wilson told him in 2006, "Don't channel me." I sit here in 2022, fifteen years after Bob's death. I have not had a sense of connection with Bob's spirit since his passing, and I have not tried to "channel" him, but I have tried to understand his books and maps of reality.

Dear Bob,

I hope all goes well. I almost wrote, "Dear Dr. Wilson." From 1982 to 1988 I thought of you as Dr. Wilson. We began corresponding in 1986, and I first met you in 1987. In 1988 you spent a week in the Phoenix, Arizona, area where you gave a talk and a seminar. I got to know you better that week, and I began to think of you as "Bob".

You told Rasa, "Don't channel me." I have mixed feelings about the survival of the individual after death. I have had some vague sense of connection to you since your death fifteen years ago but nothing overwhelming. I do want to thank you for your books and your friendship. One review of my first book said I wanted to "be" you. That has some truth to it. You seemed to have a deeper understanding of life than anyone else I had encountered, and your writings and your outlook made a lot of sense to me. Reading Nabokov's *Pale Fire* proved educational and a little painful to me when contemplating the character of Kinbote. Wikipedia says Kinbote's "writing reveals a comic mélange of narcissism and megalomania." My obsession with your thought and writing led me to become a bit zealous in my pursuit of understanding E-Prime, Ezra Pound, James Joyce, Aleister Crowley, Beethoven, etc., etc. I fear I strove too much to become your disciple which I know you never wanted. I feel grateful for all I learned in the process, but I feel a little lost. For decades I thought, "Bob said X; that seems like a good working model." I didn't always agree with you, but I thought you provided a good working model.

I tried to follow the lines of research which you found most fruitful. You had your Sirius experiences at the age of 41. I hoped that I might have a profound transformational experience around that age as well after my years of work on the exercises in *Prometheus Rising* and other lines of research you had outlined. I haven't really had that transformational experience yet.

I turned 48 in 2010, three years after you died. I decided I wanted to read Proust's long seven volume novel before I turned fifty. I did, and that turned into a bit of an obsession as well. I read it two more times and started it again. I continue to love James Joyce's writing, but I find that I prefer Proust these days. I have devoted a ton of time to studying Joyce over the past 39 years. I had *Finnegans Wake* study groups for 36 of those years. I still do weekly readings for an online *Finnegans Wake* study group, and during the Pandemic I finished reading ten books by and about Joyce. I will continue to participate in Robert Anton Wilson study groups for the rest of my life I suspect.

Anyway, I hope all goes well on your continuing journey, and thank you for everything.

Your friend,

Eric Wagner

P.S. Two mornings this week I looked up at Sirius as I took out the trash. I remember looking up at Sirius the morning after you died. Next year marks the fiftieth anniversary of the beginning of your Sirius experience. I wonder what the future holds for us all.

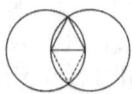

Appendix 1:
The Dogon Age of Music

And if, in whatever sense, *Dogon A.D.* marks the beginning of a Dogon age of music, in which the unity of sounds, their roots, and their potentiating energy are stressed, Julius Hemphill will play a decisive part in the developing culture of that age.
– Robert Palmer, notes to *Dogon A.D.*, recorded February, 1972

We're in science fiction now.
– Allen Ginsberg

I think sometime after 1955 rock music became the dominant paradigm of music in our world or at least in the western world. A few years ago I heard Trevor Noah say that rap had become the dominant form of music in our culture. At first I disagreed with him, but I have come to agree with him. I had lived all my life in a world dominated by rock music, so I didn't notice the shift. In the last few years I have asked my high school and community college classes what they consider the dominant form of music in our culture. Most say rap or hip hop. A few say pop or R & B or even country, but hip hop seems to have emerged on top.

Comparing the audience responses to Elton John and Eminem at the 2020 Oscars, it seemed clear that hip hop centered the musical world of this mostly under fifty celebrity audience.

Artur Schnabel commented that in the nineteenth century brides in Germany typically received a piano as a wedding gift. In the early twentieth century brides typically received a car instead. In 1950 most American homes had a piano. Popular music in America seemed largely piano based until rock music when it became guitar based. In the 1980s synthesizers and sequencers became much less expensive, and drum machines dominated popular music. I remember watching the Grammys in the late eighties, and all of the performers except Prince used a drum machine. Many artists today build music on computers from the ground up. This process seems very foreign to many of my contemporaries.

Now, I know that avant garde jazz like the music of Julius Hemphill has not played a major role in the evolution of hip hop, but I love Palmer's phrase "the Dogon age of music". Earlier forms of music created mainly by black people, such as jazz and rhythm and blues/rock and roll created much more wealth for white people than they did for black people. Rap has proved different. Although white artists have participated in and benefitted from rap music, it remains dominated by black artists, and many black owned record labels have helped shape the music. James Joyce described writing *Finnegans Wake* as drilling through a mountain from two sides and hoping the paths would meet in the middle. I suspect the two paths will not fully meet in this essay, but I will continue digging nonetheless. Tupac mapped out a history of Great Black Music in "Thugz Mansion" showing the continuity between jazz, R&B and hip hop.

Timeline

All quotes and much of this information from "The History of Hip-Hop: 1925 to Now" www.liveabout.com/history-of-hip-hop-1925-to-now-2857353

February, 1972 Julius Hemphill records *Dogon A.D.*

1972 *Mumbo Jumbo* by Ishmael Reed released.

1973 "DJ Kool Herc deejays his first block party."

Gravity's Rainbow by Thomas Pynchon released

July 23, 1973 Robert Anton Wilson begins odd Sirius experiences. Wilson would later learn of the Dogon people's knowledge of the Sirius system.

1974 "After seeing DJ Kool Herc perform at block parties, Grandmaster Cas, Grandmaster Flash, and Afrika Bambaataa start playing at parties all over the Bronx neighborhoods."

1979 "Rapper's Delight" by the Sugarhill Gang released.

1982 "The Message" by Grandmaster Flash and the Furious 5 released. I remember hearing this song all over the place when I visited New York that August. I heard Julius Hemphill with poet K. Curtis Lyle open for Billy Bang's Bang Gang at the Public Theater on that trip. One song featured Lyle chanting "Rapture is the Rupture we are looking for" while Hemphill played his silver alto.

1984 "Michael Jackson does the Moonwalk at the Grammys."

1986 Run-DMC with Stephen Tyler and Joe Perry release "Walk This Way". With this song rap reaches a large white audience. My cousins loved this song.

1988 *Straight Outta Compton* by N.W.A. released. This album, along with recordings by 2 Live Crew, the Ghetto Boys and others, mark a major change in our culture in terms of censorship. Swear words occurred rarely in earlier hip hop and rock recordings. Now explicit lyrics have become commonplace. Romantic love dominated poetry in our culture from the troubadours in the twelfth century up until the 1980s. The music of Frank Sinatra, the Temptations and the Beatles mostly focused on romantic love with occasional coded sexual references. One mark of the current paradigm seems an acceptance of sexual frankness.

> "frankness as never before,
> disillusions as never told in the old days,
> hysterias, trench confessions,
> laughter out of dead bellies."
> – Ezra Pound, "Hugh Selwyn Mauberlay", describing the response to World War I.

1988 *Yo! MTV Raps* premiers.

September 24, 1991 Nirvana releases *Nevermind*. At this point it seems to me rock remains the dominant paradigm of our culture. That changes sometime between 1991 and the present.

1992 Body Count releases "Cop Killer" with lyrics by band member Ice T. President George H. W. Bush publicly denounces the song. Ice T has played a cop on *Law and Order: Special Victims Unit* since 2000.

April 2, 1995 Julius Hemphill dies.

September 7, 1995 Tupac Shakur murdered.

March 9, 1997. The Notorious B.I.G. shot and killed.

2009 - present Rap music generates more revenue than any other form of music.

    In 2016, shortly following the election of Donald Trump, a TV special aired for the opening of the new Smithsonian African American History Museum. Common, Doug E. Fresh and Chuck D recited poems by Langston Hughes, Rakim, Chuck D, Common, and Grandmaster Mellie Mel. I found it interesting to see President Obama sitting in the balcony chanting "Fight the power" along with the rest of the audience.

    Read more. Learn more. Change the globe.
                                            – Nas

    Thanks to my friend Rob Robinson who has contributed greatly to my hip hop education.

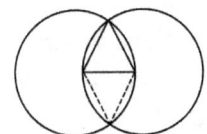

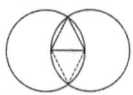

More Notes on the Influence of James Joyce on Robert Anton Wilson

– by R. Michael Johnson

Eric Wagner has shown in the previous pages how Wilson uses James Joyce, as both a character and as a thinker. But Joyce has found a critical place in almost all of Wilson's work, which among other things concerns human freedom, creativity, and deeper-than-biological levels of holism at work on our planet and in the human mind. Let the following function as an addenda, a series of footnotes to Wagner, and further elucidation of the extensive influence of Joyce in Wilson's work and what most of Wilson's critics have missed along these lines, so far, as of 2024.

Around his 27th birthday in 1959 Wilson, then scrambling as a freelance writer and supporting a family, published "Joyce and Taoism" in the *James Joyce Review*. This was later reprinted in his *Email To The Universe* as "Joyce and Daoism" (Hilaritas Press ed, pp.85-96.) Near the end of his life, into the early years of the 21st century when teaching courses online Wilson noted he'd been studying Joyce for over 50 years. The primary text for Wilson's Joyce writings is probably *Coincidance: A Head Test*, (1988), which contains extensive commentary within cabalistic musings on Joyce, especially *Ulysses* and *Finnegans Wake,* although significant statements about Joyce, his work, life, and freakish intelligence, are found in almost all of Wilson's books..

From 1959 to his first book, *Playboy's Book of Forbidden Words* (1972), Joyce's work was a near-constant presence in the – possibly over 1000 – articles he published in countless magazines, scholarly publications, and the underground press. (see German archivist Martin Wagner's collection at http://rawilsonfans.de/en/bibliography/ and Mike Gathers' archive of Wilsonia at https://rawilsonfans.org/essays/)

In *Playboy's Book of Forbidden Words* (1972), Wilson's first published book, by page 6 (paperback edition) he has already mentioned Joyce within the context of noted legal rulings that loosened censorship laws in the 20th century. Under "Bastard" Wilson notes Joyce used an intensifier: "bitch's bastard", real Dublinese. For "Blow": Molly Bloom *thinks* she *might* like to try it sometime. For the entry "Buck Naked" he quotes Buck Mulligan from *Ulysses*: "Redheaded women buck like goats." Under the extended entry for "Cock": "Joyce's Molly Bloom puns on it in *Ulysses*, saying of French erotic writer Paul de Kock, 'nice name he has,' and later, in her soliloquy, speculating that he was given the name because, 'he was always going around trying to shove it into every woman he met.'" Under another long entry, for "Cunt": "It next surfaced in Joyce's *Ulysses* where Bloom ruminates poetically about the Sinai desert: 'It bore the first, the oldest race. Dead now: sunken. An old woman's. The great sunken cunt of the world.'" Under "Fuck" Wilson notes it's the first appearance in literature, in the "Circe" episode with Private Carr saying, "I'll break the fucking neck of any fucking bugger who says a word against my king," and 200 pages later, when Molly Bloom thinks she'll confess her adulteries to Leopold: "I'll tell him yes your wife has been fucked and damn well fucked."

In a world of free Internet porn, etc: Think of the *persecution* of this book (*Ulysses*) because of such things! Published in 1922, not until 1933 did a judge allow it to be published in the US. It had to be pirated. It had to be literally smuggled into the U.S., via Canada. Wilson adds, "The censorship problems Joyce confronted intimidated other writers . . ." No doubt. Under "Masturbation" Wilson notes that Joyce seemed to seek to reduce the "terror" of it by making jokes around it: "A Honeymoon in the Hand" and "Every Man His Own Wife." The entry for "Touch" contains Molly's "Give me a touch, Poldy. God, I'm dying for it." Among others.

Wilson was not happy with editorial decisions made around this book, writing many years later that "the erudition and linguistic history were excised, along with much of the wit . . ." (*Coincidance: A Head Test*, Hilaritas ed., p.37.)

In 1973's *Sex and Drugs*, later reprinted as *Sex, Drugs and Magick: A Journey Beyond Limits*, his second book published by Playboy Press, Wilson selected quotes from *Finnegans Wake* as chapter epigraphs. For a chapter on drugs that are purported to enhance the libido or sexual performance, he selected "Hearsay in paradox lust." For a section on the history of witches, orgies, sex magick, hierogamy – mostly about the drugs from the deadly nightshade/Solanaceae family, he chose: "One must sell it someone, the sacred name of love . . . all thinking all of it, the It with an itch in it, the All every inch in it, the pleasure each will preen her for, the business each was bred to breed by . . . the law of the jungerl." For a chapter on hashish: "High Thats Hight Uberking Leary his fiery grass-belonghead all show color of sorelwood herb-green . . ." No doubt the name of his friend Timothy Leary, "grass" and "green" was too good to pass up. Heading up the chapter on "Powders Deadly and White" we read this passage from *FW*: "So that was the dope that woolied the cad that kinked the ruck that noised the rape that tried the sap that hugged the mort? . . . That legged in the hoax that joke bilked."

In other works Wilson noted that the only actual drugs Joyce was linked to that were psychoactive were alcohol and cocaine, the latter of which no doubt was prescribed for Joyce's numerous eye ailments and surgeries. However, not only had Leary said that reading Joyce prepared him for psychedelic space, but Wilson would link Joyce's prose – especially *Ulysses* and *Finnegans Wake* – to the psychedelic experience.

The ideas around later artists obtaining psychedelic effects from an earlier work by an artist known to have never ingested psychedelics before should be more discussed, as this discussion could shed light on the nature of mind. What are the best ways to describe psychedelic experience? Does having a psychedelic experience *require* LSD, psilocybin, mescaline, Ketamine, DMT, or any of the Shulgin compounds? What about cannabis? Are some minds like Joyce's genetically bent more toward what seem to be psychedelic states? Is there something particular about *writing* and *reading* and what would encourage something isomorphic to a psychedelic state, given certain texts, writers and readers? What does it say about those of us who perceive a work of art or, even an idea, as "psychedelic"? How many levels of explanation for "that's psychedelic!" can we come up with? Will it all ultimately be pinned down by ever-better neuroimaging? What might be particular values that emerge from these states/modes of perception? Etc.

Fifteen years after *Sex and Drugs* was published Wilson wrote a new Preface in which he claimed that in 1973, despite blurbs from Alan Watts, William S. Burroughs and Timothy Leary, he would give seminars and find out people couldn't find the book, and he joked that *Playboy* must have released it on a strictly "need to know" basis. He also wrote that other publishers refused to reprint it and suspected the topics were too hot during the extremely repressive period of Nixon, Ford, Carter, Reagan and Bush. Wilson also discussed in a short lucid argument that certain secrets of tantra and sex-magick, addressed in his book, which he thought probably added to the taboo and fears surrounding the book, were also (probably?) instrumental in the book being difficult to find. This socio-political "repression" of a book no doubt added to his sympathy with Joyce's 11 year blacklist in the US for *Ulysses*. In 2024 the edition put out by Hilaritas Press seems to be doing well. *Sex, Drugs and Magick* has found a new socio-political-publishing world terrain.

While waiting for the publisher Dell to put out his trilogy of novels co-written with Robert Shea, Wilson published his first novel, *The Sex Magicians* (1973), on a small press called Sheffield House in Chatsworth, California. It's a short, subversive pornographic novella that serves to lampoon all "ordinary" sex and religion-backed sexual repression, but it's also a novella filled with wild sex and the most extravagant ideas of so-called left-handed tantra, which was mostly influenced by Aleister Crowley's sex magick/Scientific Illuminism: yoga, sex, drugs, and shamanic altered states that induce telepathy and ESP in general. A comic novella which has some group sex scenes – "The Mongolian Clusterfuck" and "Flying Philadelphia Fuck" that are so baroque and extravagantly described it strongly feels like a parody of porn. This short, strange, witty and at times hilarious novella is filled with ideas and wild sex, and there is zero mention of Joyce. (Hilaritas Press has published a new edition of *The Sex Magicians*.)

Wilson had a happier time publishing his third (of three) books for Playboy Press, *The Book of the Breast* (1974), later re-titled *Ishtar Rising* (1989), it seems to be one of his most under-appreciated nonfiction works. A solidly pro-sex feminist and pro-feminine mythology work with a longing for more female-centered values in our patriarchal culture, it's perhaps best understood within the fairly urgent desire for the Return of the Goddess most famously articulated in Robert Graves's 1948 work *The White Goddess*, and a later quasi-archaeological work, Riane Eisler's *The Chalice and the Blade* (1987). *Ishtar Rising* has perhaps been burdened by academia and its warring factions and the idea of the "male gaze" since the 1970s. Wilson's "hermetic" erudition is on full display and while Joyce is only mentioned in passing, Wilson's use of G. Rattray Taylor's frame for sexual ideas, ideation and the structural unconscious throughout history, Anal-Patrist vs. Oral-Matrist values, had Wilson later remark that all three of Joyce's main characters – Stephen, Leopold and Molly – in *Ulysses* showed Oral-Matrist values. (permissive attitudes toward sex; freedom for women; women accorded high status; welfare is more valued than chastity; politically democratic; progressive/revolutionary; no distrust of research; spontaneity and exhibitionism; deep fear of incest; sex differences between people minimized; pleasure and hedonism is welcomed; "mother" or goddess-based religion).

He writes in the 1989 Introduction that the book introduced Taoist philosophy, "so disguised that nobody but the people who write commentaries of *Finnegans Wake* would ever figure out how many hidden meanings there were in every paragraph." (*Ishtar Rising*, p. xxxvii, Hilaritas Press ed.) In touching on another major theme throughout his own work: the reality of masks and the masks of "reality" and the nature of "authentic" vs. "counterfeit" and the hermetic artist (of which he includes Joyce), Wilson cites Joyce becoming Stephen Dedalus in *A Portrait of the Artist as a Young Man*, who vows to "forge in the smithy of my soul the uncreated conscience of my race," but "in *Finnegans Wake*, Joyce becomes Shem the Penman, forger (metallurgical) of alchemical transmutations and forger (illegal) of bad checks. With Shem, Joyce was no doubt parodying himself and the at-times precarious nature of the artist's life. Aristotle said art imitates nature, and what is the difference between an imitation and a counterfeit?" (ibid., xxxiv) Wilson also links the Sumerian goddess Inanna's descent and rise to Ishtar and all the subsequent "sun" gods who died and came back to life and Osiris, Dionysius, Jesus, and even Tim Finnegan. (ibid., xxv)

In a book about breasts, of course Wilson would have to get in yet another passage from Molly Bloom's "rapturous memories" from her book-culminating soliloquy in "Penelope": "And then he asked me would I yes to say yes my mountain flower and first I put my arms around him yes and drew him down to me so he could feel my breasts all perfume yes and his heart was going like mad yes and yes I said I will Yes." (ibid., xliv)

As the turbulent early years of the 1970s and the Vietnam War raged on, Wilson became probably the most energetic defender of Timothy Leary as he languished in prisons. Anyone who really looks at Leary's case will see he was a political prisoner. Wilson wrote a fairly thick manuscript that was finished around 1974, which, for reasons still not totally clear, went unpublished and the book was lost for a time until some fortuitous circumstances rescued it, and it was published 46 years later, in 2020. Titled *The Starseed Signals*, it is about the penal system, the persecution of heretics, and Leary's ideas, so Joyce was not prominent in this book and Wilson only points out by way of example that Leary's Interpersonal Grid shows that some personality types – the "Injustice Collector" and "Mama's Boy" – essentially a submissive-masochist type - can act that way at work and become a dictator or "mean motherfucker" at home with wife and children, and Wilson noted that this is "illustrated in James Joyce's unforgettable short story, 'Counterparts.'"(*The Starseed Signals*, Hilaritas Press, p.67)

Another of Wilson's "lost" texts resurfaced many years later. Around 1974 he finished a manuscript on Aleister Crowley and, like *The Starseed Signals*, it is uncertain how it got lost. It was published in 2023 as *Lion of Light: Robert Anton Wilson on Aleister Crowley* and the Joyce content is again minimal, with Wilson discussing the influence of the Hermetic Order of the Golden Dawn and noting that "Much of modern literary culture owes its symbolism and themes to this group; not only Yeats' poetry, but even that of Ezra Pound and T.S. Eliot, and the novels of James Joyce, show Golden Dawn elements, which were common currency in the London of 1900-1914, where all these writers met" (p.203). In many other places, Wilson reminds us that Joyce was interested in this occult order and read their literature, but never joined any of these Freemasonic groups and that Joyce personally preferred his own idiosyncratic aesthetic of "applied Aquinas." (This aesthetic will be discussed below, in observations about *The Homing Pigeons,* from the *Schrödinger's Cat Trilogy.*)

Wilson would return to the Molly passages in rendering a female character's inner monologue in his later fiction, including in *Illuminatus!,* where Mary Lou Servix, an intelligent African-American woman raised in racist America, begins a long unbroken threnodic paragraph containing almost zero punctuation with "No – because they broke Billie Freshette slow and ugly and they broke Marilyn Monroe fast and bright like lightning They broke Daddy and they broke Momma . . ." and ends with "that poetry Simon quoted is all wrong No it's not true that no man is an island No the truth is every man is an island and especially every woman is an island and even more every black woman is an island." (p.674 of omnibus edition)

Wilson no doubt thought Joyce had created an ideal template for writers to render the stream of inner monologue of humans (especially women?), as he also used a Molly-like passage to reveal the thoughts of a Marilyn Monroe-like character in *The Trick Top Hat,* Carol Christmas, who ponders her life as a sex goddess in the minds of millions of men and her psychic scar over having a deformed baby: "a real weirdo he is but Arab that's nice a Sultan we're in the harem it's my first time again . . . high art porn movie . . . Off-Off Broadway for me watching me watching me fuck millions . . . didn't understand at first why me why of all the millions of births on the planet that day . . . damned cruel unjust universe . . ."(See *Schrodinger's Cat Trilogy,* omnibus ed, pp.250-251; p.111-112 of Pocket Books ed. of *The Trick Top Hat.*)

In *Illuminatus!* (mostly written 1968-71, but not published until 1975), Wilson's Joyce influences flower to full bloom to the point where at times we're not sure if he's using an allusion or not. For example, after a paragraph containing characters planning a deal between enemy agents, a very short, seeming non-sequitur appears: "FIVES. SEX. HERE IS WISDOM. The mumble of the breast is the mutter of man." (p.259, *Illuminatus Trilogy*, omnibus ed.) The reader of *Finnegans Wake* may think this was a line they missed or didn't remember; it certainly *seems* like Joyce parodying Freud. Is this directly from *FW*? The proliferation of a thousand puzzles like this suffuse Wilson's fictional work. Similarly, among many other examples along these lines, another sudden break in the narrative for this: "I. THE FAUST PARSON, SINGULAR. Napalm sundaes for How Chow Mein, misfortune's cookie." (ibid., p.272) A common gloss on this among Wilson exegetes is that this is the supercomputer, FUCKUP, an advanced AI system, which has written the entire novel, and it at times uses the "mind" of *FW*. Here it seems to be trying to say something about the ongoing Vietnam war. Further use of *FW* abounds, for example on p.286: "ORGASM. HER BUBBIES FRITCHID BY THE GYNING DEEP-SEADOODLER. All in a lewdercrass chaste for a moulteening fawkin." This is followed without a break by "normal" discourse about the "plot" of the novel. Certainly the characters and their machinations do bear some resemblance to those in Hammett's *The Maltese Falcon*, but even here: the reader is taxed in the same way all *FW*-exegetes are: how many referents are here and how can we gloss them within the context of the overall kaleidoscopic narrations?

Furthermore, in a passage in which Saul Goodman is coming to revelations about his character and life, we get this short paragraph interpolated and interrupting the narrative: "QUEENS. Psychoanalysts in living cells, moving in military ordure, and a shitty outlook on life and sex, dancing coins in harry's krishna. It all coheres, even if you approach it bass ackwards. It coheres." (ibid., p.291) Whomever or whatever wrote this book seems to want to assure us to stick with it; it makes sense. This seeming fourth-wall-break, this intrusion, where the book/author seems to address the reader of difficult passages, echoes the many times this occurs in *FW*, perhaps starting with "What a mnice old mness it all mnakes!" (p.19, *FW*), or "Thus the unfacts, did we possess them, are too imprecisely few to warrant our certitude." (*FW*, p.57), Or, yet further still, "We are once amore as babes awondering in a wold made fresh where the hen in the storyaboot we start from scratch." (*FW*, p.336). There are many such breakages in *FW*, so perhaps just one more: "You is feeling like you was lost in the bush, boy?"(*FW*, p.112)

This might be a good example of, in addition to a wall-break, a "psychedelic effect" in which the phenomenology of reading a dense text, engaging all intellectual faculties *in extremis*, is suddenly pierced by the narrator, who addresses the reader directly, which can be somewhat shocking. And no, we aren't having an easy time with your book, thanks, but it's interesting, so I will keep trying to de-code you. Can we get back to business please?

On the next page of *Illuminatus!*: another abrupt shift in *Wake*-like language, in the midst of the "ordinary" narration: "NOTHUNG. Woden you gnaw it, when you herd those flying sheeps with wagner's loopy howls? Hassan walked this loony valley, he had to wake up by himself." (ibid., p.292) Richard Wagner/Wotan/Nothung/Odin, with sheep herding in a valley, and Hassan i Sabbah? Wake himself? Loony? Same page: "RAGS. Hail Ghoulumbia, her monadmen are fled and all she's left now is a bloody period." Menstruation, Hail Columbia, Minutemen, ghouls, something to do with Leibniz? (ibid., p.292) Next page - and why an influx of this *FW*-stuff crammed in here? – "UNHEIMLICH. Urvater whose art's uneven, horrid be thine aim. Harpoon in him, corpus whalem: take ye and hate." (ibid., p.293): The Lord's Prayer given a Lovecraft spin by way of *Moby Dick*? Gnosticism?

The use of *FW*-like language here seems to serve as an augmentation to the "puzzle" aspect of the novels. It had already been saturated with false leads, double and triple crosses, sundry mixes of obscure fact with wild fiction, conspiracies galore, coded language, and secret societies using mind tricks to throw off the others. To add Joycean language play would seem par for the course here, and Wilson was the far heavier Joycean of the two authors, so it seems a safe bet that much of the Joyce-play emanated from Wilson's fecund nervous system.

Joyce is referred to with the Zurich circle of Paul Klee, Hermann Hesse and Carl Jung within the context of brilliant, well-educated, wealthy, fascist madman "Robert Putney Drake": "Drake's brilliance had also been noted by Jung's circle in Zurich. Once – when Drake was off taking mescaline with Paul Klee and friends on what they called their Journey to the East – Drake had been a topic of long and puzzled conversations in Jung's study. 'We haven't seen his like since Joyce was here,' one woman psychiatrist commented. 'He is brilliant, yes,' Jung said sadly, 'but evil. So evil that I despair of comprehending him . . ." (ibid., pp.315-316) Similarly, ten pages later: "It was a famous novelist, who was later to win the Nobel Prize, who actually gave Drake his first lead on what the Mafia always called *il Segreto*. They had been talking about Joyce and his unfortunate daughter, and the novelist mentioned Joyce's attempts to convince himself that she wasn't really schizophrenic. 'He told Jung, 'After all, I do the same sorts of things with language myself.' Do you know what Jung, that old Chinese sage disguised as a psychiatrist, answered? 'You are diving but she is sinking.' Incisive, of course; and yet, all of us who write anything that goes below the surface of naturalism can understand Joyce's skepticism. We never know for sure whether we're diving or just sinking." (ibid., p.325) Wilson has injected an enormous amount of Joyce's biography into his own novels, and obviously at times Wilson felt uncertainty about "diving" over the course of his many novels and nonfiction works. Schizophrenia had indeed been evident in family members of both Joyce and Wilson.

A character quotes Joyce on the "pun is mightier than the sword," followed by pun-play between the protagonists. (ibid., p.395) The General Slocum disaster is mentioned in medium/seer Mama Sutra's conning runaround of detective Danny Pricefixer, in which she picks up "vibrations" and links the JFK murder with the Golden Dawn, paranormal beings from Lovecraft and other sources, high school physics experiments, Discordian number poetry, DNA, the collective unconscious, Abdul Alhazred, The Cult of the Yellow Sign, the John Birch Society, etc. In her "mindfuck" of the detective, Mama Sutra reels off wheels within wheels of paralogical data: "James Joyce, who studied the theosophy of Blavatski and the mysticism of the Golden Dawn Society. He wrote a novel in which all the action takes place on June 16, 1904. The novel is called *Ulysses*, and is impregnated on every page with coded mystical revelations. And, yes, now I remember, there is a shipwreck mentioned in it. Joyce made all the background details historically accurate, so he included what was actually in the Dublin papers that day – the book takes place in Dublin, you see — and one of the stories concerned the sinking of the ship, General Slocum, in New York Harbor the day before June 15." [, . .] "Let me tell you flatly, then, that what you have stumbled upon is something that could easily involve both James Joyce's mysticism and the assassination of President John Kennedy. But to understand you will have to stretch your mind to the breaking point." Pricefixer the detective is taken for quite a ride here! (*Illuminatus!*, pp.521-522)

Even moreso, it seems the line between statistical chance of a writer's use of a word or whether yet another allusion has occurred on the page, is illustrated when one character pours another coffee and we read: "Black for me, said Hauptmann, picking up a pastry with cherry filling and biting into it with relish." (ibid., p.669) Is this a nod to Leopold Bloom, who "ate with relish the inner organs of beasts and fowls"? If only because Wilson was a lifelong reader of all of Joyce's work and that in his extraordinary reverence he borrows structures, forms, and other stylistic choices from Joyce that we're never quite sure.

Similarly, "And what we're trying to communicate – the ultimate secret, the philosopher's stone, the elixir of life – is just the power of the word *No*. We are people who have said *Non serviam*, and we're trying to teach others to say it." (ibid., p. 697) Whether this "non serviam" is also an allusion to Stephen Dedalus will leave us wondering.

It seems slightly safer to catch and attribute a reference to Stephen's line to Haines in "Telemachus", "You behold in me, Stephen said with grim displeasure, a horrible example of free thought," when the now much more free-thinking Joe Malik tells Simon Moon, "I no longer claim membership in the liberal intellectual guild. You behold in me an example of creeping mysticism." (*Illuminatus!*, p.124)

As to the once very hot debate about *Ulysses* and "realism", we hear a right wing member of the Knights of Christianity United in Faith (KCUF), in a long parenthetical, rail about "realism" and "filth." It seems a temporal interpolation, as if there is a quick cut to this scene, and if it bears any resemblance to *Ulysses*, it's probably in the "Wandering Rocks" and its structure of many-things-going-on-at-once in space/time, this being just one episode:

"They fill their books with obscene words, claiming this is realism," Smiling Jim shouted to the KCUF assembly. "It's not my idea of realism. I don't know anybody who talks in that gutter language they call realism. And they describe every possible perversion, acts against nature that are so outrageous I wouldn't sully this audiences' ears by even mentioning their medical names. Some of them even glorify the criminal and the anarchist. I'd like to see one of these hacks come up to me and look me in the eye and say, 'I didn't do it for money.

I was honestly trying to tell a good, honest story that would teach people something of value.' They couldn't say that. The lie would stick in their throats. Who can doubt where they get their orders from? What person in this audience needs to be told what group is behind this overflowing sewer of smut and filth?" (ibid., p.125)

These sorts of detractors would have assailed *Ulysses* in 1930s America, and *Illuminatus!* in its time, and probably in many rural areas today. The trilogy is indeed replete with "gutter language", sexual acts, criminals and anarchists. Did Joyce, Shea or Wilson "get their orders" from the Illuminati? The idea is laughable, but in a world of Q-Anon, who knows how these passages will be read in the wake of a chaotic 2025?

Some other uses of Joyce in *Illuminatus!*: one of the main characters (George Dorn) is being held in jail and is frantically trying to imagine an escape, but keeps thinking of a monk's face he'd seen in a dream: "He began trying to re-create the face and identify it – James Joyce, H.P. Lovecraft and a monk in a painting by Fra Angelico all came to mind." A page later, rescuers with machine guns appear outside the jail, shouting, and Dorn hears, "'Earwicker, Bloom and Craft'. - I've still got Joyce on my mind, I decided." (ibid., 73-74) Wilson and Shea had concocted "Ewige Blumenkraft" : German: "Eternal Flower Power" -- for their purposes in writing about political revolutionaries and the Eris-worshiping Discordian Society in the 1960s and early 1970s. This might have been influenced by Goethe's "Ewige Weibliche Wesen": "The Eternal Feminine" - an idea that harmonizes with both Wilson and Shea's overall worldviews, and also links the Bavarian Illuminati's German language to Shea and Wilson's purposes.

"What gets me is how much has been out in the open for so long. Not just Lovecraft, Joyce, Melville, etc., or in the Bugs Bunny cartoons but in scholarly works that pretend to explain." (ibid., p.123) During a long LSD-drenched carnivalesque and absurdist section about characters real and imaginary at the

Chicago 1968 Democratic National Convention/police riot: "Abbie Hoffman went by just then, talking to Apollonius of Tyana. Were we all in Jarry's mind or Joyce's?" (ibid., 143) This is part of a very extensive employment of Joyce by Wilson: psychedelic states of mind, for Wilson, were anticipated by Joyce's work, especially certain sections of *Ulysses* and far moreso: *FW*. We will see the manifestation of mind (psyche-delicism) in Joyce's work as invoked by Wilson very many times until Wilson's death in 2007.

Some thoughts could "leak" – via psychedelics and ESP (or by the possible mysterious omniscience of the writer of the novel?) – into the heads of other characters without the narration telling us explicitly who's talking, a technique that seems influenced by Joyce, or possibly Faulkner: "The leak almost gave him water on the brain. He kept wondering where all that Joyce and surrealism was coming from." (ibid., p.145) This was "leaked" into the head of George Dorn by the free indirect discourse of a "me" of some sort.

Still in psychedelic space in Chicago, August 1968: "But acid is placid, you know, and a minute later I was on Joyce's juices again and thinking of a drama called 'Their Mace and My Gripes.' I made the first line fruity, in honor of Padre Pederastia: 'What a botch of a pair to plumb this hour's gripes.'" (ibid., 147) This obviously takes off from the "Mookse and Gripes" section from *FW*, Book 1, chapter 6, pp.152-159. Another: "Just then SDS kids who'd been teargassed across the street came running our way, and Hagbard got busy handing out wet handkerchiefs. They needed them: they were half-blind, like Joyce splitting his Adam into wise hopes." (ibid., p.148) This seems to combine Joyce's "adams and ifs" in *FW* – which Wilson thought might have referenced Heisenberg and anticipated Hiroshima – with the founder of the Bavarian Illuminati, Adam Weishaupt.

Even more: a right wing racist/sexist construction worker, Stanislaus Oedipuski, was slipped an LSD-like drug called AUM in punch one night at the Sheraton-Chicago and it completely changed his life before he was mysteriously murdered. He grew his hair long, preached tolerance, stopped watching TV and had – in less than a month – built a personal library – Sociology, Darwin, oriental mysticism, Raymond Chandler, astronomy, Lewis Carroll – and left annotations in a book on number theory. He seems to have become a habitual user of Gematria, Cabala, and the *I Ching*, leaving a long note (diary entry?), which reads in part: "Another woman just came by, collecting for the Mothers March against Muscular Dystrophy. I gave her a quarter. Where was I? Oh, yes: James Joyce had five letters in both his front name and hind name, so he was worth looking into. *A Portrait of the Artist* has five chapters, all well and good, but *Ulysses* has 18 chapters, a stumper, until I remembered that 5+18=23. How about *Finnegans Wake*? Alas, that has 17 chapters, and I was bogged down for a while . . ." (ibid., pp235-237.) Oedipuski deploys this cabalistic and Discordian-society-linked number poetry to link them with current news events and to John Dillinger, to the year 1723, when Adam Smith and Adam Weishaupt were both born (creative bluffing/license: current sources link Weishaupt's birth to 1748), to the Apple of Discord, to the defendants in the Chicago Conspiracy Trial, etc. Similarly, Danny Pricefixer flummoxes himself and goes off into a Discordian number poetry spiel while Mama Sutra is temporarily out of the room she'd been bamboozling Pricefixer in; it ends with an allusion to Leopold Bloom remembering the Law of Falling Bodies: "2422, he thought while Mama Sutra spoke to the receptionist, that's even crazier than the rest of this. 2 plus 4 plus 2 plus 2. Adds up to 10. The base of the decimal system. What the hell does that mean? Or 24 plus 22 adds up to 46.That's two times 23, the number missing in between 24 and 22. Another enigma. And 2 times 4 times 2 times 2 is, let's see, 32. Law of falling bodies." 32 feet per second per second – the formula of the fall – also shows up on the final page of the novel, before the notorious *Appendices*. This sort of cabalistic riffing would be on virtuosic extended further display in Wilson's later works, particularly in 1988's *Coincidance: A Head Test*.

Still working within *Illuminatus!*: Epicene Wildeblood tells the editor of *Confrontation* magazine that his book review – apparently of *Illuminatus!* itself – will be done "tomorrow" and Epicene talks about the book: "It's a dreadfully long monster of a book," Wildeblood says pettishly, "and I certainly won't have time to read it, but I'll give it a thorough *skimming*. The authors are utterly incompetent – no sense of style or structure at all. It starts out as a detective story, switches to science-fiction, then goes off into the supernatural, and is full of the most detailed information of dozens of *ghastly* boring subjects. And the time sequence is all out of order in a very pretentious imitation of Faulkner or Joyce . . ." (ibid., p.238)

Illuminati scaremonger, redneck sheriff in Mad Dog, Texas and member of the Legion of Dynamic Discord – he definitely Knows Things – James Cartwright – tells us the Illuminati were responsible for the General Slocum disaster, a ship that sank in 1904. 19 plus 4 = 23, etc. There are more 23s in this novel than a basketball stadium filled with 20,000 Michael Jordan fans. Cartwright, along with a couple others, seems tailor-made for the second and third decade of 21st century America and its Q-Anon-level thinking, viz: "You tell me," Cartwright said, "if all consciousness is not *one*, just how did Joyce happen to pick the very next day for *Ulysses*, so the General Slocum disaster would be in the newspapers his characters read? You see, Joyce knew he was a genius, but he never did understand the nature of genius, which is to be better in touch with the universal consciousness than the average man is. Anyway, the Illuminati were trying, with the General Slocum disaster, a new, more economical technique for achieving transcendental illumination – one that would require only a few hundred sudden deaths rather than thousands. Not that they care about saving lives, you understand, though the desire might result from the return of the repressed original purpose of the Illuminati, which was benign." (*Illuminatus!*, pp.581-582)

As the novel begins to come to a head, "a woman" has a *Finnegans Wake*-like vision of what's to come; at this point virtually every character is on LSD:

"Then I started to flip, Malik eclipsed by Malaclypse and Celine hardly serene. Mary Lou I Worship You, the Red Eye is my own Mooning, what is the meaning of moaning? and suchlike seminal semantic antics (my head is a Quicktran quicksand where *The Territorial Imperative* always triggers *Stay Off My Turf*, the Latin and the Saxon at war in poor Simon's synapses, dead men fighting for use of my tongue, turning Population Explosion into We're Fucking Overcrowded and backward also, so it might emerge Copulation Explosion, and besides Hag barred straights from his Black-and-White Mass the acid was in me, I was tripping, flipping, skipping, ripping, on my Way with Maotsey Taotsey for the number of Our Lady is an hundred and fifty and six – there is Wiccadom!), but I never expected it this way." (*Illuminatus!*, p.632) 156 is the Feminine Principle in Kabbalah, and there seems to be superfecundity here, with possible fighting for territory due to crowding and over population, but the larger context seems puzzling. "Maotsey Taotsey" does seem like a riff off of *FW*'s "Laotsey-taotsey," (*FW*, p.242) though. The issue of sex and overpopulation also shows up in one of the novel's appendices, Appendix Lamed, see discussion below.

Joyce lives on in the Appendices of *Illuminatus!*. In the Illuminati's (supposed) cyclical model of history, Hegel, Vico and Marx are hauled in. Many of these thinkers were mistaken in their ideas about tri-cyclic ideas about how all of History plays out. (The Illuminati cyclical model of history [Or is it Discordian?] is pentacyclic: Chaos, Discord, Confusion, Bureaucracy, and Aftermath, in which Chaos again reigns. The esoteric version is defined as Thesis, Antithesis, Synthesis, Parenthesis, Paralysis: see *Illuminatus!*, pp.742-756)

But Discordian five-ness (The Law of Fives) reigns, and this is where Joyce enters. *A Portrait of the Artist As A Young*

Man appears just as the 5th cycle dawns, in 1914, as if Joyce was a proto-Discordian. In that work there are five chapters with an alteration of style from chapter to chapter to draw attention to five-ness, in addition to illustrating Stephen's growth. The Illuminati Primi saw this and warned Joyce to "be more careful in the future." Now the blarney really gets laid on thick: "A battle of wills ensued, and all through the writing of *Ulysses* Joyce was still considering a novel built entirely around the Law of Fives. When the Illuminati gave him what they call 'the Tiresias treatment' – blindness – he finally compromised. *Finnegans Wake*, when it appeared, broke with the Joachim-Hegel-Marx three-step but did not include the *funfwissenschaft* ("science of fives"). Instead, the Viconian four-stage theory was resurrected, a middle path that appealed to Joyce's sense of synchronicity, since he had once taught at a school on Vico Road in Dublin and later also lived in a house on Via Giambattista Vico in Rome." (ibid., p.745) Details of Joyce's life that would seem obscure – and true – are mixed in with an entirely fictional "history."

After a tossed-off joke about Aquarians, linking Joyce to Aaron Burr, Charles Darwin, Lewis Carroll, Willard Gibbs, DW Griffith and a few others (ibid., p.748), there is a very erudite discussion of occult symbols and sex (Appendix Lamed: The Tactics of Magick, pp.768-783), in which the significations of the left-handed vs. right-handed pentagram impinge on Chapter 14 of *Ulysses*, "Oxen of the Sun": the left-handed form of the pentagram (two horns pointing upward) "is always destructive of the Holy Spirit, in a certain sense." The right-handed form of the pentagram (only one horn pointed upward) "is also destructive in most cases, especially by those practitioners so roundly condemned in Chapter 14 of Joyce's *Ulysses* – and this group is certainly the majority these days. In view of the ecological crisis, it might even be wise to encourage the left-hand method and discourage the right-hand method at this time, to balance the Sacred Numbers." (*Illuminatus!*, pp.779-780) While this is an allusion to the admonition to not waste seed and pro-Motherhood, and which is for fecundity and creativity, according to Catholic doctrine vs. the fans and readers of such a book as *Illuminatus!*, who would be pro-birth control, women's free choice about how to manage her body, pro-masturbation, pro-all forms of sex, total sexual freedom, etc. "We" are those who favor the right-handed form of the pentagram, but we must consider the "ecological crisis."

Now, we wonder how many readers of this particularly recondite Appendix knew that Chapter 14 was "Oxen of the Sun," much less knew what it entailed. Furthermore, a close reading of Wilson's gloss of both types of pentagrams seems like a sophisticated put-on: both types are "destructive" - and we're all quite well aware of the population problem, which, by the way, was 3.7 billion in 1970, whereas it's at around 8.1 billion as I write this in 2024. Which pentagram we adhere to seems quite trivial, and one wonders if Wilson is simply trying to rope in readers of occult texts and steer them over into reading *Ulysses*. This business of addressing the symbolism of the pentagrams and linking them with ideas about whether birth control is a good idea (in the early 1970s), and quasi-appearing to appeal to the "conservative" side is an ironic and hilarious rhetorical gambit from Wilson.

Two pages later Wilson is discussing the Tarot deck in relation to YHVH and noting that "the lion-man-eagle-bull symbolism also fits" (these occult correspondences) "as do Joyce's Four Old Men in *Finnegans Wake*; it can also be found in the Aztec codices and Buddhist mandalas." (*Illuminatus!*, p. 782)

The penultimate reference to Joyce in *Illuminatus!* (p.797) concerns a pseudo-clarification of an earlier section in the novel that only serves to further complicate and indeed, upend the reader's prior glossings of that section, and links the movie *Manhattan Melodrama* (1934 W.S. Van Dyke and George Cukor) and *Ulysses* to *Illuminatus!*. (Vorsicht vor dem Ablenkungsmanöver!)

For the final reference to Joyce in *Illuminatus!*: "Appendix Nun: Additional Information About Some of the Characters": an entry on James Joyce:

"After death, he met Yeats on the fifth plane and said, 'Sir, I am now willing to learn from you, since you appear to have been right about Death after all.' Yeats replied, 'Not at all. You're dreaming this.' The remark so vexed Joyce that he immediately sought reincarnation (the fifth plane was full of mystics like Yeats and George Russell and Madame Blavatsky, and Joyce knew his rational Aristotelian sensibility would be constantly abused by further conversation with them), entered the womb of Elizabeth Mullins of Vernon, New Jersey, October 11, 1942, and was aborted December 10, 1942. Entered the womb of Rachel Stein of Ingolstadt, January 18, 1943, and was gassed with her, one month before birth was due, at Auschwitz, September 1, 1943. Thereafter, he retired to a monastery on the sixth plane and wrote his funniest, most bitter book. Parts of it, which he has been transmitting ever since, have been picked up by mediums on the six continents, all of whom assumed they were flipping out and refused to transcribe it." (ibid., p.804)

In a 1976 interview dated September 5, 1976, with *New Libertarian Notes/Weekly*, Wilson was asked, "What are your favorite novels, movies, TV shows, and music? He begins his response, "The novels would be, I supposed, *Ulysses*, *Finnegans Wake*, *The Magus* by Fowles, *The Roots of Heaven* by Gary, *Don Quixote*, and anything by Mark Twain." Later on in the interview he's asked, "Any more artistic opinions?" and Wilson immediately responds: "If I must. James Joyce is more important than Jesus, Buddha and Shakespeare put together . . ."

1977 saw Wilson publish his now-classic *Cosmic Trigger vol.1*, which chronicles his self-experimentation (AKA "brain change") with yoga, magick, psychedelic drugs, cannabis, constant writing, and continued encyclopedic reading, etc. He tells of reading the early unpublished manuscript of Burroughs's *Naked Lunch* and immediately evaluating Burroughs as the greatest prose stylist since Joyce. (*Cosmic Trigger vol 1*, p.41 Hilaritas Press edition) After an exceedingly weird experience in which Wilson was seemingly contacted by intelligences from near the Sirius star system, the "dog star," he re-read *Ulysses* for the first time in many years and was "struck by the Black Mass in which the souls of all the saved chant 'Gooooooooooooood' while all the souls of the damned chant 'Dooooooooooooog.'"(ibid., p.144) He cites Joyce's nightmare of history within the context of Wilson's recently murdered daughter.

1977, in the *New Libertarian Weekly* article by Wilson on the dream of space migration, and "the human drive to escape from all restraints", he cites the first fish that tried breathing air on land, our ancestors who left Europe to escape tyranny, the lingering semi-mythic heroism of Houdini, the exemplar of escape from restraints, and that "James Joyce became the greatest novelist of the 20th century by taking as his hero the world's first Escape Artist, Daedalus, and regarding 'nationality, language, and religion' as three 'nets I must fly over.'" (January 2, 1977 issue)

In a January 12th 1977 interview with Kevin Briggs and D. Scott Apel, Wilson is asked about his influences and his reply, in part:

> "First of all, I think everybody you read influences you. Every writer I've read has left some trace on me. And I think that's true of every reader, since what you feed your nervous system today becomes your reality tomorrow [. . .] The strongest influences are certainly Joyce, the blind man who saw, and Ezra Pound, the crazy man who understood [. . .] The main influences are definitely Pound, Joyce and William Burroughs. Burroughs definitely comes in third, after Pound and Joyce. I'm much more influenced by people in this century than in previous

centuries [. . .] People like Pound and Joyce are practically my contemporaries. Pound died only a couple of years ago, actually; Joyce died in 1940. But he's still the central twentieth-century novelist. Nobody has found a way yet to surpass Joyce in cosmic, mythic, epic scope, or in sheer crazy humor." (*Science Fiction: An Oral History*, ed. Apel, pp. 238-239)

When Wilson was interviewed by *Weird Trips* magazine in 1977, he got a question about what DNA's intent is. He answers:

"Well, DNA doesn't give a damn about us. It uses us to reproduce itself. In many species reproduction is the beginning of death. That was in a biology book James Joyce had when was in university and it made a big impression on him: reproduction is the beginning of death . . ." (*"Weird Trips Interviews Bob Shea & Robert Anton Wilson"*, 1977)

Wilson collaborated with Timothy Leary on a series of books in the latter half of the 1970s, after Leary was pardoned by California Governor Jerry Brown. Because both writers were Joyceans it's not simple to discern who wrote certain passages, Leary appears to have been a Joyce enthusiast, but we can safely assume that Wilson was much deeper the Joycean.

In 1979's *Game of Life*, in a section on drug-use among Darwin, Nietzsche, Gurdjieff and Joyce, we read, ". . . James Joyce, whose painful eye problems, leading eventually to blindness, were treated with cocaine, and who created his own hilariously non-Euclidean 'in risible universe' as normal vision faded and 'it darkled (tinct! tinct!) all this our funnanimal world.' In the repeated cycle of pain-bliss-pain-bliss some especially gifted individuals can obtain neurological vistas far beyond the reflex robotry of yokel terrestrial life." (New Falcon 3rd ed, p.33) The use of "yokel" here is a strong indication that Leary had at least a finger in the pie of this paragraph.

Eleven pages later there is a discussion of the cyclical model of history, Vico and Joyce: Joyce had a jovial, Punch-and-Judy take on history's cycles in *FW*: "It is the same told of all. Many. Miscegenations on miscegenations. Tieckle. They lived and laughed and loved and left. Forsin. Thy thingdome is given to the Meades and Porsons . . . In the ignorance that implies impression that knits knowledge that finds the nameform that whets the wits that convey contacts that sweeten sensation that drives desire that adheres to attachment that dogs death that bitches birth that entails the ensuance of existentiality." Wilson/Leary add to this the robot-hero peddles along pointlessly, linking this to more *FW*: "A human pest cycling past and recycling (post) and there he is (pist!) again." It seems it's Leary's voice who asserts here that, *contra* Hindu mythology, "Joyce, as we shall see, knew better. The cycle in *Finnegans Wake* is actually an upward DNA spiral rising to the stars." (ibid., p.43)

In further musings in "psycho-archaeology" (a Wilson term oft employed), using the archetypes in the Tarot deck, there is an abstruse discussion of twelve-ness in the collective unconscious, and Leary and Wilson link this to Leary's first four "circuits" of the human brain/consciousness that arose from the depths of evolution and history: For Leary, each circuit had three stages that were analogized to the neuron's reception of a signal, integration in the nucleus, then messaging to other neurons via electro-chemical impulse, and these twelve archetypes that corresponded to the first four (times 3) circuits and the Tarot deck "are the Twelve Old Men who haunt the dreamer's sleep all through *Finnegans Wake*, reappearing as twelve customers at the bar, the twelve jurors at the trial, u.s.w. Joyce commentators have noted that they are the twelve apostles (hence the refrain, reminiscent of the Last Supper, 'Pass the fish for Christ's sake'), the twelve labors of Hercules, the twelve signs of the Zodiac, and so forth; as indeed they are in the universal symbolism of Joyce's 'monomyth.' But basically they are the twelve castes of terrestrial humanity, the twelve genetic types that keep the earthship trip dancing within the same parameters generation after generation." (*Game of Life*, p.80)

Still with Wilson and Leary and the *Game of Life*, they link William Blake to Joyce in the "creative intelligent design of biological evolution" and female "egg-wisdom." Furthermore, "To understand the Egg-Tactic one is compelled to worship the flower-insect machinery which defines God as the designer of the aesthetic-sexual game. Gaia is the ultimate pornographer, the sex-magic manipulator, the erotic-artist," and here Blake is mentioned as someone who knew this in the 19th century, while Joyce knew it in the 20th, and Molly Bloom's last lines are quoted here. (ibid., p.280)

In 1979, Wilson wrote an article on the history of censorship of Western literature for a little magazine called *Diagonal Relationship*, put out by anarchist and science fiction critic Arthur Hlavaty. This subject hearkens to Wilson's first book on "forbidden words." In it we read this paragraph: "Joyce broke through two centuries of Taboo to bring these words back into literature, in *Ulysses*, because they are present in the human psyche (even in Puritanical Ireland in 1904), and the psychological truth he was seeking could not be attained while tacitly submitting to the then-prevalent hypocrisy by pretending the words were not there. As used by Joyce, none of these words are obscene, any more than a laboratory report is obscene. Joyce *eliminated* obscenity from his world view, as he eliminated anger, pity, sentimentality, and all other subjectivities; he simply observes, with Zenlike detachment, and reports what he sees." (number 9 of this magazine) In issue number 14 of this magazine, Wilson writes, "James Joyce said he had never met a boring person, but he was a Humanist. I have never had a boring perception, because I am a Universalist."

Into the 1980s

Between 1979 and 1981, while living in Berkeley, California, Wilson put out a trilogy of novels in which different interpretations of quantum mechanics were the frames for the plots. These were *The Universe Next Door* (1979), *The Trick Top Hat* (1980), and *The Homing Pigeons* (1981). Many of the characters (or at least their names) first encountered in *The Sex Magicians* or *Illuminatus!* recur as actors here. The influence of Joyce within these novels can only be described as extensive, and the very close reader of Wilson will pardon me for inevitably giving the "complete" (impossible?) rundown mighty short shrift. We have already seen numerous quotings of *FW* and Wilson's own *FW*-influenced writing, but here it really takes off. My multiple readings of these novels has had me glossing the particular interpretation of quantum mechanics and noting many other themes in Wilson's work besides the influence of Joyce, and I tend to see the entire trilogy, the *Schrödinger's Cat Trilogy* (henceforth *SCT*, unless it's unclear) as one Big Book, much like *Illuminatus!*, and indeed, the way these novels are most read today is under an omnibus edition of all three put out by Dell, with a copyright of 1979, suggesting all three were submitted for publication by then and only released when the market seemed optimal. I will be referring to this omnibus edition (*SCT*) throughout my enumerations. The trilogy was originally released as stand-alone paperback editions that contained some material that was later cut from the omnibus edition.

On page 5 of the first novel of the trilogy, *The Universe Next Door*, we read an epigraphic quote: "History is a nightmare from which none of us can awaken," and this is attributed to "Stephen Prometheus" as quoted in Carl Jung's *Odysseus*. Right off the bat we know what we're in for here: in a "universe next door" a character in a novel named Stephen Prometheus (instead of Dedalus) existed, in some sense, and Carl Jung became a theologian and great novelist. Obviously this quote paraphrases from the "Nestor" chapter of *Ulysses*, where Stephen tells Mr. Deasy that history is a nightmare from which he is trying to awake. A heavy reader and student of G. Spencer Brown's *Laws of Form* (1969), Wilson tells us in this first novel of the trilogy, *The Universe Next Door*, has a "form" that was taken from the interpretation of quantum mechanics known as the Everett-Wheeler-Graham model (EWG) first proposed by Hugh Everett III in 1957 and now very widely accepted by physicists deeply involved with quantum mechanics. As Wilson understood it then, "everything that can happen to the state-vector does happen to it." This means there are probably an infinite number of universes in which we all exist. Today it's often called the "Many-Worlds Hypothesis" and the disagreements among scientists are robust to say the least. In an odd glitch, Wilson tells us that that this interpretation was the form/frame for *The Universe Next Door* in the "Glossary: A Guide For The Perplexed" that appends each of the single-volume editions of the trilogy, but this information is (conspicuously?) missing in the omnibus edition, which contains the same "Glossary" but omits naming *which* interpretation of QM each novel uses. Perhaps Wilson wanted to make readers of the omnibus edition work even harder to decipher the scads of puzzles in each book of the trilogy? Onward . . .

One further note about the *Schrödinger's Cat Trilogy*: in what is emblematic of Wilson's fiction, these novels represent other worlds, which themselves include many discussions of other worlds, including "our" universe – and novels from other worlds – with himself appearing in very minor roles, sometimes with the same name, others times under a character's name, with many biographical facts from "this world" but also from other universes. Quotes from books or articles about other interpretations of the quantum theory will appear and characters will discuss the absurd idea of characters in books in other universes discussing different interpretations of quantum reality. Furthermore, a character will discover he's in a novel and will try to tell others this and will usually not be believed. And in this trilogy, one character gets so high on cannabis he "remembers" what happens in other of Wilson's books, which are other universes/worlds. Got that?

This play/perception of multiple realities that are always with us, even in this world, the world right where you are sitting now, is at the core of all of Wilson's work. In addition to quantum "Many-Worlds" in which we might exist, mental states are worlds. Other languages are worlds. Different disciplines and forms of media are worlds which we inhabit for bracketed-off portions of the day. The quality of discreteness with each of these worlds seems beyond the present study, but they have to do with an interpretation from the psychology of perception. How are worlds combined? Why do some clash so strongly with others? How does the world look different from the point of view of people in remote places vs. those who live in cities with a population over five million? Your freelance artist/California vegetarian " reality" vs. The "reality" of some farmer in China or even Nebraska? What is "reality"? How do we make "reality"? Etc. . . .

For Robert Anton Wilson, the works of James Joyce were vast, endlessly fascinating, dense with language, intellectually sophisticated, musical and humorous. They were worlds he lived in, especially *Ulysses* and *Finnegans Wake*. In the *Schrödinger's Cat Trilogy* Wilson plays with Joyce's work and biography while exploring what other worlds and James Joyce could look like from the multiple interpretations of Erwin Schrödinger's wave equation.

The character Benny "Eggs" Benedict -- who, like many of Wilson's characters, displays conspicuous aspects of Wilson's own biography or disposition -- is heavily influenced by Jung's profound book, *Odysseus*. The most "shocking" thing about this book "aside from the searing indecency of its language" is that it came from a Swiss theologian. Clearly Carl Jung plays the role of Joyce in this universe: the book has 14 chapters and is about an ordinary day and ordinary characters wandering about Zurich. The 14 chapters mirrored the Stations of the Cross and "academic exegetes adopted *Odysseus* as the very model of a modern novel and wrote endless studies proving it was an allegory on everything from the evolution of consciousness to the rise and fall of civilizations." (*Schrödinger's Cat Trilogy*, p.17) For Benedict, he loves the novel because it was the only book to make "the daily seem profound." Then Wilson describes *Odysseus* in a way that he would see *Ulysses* (in "this" universe?), but Jung's *Odysseus* also seems like it was influenced by Wilson's own particular valuations of marginalized discourses: "If Jung's characters, or some of them, happened to defecate, urinate, masturbate and fornicate during the fourteen hours, that was not because the theologian was trying to write pornography, but because the miracle of daily life could not be shown without all of its daily details. Benny didn't give a flying Philadelphia fuck about the novel's parallels with the *Odyssey* and the Stations of the Cross, which Jung admitted, or the other correspondences with body organs, colors, Tarot cards, *I Ching* hexagrams, and the romantic triangle in *Krazy Kat*, which his admirers claimed to have found." (ibid., p.18) The tarot, *I Ching* and *Krazy Kat* seem pretty much Wilson here.

Further description of Jung in this alternate universe makes him sound not only like Joyce, but also like Timothy Leary, at times quite explicitly: "Jung, who regarded himself as a better psychologist than the psychologists – this was a conceit typical of theologians – claimed to have found three more circuits in the nervous system beyond Freud's oral biosurvival circuit and anal emotional-territorial circuit. Jung said that *Odysseus* demonstrated also a semantic-hominid circuit which created a veil of words between domesticated primates and their experience, thereby differentiating them from the wild primates. He also claimed a specific socio-sexual circuit created by the process of domestication. And he added a fifth, neurosomatic circuit typical of mysticism and music, which causes primates to feel High and spaced-out." (ibid., p.18) Obviously, these are Leary's metaphorical inventions from his Eight Circuit Brain Model of evolution and consciousness. So: a Jung/Leary/Wilson character is combined with the (hidden) Joyce character. And all four – Joyce/Jung/Leary/Wilson – are interested in psycho-archaeology, in greatly overlapping ways.

In the chapter, "Louses In The Skidrow Dimehaunts," a common Wilson scene plays out: a crowded, multivocal cocktail party in which snatches of dialogue from many speakers, many with pressing ideological agendas, occur one after another in rapid succession, as if the reader is hearing a cacophony of talkers amongst the din of a crowded gathering of artists, poets, actors, critics, editors, intellectuals, and Beautiful People. The assemblage of baroque-like counterpoint of voices seems, at these parties, to function similarly to Burroughs's cut-ups. It's as if Wilson had written scraps of dialogue for many characters, then assembled them randomly on the page, although there is a logic at work in the overall accumulation of data about certain typological characters. Among the attendees of Epicene Wildeblood's party is Simon Moon, a mathematician/poet/computer scientist/hacker/covert "insider" working on the supercomputer GWB-666, who has "almost as much hair as Bigfoot", and who has written reams of *FW*-like poetry, from which he reads aloud, broken by many other conversations. "Louses in the Skidrow Dimehaunts" forms part of one line, and it's easy to parse the initials here. One line sounds like a parody of the first line of *FW*: "Elverun, past Nova's atoms, from mayan baldurs to monads of goo brings us by a divinely karmic Tao-Jones leverage back past tallchief tactics and azlantean tooltechs to Louses in the Skidrow Dimehaunts. This way the Humpytheater." A lot of ancient civilizations there, driven by the Big Bang, karma or the Tao? In other *FW*-lines by Moon, we seem to read yet more about the JFK assassination: "Wet with garrison statements, oswilde shores, daily blazers, tochus culbook depositories, middlesexed villains and fumes. Fict! The most unkennedest carp of all. Fogt. Veiny? V.D? Wacky? His bruttus gypper." Later in the party, and usually without much enthusiasm from the party's members, Moon is heard to utter a *FW*-like line from yet another of Wilson's topics: the 1968 Democratic National Convention: "where yippies yip and doves duz nothing, to the hawfullest convention ever." NB this uses Joyce's recurring HCE riff, as if the mind of *FW* has leaked into this other universe. (ibid., see pp.46-50 for these *FW*-like lines and others by Simon Moon. See also one line, from the same party, p.57; on p.64, same party, Moon's *FW*-spiel describes Chicago and the US at the time of Nixon, Agnew, Hoover, Daley, even Capone, but the reader should parse for herself; in this and other passages using *FW*-like language it seems to function as a code for radical dissent, but not always; p.179: from Moon's poem "Hawkfullest Conventions Ever": "Rolypolyboys tell lasses.")

We mentioned earlier how Wilson thinks of Joyce's use of language and particularly *Finnegans Wake* as isomorphic to mind-manifestation, or psychedelic states. He will use *FW* or certain musical writing from *Ulysses* to simulate drug and dreaming states, and this seems apposite in a character waking up from anesthesia from a sex-change surgery, male to female: "A gay swish of starched cloth moved queerly and a nurse's bland blond face appeared looking down at hir." After waking, she asks the doctor a question, then sinks back into anesthesia, and *FW*-language: "And SHe went, she went, into the great ether drift, into the cosmic void again, from dina shaur to turban bay in a michaelsonmorley regurgitation to the Hawkfouldest Convention in Elveron. Yes a forty-four-year-old male rising like Venus on fours out of the waves but aglow gleaming as in Botticelli: hir Self surprised at this astonishingly female body a really successful crossing and one hand crept as she slept toward the crypt rested there happy: yes: it was true A female body. She snored hoarsely." (*Schrödinger's Cat Trilogy*, pp.86-87) We see HCE again, and we seem to see Dina Shore and Turhan Bey? The famous Michaelson-Morley experiment showed in physics that the previous idea of light moving through a luminiferous ether wasn't quite correct; however, the "ether" as anesthesia seems to be working just fine. Your glossing may vary, of course. This now-female character will use a dildo named "Ulysses" later, and it's named that in part because it has "Greek proclivities."

Richard Ellmann is quoted from *Ulysses On The Liffey*: "Being keys themselves their keylessness does not matter." (*Schrödinger's Cat Trilogy*, p.182) We will see Wilson quote or cite, mostly approvingly, many Joyce scholars later.

As *The Universe Next Door* ends, very badly due to the nuclear weapons planted by the Purity Of Essence party – who wanted men and women to live equally and for everyone to eat uncooked vegetables – a line about "historical and neurogenetic forces" that led to the end of the world reminds us of Vico's cycles of history, which of course were part of the form Joyce took on for *Finnegans Wake*. (*Schrödinger's Cat Trilogy*, p.189)

In *The Trick Top Hat* (1980), the second novel in the trilogy, the frame/form Wilson uses is from Bell's Theorem (1964): any particles that have ever been in contact with any other particle remain in contact and influence each other, no matter how far apart they are in space/time. And this violates Special Relativity, unless the influence between the particles is not using any known energy. By the time this was written, two candidates for what accounted for this interaction that had to be faster than light were information and consciousness. Since 1980, what is now referred to as "entanglement" seems to have only gotten weirder.

In this universe, James Joyce, who in "our" universe actually had a great singing voice and almost made a career of it, became "the greatest tenor of the twentieth century." Joyce is the personal hero (or "god") of pretentious music critic Justin Case. "Case owned every record of every Joyce concert preserved on wax, and regarded the man as having the most subtle musical sensibility since the great Ludwig himself. If only he had been a composer instead of a singer, Case sometimes thought, with that ear . . ." In this universe, Joyce had considered a career in writing, the priesthood and medicine before he settled on music, and "thrilled audiences in Europe and America." Then there was a scandal that ruined his career. It appears once his salacious letters and kinky sexual proclivities came to light, he was done, shamed and humiliated. Joyce drank himself to death, comparing himself to Wilde and Parnell. Case once had a sexual affair with the sexologist Marilyn Chambers, simply because she was also crazy about Joyce's music. Once, after sex, "he had even allowed her to explain the parallel universe theory" and asked if she actually meant there might be another universe in which Joyce's kink about women's underwear might have never been discovered and his career not ruined? Chambers says yes, if Wheeler is correct, there would be another universe – a universe next door – in which Joyce indeed went on and had a career as a priest instead of a singer. (*SCT*, pp.202-203)

A very similar cocktail party scene plays out in this novel that did in *The Universe Next Door*, and a brief recapitulatory passage seems to bear a structural similarity to the "Circe"/ "Nighttown" section of *Ulysses*, in which Justin Case "began to think he was in a play, with everybody reading from a different script" and the snippets of dialogue are set off like a "play", similar to "Circe" and with a quasi-Burroughsian cut-up feel. (*SCT*, p.207)

Three paragraphs of *FW*-language appear as Justin Case nods off to sleep, with George Washington, the dollar, Presidents Tyler, Adams, Lincoln's Emancipation Proclamation, the cherry tree, the "dawn's early light" and other Americana showing up in his dream, then Ra/Shiva/Indra making an appearance before the Marx Brothers and Moby Dick. Case's apparent subconscious fear of the Internal Revenue Service ends that dream section. (*SCT*, p.284)

Similarly, another character, Marvin Gardens, falls off to sleep after popping "a downer" to level off the cocaine jitters, puts on some Beethoven and recalls watching *Deep Throat* as sleep descends and his quest to understand the multiplicity of amoebas mixes into: "Linda's mouth two inches four inches six inches nine goddamned inches gorgeous splat splat splat always splitting but always one, is it really? as Ludwig answers yes I will yes " (ibid., p.295) Finally, Sput Sputnik falls asleep while someone wearing chains has broken into his house, and the sounds of the chains enter into his *FW*-like rendered dream-world, much like the sound of a tree hitting the window makes the sound "tip" in *FW* and HCE hears it; here Sputnik dreams of Ra Hoor Khuit, Nuit, and the film *Casablanca* before waking to the sounds of the chains. (ibid., p.326)

At the beginning of the third volume in the trilogy, *The Homing Pigeons* – based on an alternative to the Many-Worlds interpretation, and said to be preferred by John Archibald Wheeler himself: "Non-Objectivity" – probably first thought of by the British Empiricist George Berkeley – *esse es percepi*: to be is to be perceived, or roughly, there is no reality unless it is being perceived. Everything seems in a "maybe" state, until some observation is made and it becomes "real." As the novel starts, a character thinks he's one person, while his kidnappers are sure he's someone from another Wilson novel, and the oddness of this situation is peppered with two three-word lines that sound like *FW*, uttered within "normal" kidnapper/kidnapped dialogue: one character is toying with a gun like the "ghoats in hammelts." Another says that the kidnapped character was "rescued" like the "gauds in ambers." (*SCT*, p.353) As the character – Francis Dashwood, who is living the life George Dorn lived in *Illuminatus!* when the Discordians broke him out of prison – turns down a sexual opportunity, he's warned that he's about to "walk into a completely different universe, one you might not like at all." (*SCT*, pp. 358-361) This opening surrealistic scene seems very much influenced by "Circe" and the character of Dashwood feels like Bloom.

For our purposes, this universe's Joyce character is "Pope Stephen", the most progressive Catholic leader ever known. That noted – and more on Pope Stephen below – this novel's world seems so surreal that *FW* language and allusions to Joyce and *Ulysses*-like prose happens frequently. Therefore, in addition to fostering mild psychedelic states and rendering dreams and hypnagogic imagery in *FW* prose, Wilson also uses *FW*-like language to increase the feeling of living in a surrealistic world in which non-objectivity is "on", full-blast.

At a bizarre multivocal cocktail party we first hear of Pope Stephen when someone asks, "I wonder . . . if there's a universe where Pope Stephen became a singer instead of a priest?" And a theologian wonders who had "started all those rumors about Pope Stephen." (ibid., 397-398) We receive a quote from Pope Stephen's book *Integritas, Consonantia, Claritas*: "The apprehension of the Real can only be compared to a radiance or illumination because it is a revelation of part of the Divine Act of Creation." (ibid., p.409) It's as if this Pope has been influenced by Bishop Berkeley, and has articulated the quantum reality – "normal" for the characters who reside there – in the world they live in. Another quote from Stephen's *Integritas*: "The first entry of sin into the mind occurs when, out of cowardice or conformity or vanity, the Real is replaced by a comforting lie." (ibid., p. 433) Pages 433-440 reveal a Catholic world that Wilson might have never left: consensual free love is a virtue, but when a character confesses to a father in church that she might be getting money from slum properties, though it's difficult to tell, this is a grave sin, and the first moral law about money reads like this: "To ensure that no human being was hurt in acquiring it, and if anyone was hurt, to return the money to them and make whatever other restitution is morally necessary." (ibid., p.436)

The Stephenites of the Catholic Church "were the most radical of all the Catholic clergy and made even the neo-Jesuits, under General Berrigan, seem like milkwater liberals by comparison." Stephenites were held in jails throughout the world, because they obeyed the laws of God and not man . . . mostly the encyclicals left by now-dead Pope Stephen, who, in five years, had changed the Church from the most reactionary to the most progressive, according to French feminist Jeanne Paulette Sartre. Pope Stephen was the first to denounce Hitler and Mussolini and excommunicated the fascist's supporters, and 70% of the Catholics followed Stephen, leading to the downfall of fascism. In five years, up to the time of Pope Stephen's death in 1940, the Church had spent 90% of its wealth on projects to abolish poverty, disease, and ignorance. While the Church became poor for the first time in aeons, its prestige was 1000% higher.

Pope Stephen, the first Irish Pope, wore a black eye patch over a blind eye and was arrogant in that he thought he had the best literary style in Latin since Cicero, and had displayed some vanity over his command of English, Italian, French, German, Spanish, Danish, and Hebrew, and it was known that he considered himself a greater Psychologist than James or Jung. Stephen mostly listened, and spoke little. "Actually, he spoke little because he was so busy *observing*. This passion for studying other human beings had gradually turned him from a disputatious young intellectual into an almost pathologically sensitive middle-aged man, because the more he observed people, the more he liked them, and the more he liked them, the less able he was to bear seeing or hearing of injustice to anyone anywhere." (ibid., p.438) The only time he "pontificated" was once, when he said he had never met a boring human being. Pope Stephen not only allowed, but encouraged, priests to marry, and he himself had married a peasant girl from Galway. Conservative Catholics hated his sexual liberalities and were forever trying to get him posthumously excommunicated, and frequently they brought up his alleged penchant for women's underwear, especially garters. Likely these were the members of fascist True Holy Roman Catholic Church splinter group that arose during Pope Stephen of Dublin's reign. (ibid., pp.

449-450) Apparently Stephen had something of a sense of humor, as he was known to say, "What – *me* infallible?" (ibid., p.437)

"Pope Stephen's whole philosophy was derived from a single sentence in Aquinas:

>Ad pulchritudinem tria requiruntur:
>Integritas, consonantia, claritas.

Which may be rendered:

>Three things are required for beauty:
>Wholeness, harmony, radiance."

(ibid., pp.438-439) ("Applied Aquinas" indeed!)

The reason so many of the humans in the universe of *The Homing Pigeons* didn't perceive wholeness, harmony and radiance was because they were not paying enough *attention*. When he died, obituary writers compared Pope Stephen to Buddha, Whitman, Plotinus, Rumi, Dante, Eckhart, Joan of Arc and Saint Terrence of Avila, but one "obscure Canadian professor of literature" came closest to actually describing how Stephen's mind worked: "The only mind in history comparable to Stephen's was that of a fictitious character – Mr. Sherlock Holmes of Baker Street." (ibid., p.440) (Wilson was a fan of Hugh Kenner's criticism.) Later another character, Indole Ringh, a yogi, is described as being as "conscious of detail" as Pope Stephen "because he smoked a great deal of *bhang*" (ibid., p.468), another theme that runs through most of Wilson's work. (Bhang is much more commonly thought of as a cannabis *drink* in India, although we seem safe to assume Wilson had his sources.)

A recurring character, Blake Williams, is very much a stand-in for Wilson himself, and in this book is described as lecturing on "How To Tell Your Friends From the Apes", which is literally the title of a Wilson lecture he gave many times, where he talks about Zen and General Semantics, how money is symbolism and not value and a collective hallucination, about Ethnomethodology, the latest theories in the psychology of perception, McLuhan's media probes, and "He quoted Hume, Einstein, Korzybski and Pope Stephen." (ibid., pp.484-485)

After one lecture, when most had left, five remained and Williams recalled the little-known story of Pope Stephen's parable to the Spanish Cardinal. Stephen told the Cardinal that "seeking for the Real" was pointless because the Real is "palpably right in front of our noses," an idea that receives major play in Wilson's entire oeuvre. Williams goes on, recalling that Stephen said everyone knew he'd thought about being a singer or doctor before deciding on the priesthood, and "What few know is that I also considered becoming a novelist. I often wonder, myself, if I ever abandoned that last ambition. Sometimes I feel like a novelist pretending to be a Pope, to see what it's like. And sometimes I even think the whole Church is a very old novel which I've revised and modernized. And, my reverend brother in Christ, sometimes I even think that I'm not alone in this novel-writing business; I think that every man, woman, and child on this planet is writing a novel inside their heads, all day long, every day – editing, rewriting, touching things up, improving a page here and throwing a page out somewhere else. The only difference is that when I write a novel, it becomes an Encyclical, and is therefore Reality for millions of believers." (ibid., p.488) Not only does this touch on a favorite theme of Wilson's: the blurring of book-reality and non-book reality, but this seems very close to what Wilson thought of *Ulysses* and *Finnegans Wake*: they are holy books, and he'd even called *FW* "the good book."

It's difficult not to see the joy Wilson had in re-writing the Church's history – Wilson was raised Catholic but became estranged at the age of reason – with Joyce as its leader, and idealizing what might have been, a truly utopian vision in this, essentially a work of counterfactual history, albeit an ultra-imaginative counterfactual.

"Shem the Penman" from *FW* also lives in this world as "Shemus de la Plume, Naval Intelligence's ace handwriting forger." (ibid., p.449) And a "stately, plump young Irishman" (Buck Mulligan), not named, appears as a snide dissenter upon the ascendance of Prince Charles to King of England, with quotes straight from *Ulysses*: he sings "O won't we have a merry time/Drinking whiskey beer and wine/On coronation/Coronation day", and a half-quote: "The sacred pint alone is the lubrication of my Muse." Someone calls him a "drunken Irishman" and he replies, as if the quote was meant for Charles, "What, what if he is? He still looks like a king, and is that not what really matters?" And the Irishman asks about another's "lean, unlovely English" from "Scylla and Charybdis" (ibid., pp.462-463)

In *The Illuminati Papers* (1980), Wilson answers a question from *Conspiracy Digest* by talking about a passage in *Illuminatus!* where the Laurel and Hardy routine in which Hardy tells Laurel, "Now look what you made me do!" functioned as "a profound epiphany in the Joycean sense," a "synecdoche of how people are always trying to blame somebody else for their own behavior." (ibid., p.23) In an essay about Beethoven's struggle to assert personal freedom in both life and art, Wilson links this to Joyce and active perception: "But the artist, as Joyce has dramatically demonstrated in *Ulysses* and *Finnegans Wake*, is fighting the struggle which every human must fight if we are not to relapse into total robotry: the struggle to see and hear with one's own eyes and ears, not with the circuitry of social conditioning." (ibid., p.62) In an interview with *Science Fiction Review* Wilson answers another question about his influences: "My style derives directly from Ezra Pound, James Joyce, Raymond Chandler, H.L. Mencken, William S. Burroughs, Benjamin Tucker, and *Elephant Doody Comix*, in approximately that order of importance." (ibid., p.66) In an essay about "Mammalian Politics" and Thackeray and Kubrick, Wilson wrote, "I once claimed that Joyce invented the 'alienation effect' before Brecht; but Thackeray had it even before Joyce. Both *Barry Lyndon* and *Vanity Fair* are classic examples of Brechtian-Joycean artistic judo, constantly moving the reader into highly charged emotional-political situations and deftly diffusing audience identification at the most crucial points." (ibid., p.69)

The essay "Coex! Coex! Coex!" is an entire piece devoted to *Finnegans Wake*, which Wilson bought on his 16th birthday in 1948 and never stopped reading. He cited an essay by James T. Farrell, who had defended *FW* from his fellow Marxists, who thought it was devoid of social significance. Wilson parses and glosses "thuartpeatrick" from p.1, and "goddinpotty" from chapter 4. Wilson agrees with psychedelic researcher Stanislav Grof, who in his *Realms of the Human Unconscious*, described his idea of "coex" – a *co*ndensed *ex*perience montage – in terms Wilson thought apposite for the readers of *FW*. "Critics have tried to explain *Finnegans Wake* by means of Freud and Jung, but Joyce was a quantum jump ahead of the psychology of his time." "To learn to read *Finnegans Wake* with ease and pleasure is to learn to think with your whole brain, conscious and unconscious circuits included, in a holistic *coex* system." (*Illuminati Papers*, pp. 31-34)

Masks of the Illuminati (1981)

Eric Wagner points out that Wilson saw that one thing his critics and commentators had missed about his work was the heavy Joyce influence. So now, finally, someone has begun to address this lacuna and to document that influence here, with Wagner's examinations in *Straight Outta Dublin*, especially with Wilson's explicit use of Joyce as a main character (with Albert Einstein, Sir John Babcock, and Aleister Crowley) in Wilson's detective story and lodge novel, *Masks of the Illuminati*.

I'm borrowing the term "lodge novel" from academic scholars and literary critics Marianne Thalmann and Theodore

Ziolkowski, who say this form arose in Germany in the latter half of the 18th century and was a counterpart to the Gothic novel in England. This form arose when the power of Freemasons and the Illuminati was in ascendance, and "central to the genre is the idea of a secret society that somehow guides – or seeks to control – the life of the hero and enlist him in its cause. This produces a constant tension between the central figure and the order, which traditionally represents an ideal to which the hero is being educated." (*Lure of the Arcane*, Ziolkowski, pp.69-70.) While the "central figure" in *Masks* seems more oblique and his influence indirect, the basic structure of the lodge novel narrative holds, at least for that particular play with form/genre. Wilson is always playing with genre in his novels, comically combining them to destabilize the reader, asking them to wonder about the continuity of genre, form and tone with their own states of mind and reality-tunnels.

In a 1990 interview with Sander Wolff, Wilson said he knew Aleister Crowley had sought initiation techniques that were stronger than the Freemason's. While Crowley lurks in the background of the novel until the end, a very real, very "strong" initiation is undergone by Sir John Babcock in this book.

This is the form Wilson uses – an elder mage educates a younger person in occult matters. He also uses it in his three-part *Historical Illuminatus Chronicles*, and Ziolkowski thinks it's used in *Illuminatus!* also. On top of this late 18th century form, Wilson superimposes another favorite form: the detective novel, and his two detectives are Einstein and Joyce, and this allows Wilson to playfully display his erudition around the knowledge and thought processes of three of the 20th century's great geniuses: Joyce and Einstein, with Crowley always lurking here, until the end. However, describing *Masks of the Illuminati* as a lodge novel that becomes a detective novel seems far too simple, as play with genre and style was a central aspect of Wilson's literary style, much like Joyce's *Ulysses* contains at least a different style or form for each section throughout the day of June 16, 1904. Einstein and Joyce are listening to terrified Babcock describe how he arrived at wit's end, and the geniuses use their powers of intuition and ratiocination, based on their biographical facts, to try to help the young man, or at least assuage his now-crippling fears. So the detective work done by Joyce and Einstein is interwoven with the chronicle of Babcock's apprenticeship to the mage George Cecil Jones, a colleague of Crowley's, though Babcock doesn't know this.

Wilson told Dr. Jeffrey Elliot in a 1980 interview just before *Masks* was published that it's "something the publisher is going to have a hard time finding a label for, because it deliberately starts out as one kind of novel and turns into an entirely different type of novel. This, to me, is realism," adding, "I've always wanted to write novels in which the reader doesn't know what kind of script he's living in. Publishers can't stand this approach." The reason Wilson thought publishers wanted a straightforward genre was due to marketing, which violated Wilson's aesthetic ideals. The play with genres was a significant strategy for Wilson, who asserts that humans create the worlds they live in – "reality tunnels" – by acts of will, or they don't understand their own agency and fall into default modes of living soap opera or mechanical, habitual, melodramatic lives. This too is "realism" (NB the passage from *Illuminatus!* By a right-winger railing against certain types of "literary realism", above) but the reader will notice I'm conflating literary typifications with the existential-phenomenological lives we all live . . . which is also a significant trope in Wilson's work: that we live inside of books, and it's up to us to notice this, and change the narrative style and genre at will, using a variety of techniques, some of which were taught to the fictional character Sir John Babcock by the real-world character, George Cecil Jones, chemist and mentor in magick and fellow conspirator with Aleister Crowley.

To extend these literary genre vs. real life metaphors, in another 1980 interview, Michael Hollingshead asked Wilson what a "psychedelic novel" was and Wilson replied that "*Illuminatus!* is a psychedelic novel in the sense that it's a novel of initiation and revelation in which the characters go through various forms of brain-change." This seems isomorphic to what Ziolkowski called a "lodge novel" but what's in a genre? On another level, they are merely convenient reifications and every work is unto its own. Wilson considered our lives as initiatory in some sense, and our initiations often led to humility. In *Masks*, "A real initiation never ends, Jones had said cryptically, before the physical-plane initiation. Sir John understood: the dream, in its own language, was indeed a continuation of the initiation, but on another plane." (ibid., p.62) More famously, Wilson had intentionally undergone a self-invented long series of self-experimentation with yoga, drugs, magick and other brain-change gimmicks, for 14 years, between 1962-1976, and wrote about his findings in *Cosmic Trigger vol. 1*, calling the entire period of experiment an "initiation."

In *Masks of the Illuminati* Joyce appears as himself, of course, as filtered through Wilson's lifelong reading of Joyce's works, critical studies, letters, and biographical details found in Ellmann's biography and others. *Masks of the Illuminati* seems to be one of the two "must-read" books from Wilson for any Joycean, along with *Coincidance: A Head Test* (1988), which includes extensive critical commentary on Joyce's work, especially *Finnegans Wake*. In *Masks*, Joyce is trying to find a framework and ideas for his next novel, which would be *Ulysses*. He happens onto some ideas during the narrative, but – however fanciful – an actual psychedelic experience clarifies and solidifies the general scope for what would be that novel, *Ulysses*.

There is no reason to think the biographers have missed that Joyce tried mescaline or peyote; he probably didn't use any psychedelic drugs to help him get ideas for writing. But Wilson here is not only using counterfactuals, but linking the general state of extreme creativity and a mind open to all possibilities, which he thinks we can all access, with or without mind-altering drugs. Certainly the history of extraordinary states in religion, among artists, and scientists – no drugs involved – supports this idea.

However the reader assigns genre status to *Masks*, it is in part embedded in psychedelia (though the timeline of the novel is pre-*Ulysses*, and Wilson drops some ideas about Joyce getting ideas for that novel), in keeping with a general theme in Wilson's work overall and much of his reading and writing around James Joyce. Despite any additions I may make here, Eric Wagner's excursus about *Masks* above should suffice.

"Araby" from *Dubliners* is referenced when Joyce tries to puzzle out the bizarre story of Sir John Babcock, who believes he is being stalked by someone or something, for some reason having to do with his initiations. Joyce remembers, around age 10, reading of the dervishes and Ali Baba, Aladdin and Sufis, but then actually visiting the fair and finding it something of a cheap clip joint. Here he links his own memory of "Araby" as a boy to what he assumed would happen to him when he first visited the Red Light District, and then to the romantic world of Yeats and his friends, who "live in Araby. It is real to them. More real than their servants, certainly. We go forth each into the world of experience but we do not go mentally naked like Adam and Eve." This leads to a discussion, with Einstein, of what Wilson would call "reality tunnels": "If a pickpocket enters a room he'll see pockets to be picked. If Socrates were to be ushered in [. . .] Socrates would see minds to be probed by annoying questions . . ." And "I am saying," Joyce replied, "that I can see the world as Yeats and the occultists do – as a spiritual adventure full of Omens and Symbols. I can also see it, if I choose, as the Jesuits taught me to see it in youth: as a vale of tears and a web of sin. Or I can see it as a Homeric epic, or a depressing naturalistic novel by Zola. I am interested in seeing all its facets." (ibid., pp.171-172) This functions as a paraphrase of perhaps the central point in all of Wilson's work: that we should train ourselves to see the world from a multi-model point of view, using "maybe logic", and to be ever-agnostic at least a bit, even about our "favorite" "reality."

In *Masks of the Illuminati* there are many details about Joyce in the work that would only be known by those who had read biographies or other secondary literature on Joyce. For example, as Joyce and Einstein begin to try to solve Babcock's mystery, thunder cracks at night in Zurich and Joyce recalls Vico and Joyce's own fear of it, and suddenly he remembered Mr. Popper asking him, in Trieste, how can a man with as much moral courage as himself be afraid of such a natural phenomenon? And Joyce thinks, "You were not raised an Irish Catholic." Then Joyce's inner monologue around thunder is rendered in *FW*-style language. Joyce thinks, for his next work, maybe have a good man, a good Samaritan-type raise these questions. He thinks the character will be "Hunter" or Einstein himself. (ibid., pp.152-153) Only the Joycean would know that Mr. Popper here was Leopoldo Popper, whose sexually attractive daughter Joyce had taught at the Berlitz School in Trieste, and Joyce had felt the agenbite of inwit over this. (see Ellmann's *James Joyce*, pp.342-345) Only the Joyceans know that "Hunter" was probably a Dublin Jew who helped Joyce after a drunken bout, and who was rumored to have an unfaithful wife, and that Joyce first thought about Hunter as "Ulysses" in the fall of 1906, while in Rome. (*James Joyce A to Z*, by Fargnoli and Gillespie, p.106. *Letters*, vol II, p. 168 and p.198)

Masks of the Illuminati abounds with such tidbits. And the final section of psychedelic space/time experience seems to combine "Circe" with *FW*-like language and imagery, and employs many Joycean motifs, forms, and in-jokes to keep the scholars busy for a while.

Wilson In Ireland: 1981-1987

In an article titled "Cabala: Tasting the Forbidden Fruit of the Tree of Life," published in *High Times*, July 1981, Wilson cites the Biologist Lyall Watson, who had collected examples of Jung's "collective unconsciousness" – synchronicities and dreams, from results of automatic writing, hypnotic states, etc. And he quotes from Watson's book *Lifetide*: ". . . there is a sameness in the tone, the word structure, the feeling and the delivery of almost all the material. It has a dreamlike quality, and my feeling is that the vast majority of all the evidence I am looking at is a series produced by *one* prodigious dreamer." (*High Times*, July 1981, p.104) This would be a major reason for Wilson's enthusiasm for *Finnegans Wake*; Wilson seems to have been thinking about *FW* and the collective unconscious since at least the late 1950s.

Wilson wrote an Introduction, in 1982, to a new edition of Dr. Israel Regardie's analysis of Aleister Crowley's life and work, *The Eye In The Triangle*, and Wilson compares the work to the first books that introduced Einstein, Picasso, and *Finnegans Wake* to new audiences. In comparing Crowley's occult work to Modernist movements in other arts: Cubism, Pound's ideogrammic method in poetry, Freud and Jung, Leo Frobenius's new framing of African art, Einstein and Anthropology and cultural relativism: "Joyce's *Ulysses* mutated the novel by introducing this relativity into the very structure and style of the narrative; we never see the 'real' Dublin of Berkeley's 'God' in *Ulysses*; we see the Dublin that impacts on the brain of Stephen, the Dublin that impacts on Mr. Bloom, the Dublin of the barflies in Barney Kiernan's pub, the Dublin of Molly Bloom's sleepy reveries. Each 'Dublin' is equally real: that is the essence of the Relativity Revolution." (ibid., pp. xi-xii)

Right Where You Are Sitting Now (1982), a pastiche of past articles, interviews, a short story, a quiz, and much experimental prose using William S. Burroughs's cut-up method of text generation, this book bears a formal similarity to a Modernist "little mag" in layout, and seems to take a page from something like Ezra Pound and Wyndham Lewis's *BLAST* and popular magazines of the 1970s. Dedicated to Burroughs and Philip K. Dick, "pioneers," Joyce appears in a cut-up: "'What you don't like . . . somebody else's prose blowing in the streets,' Joyce commented ironically." (ibid., p.64, Ronin ed.), and in a section on how language manipulates us, Wilson used a quote from the "Lotus Eaters" section of *Ulysses*, where Leopold Bloom observes the Catholics in their church: "Mass seems to be over. Could hear them all at it. Pray for us. And pray for us. Good idea the repetition. Same things with ads. Buy from us. And buy from us." (ibid., p.161) In a profusion of writing on techniques of magick and altered consciousness, Wilson noted how central *repetition* was to ritual.

Within a speculative essay about the future effects of technology upon the human mind, and especially human sexuality, Wilson hits on another common theme in his Joyce-reading: "A great deal of the erotic realism of such writers as Joyce, D.H. Lawrence, and even, at times, Hemingway, is an attempt to get inside the female mind and see men – in the sex act and in other relationships – as women see them. Presumably, many gynecologists and obstetricians share empathetically in the female functions they tend to, and many an artist has decidedly fused into the glorious nude female models he paints." (ibid., p.185) Wilson then goes on to speculate about sex-change in the future, from an article first published in *Oui* magazine in 1976.

While many prominent liberals in the US announced that upon Ronald Reagan's election in 1980, they would leave the country, Wilson and his wife Arlen actually did. Wilson relocated to Ireland in 1981, living for a time in Dalkey, near the Martello Tower (now the Joyce Tower/Museum), until 1987, when they moved back to the US, and Los Angeles. In a long series of letters Wilson wrote to a friend and benefactor,

Kurt Smith, Wilson very often referred to Joyce and Joycean topics. These letters will one day be published (one hopes!), but for now we shall cite some of Wilson on Joyce from personal correspondence with the magnanimous Kurt Smith:

••• December 1st, 1982: "You really oughta read *Joyce's Politics* by Dominic Manganiello. Full of fascinatin' info about Irish politics 1880-1940 and Joyce's analysis of same; and how he combined individualist anarchism, pacifism and Blake into a unique political stance all his own."

••• May 19th, 1983: Wilson tells of how the bureaucracy finally got around to honoring Joyce with a stone and a tree near where Wilson was living in Sandycove, and how he and Arlen ate at Bloom's Hotel and at Nora Barnacle's (Finn's Hotel?). He'd visited the Mullingar House at Chapelizod and, as "predicted" in *FW*, there was a huge TV on the wall. And Wilson discussed the "Ithaca" chapter of *Ulysses*: if it "sounds like WC Fields" that's because Joyce was parodying the same sort of "pretentious pedantry" that Fields did: "We have seen Bloom from every other angle Joyce could think of; in that chapter we see him as he appears to a humorless professor who is actually more interested in the plumbing system. Oddly, this authoritative voice is actually as crooked as Fields always was. He collaborates with Bloom in contouring the day's budget to conceal the money spent in the whorehouse . . . and in general, if one is not snowed by his vocabulary and his pretentiousness, it is easy to see that he is as prejudiced and untrustworthy as all the other narrators in the book."

••• May 31st, 1983: Wilson tells Smith he's been "working on a book explaining or translating *Finnegans Wake* and the *I Ching* and quantum mechanics. That is, explaining each by illustrations from the others, until all three serve to illuminate each other. It's lots of fun to write, although I have no idea who would publish such a book. Maybe I will sell Xerox copies on streetcorners." (This book would become *Coincidance: A Head Test*, and would be published in 1988 by Falcon Press in Arizona, and is now published by Hilaritas Press and is indispensable for those interested in Wilson's use of his Joyce reading.) Wilson then goes on at substantial length about the sigla of HCE: the four "E" sigla, rotated and what they mean: "The 'hero' of *FW* is not Earwicker; he is just the local manifestation. The 'hero' is the system." This letter will no doubt be of some substantial interest to certain *FW* exegetes.

••• January 1st, 1984: "Arlen and I spent the Xmas holidays at Tigroney House, a kind of Irish Esalen in the Wicklow mountains. Very pretty, very rural and colorful, very cold. I met a Druid there who knows more about *Finnegans Wake* than anybody else I've ever talked to, and he claimed Joyce was a Druid, too. Almost convinced me."

••• March 29th, 1984: Scads and abundance of erudition on *FW*: linking it to stochastic processes in the universe and Jastrow's book *Mind in the Universe*; the idea that human consciousness can be downloaded into silicon "which can rove the spacetime continuum forever"; the Buffalo notebooks and sigla; Evan Harris Walker's interpretation of quantum mechanics and how this might relate to Earwicker; how Chinese ideograms, Sheldrake's morphogenetic fields, Leary's neurogenetic circuit, and Jung's collective unconsciousness all play with *FW*; shamanism and Shem the Penman, etc., etc., etc.

••• May 29th,1984: Wilson tells Smith of the synchronicity of giving a talk at the Dublin Theosophical Society on "Isomorphism and Synchronicity in *Finnegans Wake, I Ching* and Quantum Mechanics," then he and wife Arlen got home and turned on RTE for the nightly reading on Irish history, which was about the final battle of O'Sullivan Beare in the 17th century, which links to all the bear-god and bear-man references in *FW*, and then the radio-reader quoted a schoolteacher named Joyce who lived at the site of that 17th century battle, and then there were quotes from both Napoleon and Wellington, who figure in *FW* as well. Another very bookish thing about Wilson was that he identified certain cities and places with authors and books and Dublin was a "Joyce Theme Park" while, say, Raymond Chandler's books made Los Angeles feel like a Chandler Theme Park.

••• October 8th, 1984: Wilson uses as an epigraph to this letter a passage from Seamus Heaney's *Station Island*, in which the ghost of James Joyce is talking: *You lose more of yourself than you redeem/Doing the decent thing/ Keep at a tangent.* Wilson tells his friend: "The above quote from Seamus Heaney is spoken, in a poem, by the ghost of Joyce. Said poem is about the death of Heaney's cousin, killed by the Protestant para-military Ulster Volunteers. Joyce's ghost appears at the end and tells Heaney to stay out of politics." Wilson writes at great length about all the books he's been reading, with a lot of material on Ireland, including Eileen O'Casey's book *Sean*, in which Oliver St. John Gogarty (AKA "Buck Mulligan") appears. Wilson loved the line from Sean O'Casey: "Life contains tragedy, but life itself is not tragic."

••• October 30th, 1984: Wilson relates how he visited Bray via the DART rapid transit system, and Bray Station "is on the same block with the old house where JJ lived as a small boy, where the Xmas dinner in *Portrait* is set."

••• November 29th, 1984: Among many things, Wilson tells how he went to Cornwall to interview Colin Wilson for the magazine *New Age* at Colin's house there, which of course reminds him of Tristan and Isolde: "lovely place." Among the things they discussed was that our "I" is fictional and that "we are all several persons, one of whom is a lot like Joyce's" (backwards "E" symbol) in the *FW* sigla for the system-function: "the timeless–spaceless Absolute Self." Robert Anton Wilson says that Colin Wilson doesn't really like Joyce nor mention him. Later, Robert Anton Wilson tells Smith at some length about Ulysses S. Grant and how he's found him hidden in *FW* in "unexpected places" and then elaborates. Even more elaboration of the US Civil War, Ulysses S. Grant, Abraham Lincoln, and the Blues and the Grays, etc., as found in *FW*, later appears in *Coincidance: A Head Test* (1988, Hilaritas Press, p.187)

••• January 7th, 1985: Wilson relates how he'd recently seen the play *Arrah na Pogue*, where Joyce got the character of Shaun the Post in *FW*. He goes on at length about this play and how it relates to Joyce.

••• May 2nd, 1985: Wilson and Arlen have moved to "a few steps from Howth Castle" to a road named The Haggard, and notes this date (May 2nd) is the same day in which, in 1934, Joyce wrote to Frank Budgen: "I have a grocer's assistant's mind." (Four days later Wilson would embark on a magickal operation of free writing that would prove embryonic to much of his Joyce writing in 1988's *Coincidance*.)

••• July 10th, 1985: Arlen's health issues begin to be a major factor in Wilson's life. With regards to Joyce, Wilson has a couple of paragraphs on "baken head" on p.7 of *FW*; how it relates to the Baily lighthouse, Danish "bakken", and of course Francis Bacon/Shakespeare/Hamlet, Shakespeare's boar's head coat of arms, occupation as butcher, Cain and Abel, etc. "The weirdest one is 'now let the baxters and fleishmanns cease bedivil uns', which combines Bacon and Shakespeare, baker and butcher (fleshman), Cain and Abel, and Ms. Martha Fleishman, with whom Joyce was enamored in 1918. (Martha, thou lost one: *Ulysses*, chapter 12.)" Other riffs are on Poolbeg lighthouse, gaelic "kis", and wicker, etc.

••• November 9th, 1985: Enclosed in this letter was a photo of Wilson with Fritz Senn, head of The James Joyce Society in Zurich, at the Fluntern Cemetery, at Joyce's grave. Wilson thinks the statue there "makes him look like a grass-hopper, commemorating his final self-portrait as the Gracehope in the *FW*." In a radio interview with Cliff Walker in 1990, Wilson mentioned that whenever he visited Joyce's grave in Zurich he always brought along a couple of friends and a bottle of Jameson's: "We each have a drink and then we pour the rest of it on – well, maybe we have two drinks –

well sometimes three – er, well maybe four [laughs] on rare occasions, we drink most of the bottle we originally bought for the occasion, and then we pour a drop or two (or whatever is left) on the grave for Jim. He was a great fan of Jameson's. No, what I love about Joyce (besides introducing me to Jameson's and Guinness Extra Stout – the two greatest products that ever came out of Dublin) is he wrote the first relativistic novel, *Ulysses*. *Ulysses* seems to me the only realistic novel of the twentieth century, because it's the only novel that contains at least a hundred different interpretations of itself, within itself. Therefore it's contemporary with quantum mechanics and Gödel's proof in mathematics and Cubist painting and movies like *Citizen Kane*, where you get five versions of the same story; Joyce anticipated all of modern science, modern philosophy, and modern art. And he was very funny, too, like most Irish writers." Wilson is then asked why Joyce was censored and Wilson adopts an Irish brogue and quotes Joyce's response to an Irish Times interview: "I don't know what tha fook improper language is!" (see *Natural Law*, Hilaritas Press, pp. 193-194; Eric Wagner has told me he thinks Wilson got the line about "what tha fook improper language is" from Bob Geldof.)

••• December 6th, 1985: An excursus on Joyce's feminism: "Joyce told Arthur Powers that the most important event of this era is feminism and Ibsen was the greatest writer of the 19th century because he realized the importance of woman's refusal to be defined by man." Wilson also discusses Joyce's conversations with Mary Colum, Harriet Shaw Weaver, and his takes on Ibsen's Nora and Molly Bloom: "Ibsen's Nora was too bloody heroic; Joyce's Molly, like Leopold, remains REAL with real faults and defects, but still transcends all the other characters in Nietzschean freedom from bullshit. Joyce's hints that Molly is the final revelation of evolution include the concentric lights above her bed (from Dante's *Paradiso*), the lovely irony of giving her the same birthday as the Virgin Mary (Sept. 8), the parallels with geology in her monologue, the Nietzschean affirmation of her last words, etc." Wilson also comments on Fionnula Flanagan's interpretation of Molly; how the interior monologues in *Ulysses* often conceal as much as they reveal (EX: Bloom thinking of Boylan). Wilson also comments on what Martin Cunningham, Stephen, Molly, Leopold and Earwicker "represent" as characters. "One innkeeper's repressed sexual drives become in *FW* the whole battle of class and caste throughout history."

••• July 3rd, 1986: Arlen and Wilson recall listening to the 30-hour radio broadcast of *Ulysses* in 1982, "and loved it." "RTE is currently rebroadcasting it in 18 episodes on Saturday afternoons. I'm going to make tapes of it, or most of it, since I didn't hear about it until after they broadcast the first two chapters." This year he and Arlen saw actors give readings of sections of *Ulysses* at the Ormonde Hotel, for Bloomsday. Wilson's watch stopped at 2 PM on Bloomsday, where Bloom's watch stopped at 4 PM. Wilson got a new battery at a jeweler's not far from where Bloom bought *Sweets Of Sin*. He was at the Joyce Tower for the release by Penguin Books of the new edition of *Ulysses* and met one of Joyce's nephews, who said he "liked *Ulysses* but cdn't make heads or tails of *Finnegans Wake*. He also said, in response to a question by me, that his collection of JJ photos does not include any of JJ in a brown mackintosh, thereby setting back a bit my latest attempt to answer the question that left Bloom puzzled even after he figured out where Moses was when the candle went out."

••• November 12th, 1986: Wilson is engaged in buying a house in Ireland, and Arlen had to have bypass surgery, and he's kind of freaked out and is now composing his letters on a Mac. In response to a pamphlet on schizophrenia that Smith sent him, Wilson has a lot to say about E. Fuller-Torrey's ideas about the disease, and Irish genetics and schizophrenia, and goes off on a wild bit about Type O blood, the Irish and North Africans, County Clare (where Wilson's ancestors came from), and the North African sounding indigenous music of

West Ireland, and Bob Quinn's ideas about many of the Irish being from Asia. Quinn, says Wilson, argued that "West Ireland is more Asian than European in genes, music and culture generally." Quinn quotes Yeats as saying Ireland was part of Asia until the Battle of the Boyne. "Shem the Penman, you may remember, lives at the Haunted Inkbottle, No Number, Brimstone Walk, Asia in Ireland." Both Wilson and Joyce had offspring with schizophrenic symptoms.

In 1984 Wilson reviewed *Ulysses: The Corrected Text*, AKA the "Gabler edition", for, it seems, the *Irish Times*: "Five Masters Make A Mess." In a letter to Smith he says the review comes off as far more negative than he meant it to be and that the editor had an agenda. The first line of the review: "*Ulysses*, the saddest funny book in the world, remains, after 64 years of damnation, beautification, pontification, and general consternation, still the funniest sad book in the world; and that is why people still read it, despite the attempts of academics to turn it into a glorified theosophical crossword puzzle."

Wilson even included Joyce in his historical novels - The *Historical Illuminatus Chronicles* - which turned out to be three novels: *The Earth Will Shake* (1982), *The Widow's Son* (1985), and *Nature's God* (1991). Very much in the tradition of the "Lodge Novel" (see notes on *Masks of the Illuminati*, above), they take place in Europe and the America of the Revolutionary War, roughly between 1764 and the early 19th century. In *The Earth Will Shake*, the young Neapolitan hero, Sigismundo Celine, traveling to northern Europe under the tutelage of his wise Uncle Pietro, visits a factory in Westminster and talks briefly to a an ex-peasant worker there: "This ex-peasant was named Joyce, and he was Irish. Our host told me later to believe nothing he said because the Irish are all liars, scoundrels, ignorant and superstitious. It sounded just like what everybody in Napoli said about Sicilians. I keep thinking about that man named Joyce, and I feel there is a specter haunting Europe: but I do not know its name." (*The Earth Will*

Shake, p.217 Hilaritas Press ed; p.223 Lynx Books paperback ed.) Here it seems "Joyce" is an Irish stand-in for all Irish, and the deformed communication that comes from politically oppressed peoples and their local variations on the law of Omerta. Wilson wrote a lot about the puzzling, elliptical speech of the Irish, who were trained over hundreds of years to speak in code to evade the invaders.

In *The Widow's Son* (which Wilson once told an audience of young writers in San Francisco was his favorite of all his own novels, because he mixed up fact and fiction and interwove the two so deftly even he wasn't sure what was "real"), one of his main characters, an Irishman named Seamus Muadhen, narrates an historical Irish consciousness that dovetails Wilson's own deep reading of Irish history and the historical consciousness of Joyce. (See, for example, pp.107-123 of the Hilaritas ed.) Seamus is considering his current plight and thinks of course an Irishman would be the one who said, "History is a nightmare from which I am trying to awake." (ibid., p.111) That this occurs in the 19th century is certainly License, but it's a trifle compared to how Joyce is woven into this text via the extensive footnotes throughout the novel, many of which function as a surrealistic counter-narrative to the main novel. Wilson never tired of satirizing academics and their vicious ideological turf wars, and one of Seamus's friends, Sean O'Lachlann of Meath (Wilson is related to the O'Lachlanns) who had read more than he, told Seamus a lot of lore that had not gotten into books yet but was instead passed on in the oral tradition: that James II was known as Shem the Shit; that "Puck in Shakespeare was actually the old Celtic pookah, or woodland spirit" – proof that Shakespeare had come to Dublin to "learn how to use English properly" and that the real Hamlet had not died after he killed his uncle but came to Dublin and "was governor during the Danish occupation" (ibid., p.112), which leads to a very large footnote that cites Brendan O'Hehir's *Gaelic Lexicon for Finnegans Wake* and Dounia Bunis Christiani's *Scandinavian*

Elements of Finnegans Wake, but also: Saxo-Grammaticus and a bevy of fictional authors, professors and books, including books on Flann O'Brien's "De Selby", who is a major character throughout the footnotes of this book.

In another antic footnote describing de Selby's relationship with Sophie De Neuve, we read this passage: "It is a tribute to both de Selby's mental resilience and his unique capacity for transmundane states of consciousness that he soon recovered and became convinced that he was deeply in love with Nora Barnacle, whom in fact he had never met. His letters to her, attempting to woo her by demonstrating his intellectual agility – he was under the misapprehension that Nora lived with James Joyce because she admired macaronic metaphysics – contain many ingenious and piquant passages, such as his famous argument that the mysterious number 1132 which occurs monotonously and tantalizingly throughout *Finnegans Wake*..." and it goes on and on from there. This novel is Wilson at his most playful heights, surely. (ibid., 231-232)

Yet another footnote links the "bear" archetype to Dagobert II, the last Merovingian king, to the Priory of Sion and de Sede and Pierre Plantard; from there to anthropologist Weston La Barre's *Ghost Dance*, which links – via the bear-god archetype – to de Selby's "remarkable letter (*De Selby/Barnacle*, closed shelves, Cornell University James Joyce Collection)" to Joyce in *FW* (p.66) on "Arthur" and all the bear-god types, to some rather fanciful citations, to Adeline Glasheen's quite solid *Second Census to Finnegans Wake*, and finally to *Holy Blood, Holy Grail*. (ibid., p.322)

Later the hero Sigismundo falls asleep and *FW*-language takes over: "Mark my words, you will come to know God." And a bell bellowed, "Look, look, look: to leaf is to sea." And a seagull sang, "John peeked with his goat so grey and a hney nonny nonny hney!" And the angel mermaid said, "Matter of space, matter of time, matter of mind. You will come to new good." (ibid., pp.329-330)

Due to a very unfortunate series of events with publishers, the third novel in the trilogy, *Nature's God*, was far less playful and expansive than *The Widow's Son*, though it has many moments. Wilson shows a particular deftness with the aphoristic style, using the main character's "Wilderness Notebooks" as a vehicle for these quasi-Nietzschean aphorisms. The entirety of chapter 6, "The Marquis de Sade and Other Libertines: England-France-America 1776-1986" is in the form of the "Aeolus" chapter of *Ulysses*. (*Nature's God*, Hilaritas Press ed, pp.71-108) The hero, Sigismundo, writes in his notebook an idea that seems derived from Joyce: "The greatest thing about masturbation is that it is always available. I wager that many a condemned man has consoled himself this way during the night before his execution." (ibid., p.117) Joyce on masturbation: "The amazing availability of it." The Stephen-like Sigismundo is living alone in the woods in southern Ohio and sees a dead dog, which seems to be linked to "Proteus": "A dog's dead body in the woods. The blood looks like human blood. I think: The clues are everywhere but we do not see. Is it mere foppery that makes us think that we are not animals, or is it that the noise & commotion of human society keep us from thinking clearly until we deliberately go into isolation?" (ibid., p.122) Another line that makes us wonder how conscious Wilson was of Joyce occurs when he wrote, "I had just enough Jesuit education to make my honesty doubtful even to myself." (ibid., p.123)

The heroine, Maria Maldonado slips into sleep with *FW*-language: " . . . and the thirteen, and the Last Supper and the sun, which is One, moving in eternal circle through the twelve Houses, one plus twelve being thirteen, and why did the Order of the Garter have one hundred sixty-nine or thirteen times thirteen members? And if all this could be coded, as John said Leibniz said, into the one and the zero, the upright 1 and the cauldron-like zero, the wand and the cup, one l'oeuf one vier, on love on wir, ein loaf ein vir, and she sloped down and slooped up and slipped round into sleep." (ibid., p.157)

Similarly, spy-master Sartines's consciousness falls into dream *FW*-language later in the book: "He dozed off dreaming of the ramifications of the consternation of the fornification of the population in the cooperation of the procrastination of the monsturbation of the castroidclownation of the incamination for the phartification on the pantification with the hulahulalation of a warp in process." (ibid., p. 227)

While living in Ireland, Wilson often made speaking tours throughout Europe and the US, and on August 30, 1985, while in San Francisco, V. Vale interviewed Wilson and asked him about his influences. While we've gone over this question, supra, here he links American individualist-anarchist Benjamin Tucker, whom Joyce also admired, and after discussing the influence of Nietzsche, Wilson talked about Tucker and Joyce:

"And another major influence is somebody that hardly anyone has heard of. Whenever I run into somebody who's heard of Benjamin Tucker, I'm astonished. Very few people have read Ben Tucker. Strangely, two of my favorite novelists have read him and mentioned him: Henry Miller and James Joyce both read Ben Tucker. I don't know who else has ever read Ben Tucker. He wrote one book in his whole lifetime – it's called *Instead of a Book, by a Man Too Busy to Write One*. It's a fantastically logical book." Wilson then talks about logical traps, and how Tucker at times called himself a "philosophical anarchist" to avoid being linked with the bomb-throwers, but Wilson thought it was the best defense of individual rights ever. Wilson then adds to his influences, "Joyce's experiments with language in *Ulysses* and *Finnegans Wake*. And Korzybski's *Science and Sanity*, which encouraged me in my Joycean tendency to suspect that language is full of traps and it's the job of the writer to find his way around the traps in language and not just fall into them [. . .] I see language as a means of human liberation, potentially – and the main mechanism of human slavery most of the time. It depends on how you use language." (This interview was lost for a long time, then found and published in 2019 under the title: *Robert Anton Wilson: Beyond Conspiracy Theory*, by Re/Search Publications; the above quotes are on pp.36-37).

Wilson published an occult experiment he did while living in Howth, with his own nervous system beginning at 11:54 on May 6th, 1985, in *Semiotext[e] USA*, edited by Jim Fleming, Peter Lamborn Wilson, and Sylvère Lotringer. This book appeared in 1987. Titled "Coincidance" it prefigures and seems to function now as the ur-text for the extensive essays on *Ulysses* and *Finnegans Wake* that later appeared in *Coincidance: A Head Test* (1988), but this 1985 piece seems to be a marathon writing session (the book is in large format size and the essay runs from pp.155-188) which went on for around a week, linking *Finnegans Wake* and the Buffalo Notebooks sigla, via his own cabalistic ingenuity to the nonlocality of quantum mechanics, Irish history, I Ching, Leibniz's binary system, the genetic code, mythology, etymology, symbolism in Freemasonry, the coincidence of opposites which reveal a third, UFO and Fortean phenomena, ideas from *Holy Blood, Holy Grail*, the P2 conspiracy and Roberto Calvi, Flann O'Brien as a reader of *FW*, Wilde's idea of the "reality of masks," and Hitler and the Thule Society. Among many other things. The piece overall feels both brilliant and manic, and this was the same year he published the even more manic and dazzling *The Widow's Son*. In the letters to Kurt Smith (supra) there seems some indication of a deep depression from near the end of his run in Dublin (1986-87) before moving back to the US. Neither he nor his friends or family – as far as known to the present writer – have said Wilson was bipolar/manic depressive. Wilson was very candid about his bouts with polio as a child, his poverty, anxiety, and short depressions, but no one has ever said he had a pronounced mental illness. This is only speculative on my part, born of my reading of various books on genius and mental illness (such as *Touched With Fire: Manic Depressive Illness and the Artistic Temperament* by Kay Redfield Jamison) and probably further biographical writing on Wilson will yield more on this, if there is anything to it. Of 1985, Wilson once said in a talk that "I was very hot that year." We should say so!

Wilson begins this occult experiment by telling us that May 6th is the birthday of Orson Welles, Freud, and the Phoenix Park Murders that figure so largely in *FW*, and that 11:54 = 1+1+5+4 = 11, that May 6 = 6+5 = 11, and that 1985 = 23. The 23 Enigma, introduced to Wilson by his friend William S. Burroughs, runs throughout Wilson's work, and "Looking into the Good Book, we find that 11 runs through it like a refrain, usually as part of the mystery number, 1132, which has largely baffled commentators; 11 also appears as part of 111, which Joyce always identifies with his heroine Anna Livia Plurabella, because her initials, ALP, Cabalistically add to 111 . . ." There are 6/5 correspondences that link to ceremonial magicians and the ultimate goal of the Knowledge and Conversation with the Holy Guardian Angel. 65 = ADONAI; 56 = Nu, Egyptian goddess of the stars, several of the 56 signers of the Declaration of Independence were Freemasons, the Roman historian Livy=Liffey = LVI = 56, Mark Twain's wife was called "Livy" 56 = 50 +6, but 50 x 6 = 300 is "shin" and the number for the resurrection of the dead: Jesus, Osiris, Tim Finnegan, many many more, etc.

On p.162 of the *Semiotext (e) USA* piece Wilson quotes from *FW* (p.263): "The task above as are the flasks below, saith the emerald canticle of Hermes," and he then links this to Philip K. Dick's *VALIS*, Giordano Bruno, holograms, and David Bohm's Implicate Order, which not only prefigures the essays in *Coincidance*, but might have formed some of the ideas in a text that was announced by Wilson but never appeared, death intervening, *The Tale of the Tribe*, although this is mere speculation on my part. (See *TSOG*; Hilaritas Press, pp. 215-228)

The above gives the tenor of the piece, which is overwhelming and reminds the present writer of John

Coltrane's improvisations near the end of his life. Given a structure, a superabundance of esoteric and erudite riffing ensues on a theme. More about this kind of writing from Wilson in the discussion of 1988's *Coincidance: A Head Test*, below.

In 1978-79 Wilson wrote a PhD dissertation for an alternative university, Paideia, titled "The Evolution of Neuro-Sociological Circuits: A Contribution to the Sociobiology of Consciousness," which he later re-worked into *Prometheus Rising*, sans excess scholarly apparatus. First published in 1983 by Falcon Press, it's now - as of this date (2024) in its Third Edition and has gone through at least 24 printings. It's now published by Hilaritas Press. Largely an expansion and interpretation of Timothy Leary's Eight Circuit Brain Model of consciousness – which Wilson helped Leary build throughout the 1970s – it's still the *locus classicus* for the 8CBModel, and in the chapter on the Oral Bio-survival Circuit, there is much that goes into biological and historical depth as to why Stephen Dedalus told Mr. Deasy that "History is a nightmare from which I am trying to awake." While not mentioning this line in that chapter, the analysis has everything to do with why history would be seen like this, by Joyce and Wilson. Wilson considers Stephen's line as a classic Gnostic take, and indeed, Wilson quotes from the 1st CE gnostic text *The Gospel of Truth*, which says very bluntly that history is a nightmare: " . . . as if (mankind) were sunk in sleep and found themselves in disturbing dreams. Either (there is) a place to which they are fleeing . . . or they are involved in striking blows, or they are receiving blows themselves . . . sometimes it is as if people were murdering them . . . or they themselves are killing their neighbors." (*Prometheus Rising*, 3rd edition, Hilaritas Press, p.30; see the entire chapter, pp.25-39)

The psycho-archaeology Wilson found in Joyce was employed to weighty effect in the dialectic between the 1st (matrist-oral-biosurvival) circuit and the 2nd (anal-patrist) circuit, with examples from Dickens and Joyce. In *Finnegans Wake*, "the Father and Father-God" are always associated with war and excretion, as Joyce scholar William York Tindall has noted. As 'Gunn, the Farther,' the terrifying anal monster combines pistol, deity and flatulence; as 'Delude of Israel,' he is the jealous (territorial) Old Testament 'Lord of Hosts,' i.e., of battles. His insignia, hundred letter thunder-word which recurs ten times in the dream, always combines Fatherhood, menace, defecation and war . . ." (ibid., p.68) Wilson goes on at length in further elucidations here. Regarding Joyce's use of Vico in *FW*: "This cyclical view of history, whether in Joyce, Rattray-Taylor, Vico (Joyce's source), Hegel-and-Marx, etc., is only part of the truth, but it needs to be stressed because it is the part that most people fearfully refuse to recognize. Whether we speak in terms of Taylor's Matrist-Patrist dialectic, Vico's cycle of Divine, Heroic and Urbanized ages, the Marx-Hegel trinity of Thesis-Antithesis-Synthesis, or any variation thereon, we are speaking of a pattern that is real and does repeat." (ibid., p.69) This further informs Stephen's nightmare of history.

In describing how the 3rd circuit – the time-binding semantic circuit – works, Wilson tells how "The semantic circuit allows us to sub-divide things, and reconnect things, *at pleasure*. There is no end to its busy-busy-busy labeling and packaging of experience. On the personal level, this is the 'internal monologue' discovered by Joyce in *Ulysses*. On the historical level, this is the *time-binding function* described by Korzybski, which allows each generation to add new categories to our mental library . . ." (ibid., p.75) (No doubt Wilson knew of the time Joyce inscribed a book to Édouard Dujardin, who is often cited as the actual discoverer of the internal monologue/ stream of consciousness, probably in late 1880's novella *We'll To The Woods No More*. Joyce inscribed Dujardin's copy of *Ulysses* from "the impenitent thief.")

The Collective Neurogenetic Circuit is a post-history-as-nightmare circuit and not activated by everyone on the planet, but only by happy accident and is referred by Wilson in terms of Jung's collective unconscious, as Atman, Tao, the Akashic Records, Pan, and more recently in history, the Gaia Hypothesis. Leary's idea was that it was our minds in contact with DNA-RNA-Central Nervous System-Nature feedback loops. Wilson says "the language of this circuit is the multi-level language of *Finnegans Wake* . . ." and goes on at great length to describe how this works in *FW*. It's perhaps this level of writing about *FW* in which Wilson shines most brightly, and his entire aggregated oeuvre contains a fairly sophisticated exegesis in these regards. (ibid., p.187)

This is the level in which synchronicities occur, and they are "a sure sign that you are dealing with the neurogenetic circuit. For instance, in a *Finnegans Wake* study group we were all convulsed with laughter when noticing that 'Toot and Come Inn' is not just a parody of American cutesy-pie motel names but another of Joyce's countless puns on Tutankhamen. At this point, my wife entered the room to enquire what was so funny. When we explained, she said, 'That's a synchronicity – I was just watching a TV program about Tutankhamen.' And, of course, Joyce put the boy-king into the dream because the main theme of *Finnegans Wake*, the main theme of the neurogenctic circuit, is the survival of genetic memory through time, symbolized by the Resurrection myth; and Tut was dug up (resurrected) synchronistically, just after Joyce started work in this epic." (ibid., pp.187-188)

In *Prometheus Rising*, Wilson also links the symbolic names of the Four Old Men in *FW* (p.53); uses *FW*'s "being humus the same roturns" to illustrate the 2nd circuit (p.62); uses *FW*'s "that why all parks up excited about his gunnfodder. That why ecrazyaztecs and crime ministers preaching him mornings" as an epigraph for the 1st-2nd circuit dialectic; quotes ALP at length illustrating how she is as "oral and loving as the 'Omniboss' is anal and threatening" (pp.68-69); how the nightmare of appearing naked in public – HCE in

Phoenix Park – is related to processes of brainwashing and initiation into new realities, via neurological shocks to the system (see p.135 of *Prometheus Rising* in this context, ibid.); Wilson quotes from *FW* in illustrating how the 5th circuit – the Holistic Neurosomatic – is limned with "Calling all downs. Calling all downs to dayne. Aray! Surrection! . . . It is just, it is just about to, it is just about to rolywholyover." (ibid., p.162) In elucidation of the Meta-Programming Circuit and a short discussion of how Strange Loops work, Wilson assures us this circuit is "*not* a trap. As Joyce would say, it only looks like it as damn it. Simply accept that the universe is so structured that it can see itself, and that this self-reflexive arc is built into our frontal lobes, so that consciousness contains an infinite-regress, and all we can do is make models of ourselves making models . . . "(ibid., p.211) There is a discussion about the "logic" of schizophrenic thought that seems to bleed into our non-schizophrenic thinking, which Wilson links to the logic of *FW*. (ibid., pp.221-222) And finally, Wilson quotes Mr. Deasy with extreme irony at the chapter head to the Non-Local Quantum Circuit: "The ways of the Creator are not our ways, Mr. Deasy said. All history moves toward one great goal, the manifestation of God."

Wilson's friend D. Scott Apel wrote and edited *Philip K. Dick: The Dream Connection* (1986, Atomic Drop Press) which also included interviews conducted with Kevin C. Briggs, a short essay and letter by Philip K. Dick, an essay by Ray Faraday Nelson, and an "Afterwards" essay by Robert Anton Wilson, in which Wilson muses on PKD's otherworldly gnostic experience of interacting with what he called "VALIS" or the Vast Active Living Intelligence System: "Since Phil Dick often referred to *Finnegans Wake*, a book which impressed him greatly, it is profitable to note certain parallels between Joyce's masterpiece and Phil's own masterpiece, *VALIS*. This can be demonstrated by the handy notation which Joyce invented and used in his own notebooks." And Wilson goes on to instrumentally link PKD's experiences with each of the four "E" sigla, describing the functions of each, and how they might be mapped onto Philip K. Dick's experience, and Apel's uncanny dream experience involving PKD; Wilson suspects Apel tapped into the Jungian collective unconscious and also the *wu-hsin* levels that had also communicated through PKD, but he wasn't about to dogmatize about it. (see *Philip K. Dick: The Dream Connection*, pp.257-260; the entire piece by Wilson: pp.244-267, including an appendix.)

The New Inquisition: Irrational Rationalism and Citadel of Science (1986) functions as Wilson's philosophy of science. Somewhere in the interstices of Feyerabend, Popper and Charles Fort, it's largely his critique of the professional debunkers of phenomena of so-far unexplained anomalies and those small-minded scientific fideists that want to police official scientific discourse. It's also an exercise of his almost Pyrrhonic skepticism, grounded in his Transactional Psychology, in which every act of perception by humans is active and "creative" in the widest sense: we do not passively receive signals from some block-like "reality" which is "out there" and react to them. We are constantly editing our perceptions and we all have preconceived ideas that box in our perceptions, but it takes knowing this fact and much training in doubt to begin to see more clearly.

In an epigraph to the first chapter Wilson quotes Roger Jones, from his *Physics As Metaphor*: "How is the quark more real than figurative? And is the very term *quark* coined from that most metaphoric and creative of works, *Finnegans Wake*? And when physicists, with tongue in cheek, apply terms like *color* and *charm* to quarks, can we believe they are oblivious to their own creative acts?" (*The New Inquisition*, Hilaritas Press ed, p.1)

In illustrating relativity in perception, Wilson uses the dog Garry Owen from the "Nausicaa" and "Cyclops" episodes of *Ulysses*: Garry Owen, if we can believe the records, was an actual Irish Setter owned by a dog breeder named J.J.

Giltrap. Garry Owen is cited twice in *Ulysses*. 1.) he's an ugly, ill-tempered, dangerous, mangy hound as described by the ("drunken"?) narrator in the "Cyclops" episode; and 2.) Garry Owen is described by the sentimental adolescent Gerty McDowell as a sweet dog, "so human he almost talked." So which is it? "Joyce's text sayeth not – which may be one reason *Ulysses* increasingly appears as *the* archetypal 20th Century novel. We can believe the drunk, or we can believe the sentimentalist, or we can believe a little of both, or we can believe neither." (ibid., pp. 240-241) Just after this passage Wilson unpacks various characters from *FW* using the sigla system (Cain/Abel; Brown/Nolan; Shem/Shaun; Michael/Nick, and their interweavings); by 1986 he had become adept at using this system. Wilson makes a plea for John von Neumann's quantum logic and Transactional Psychology – what he would later simplify as "Maybe Logic" – by using Joyce's *FW* sigla here. (ibid., pp.241-242)

If we only knew more about our perceptions and reifications of "reality" we'd notice how our own reality-tunnels are not "reality" but more like works of art, "as varied and imaginative as the paintings of Rembrandt and Van Gogh and Picasso [. . .] as miscellaneous as the novelistic styles or 'frames' of Jane Austen and James Joyce and Raymond Chandler and Leo Tolstoy and Lewis Carroll and Samuel Beckett." (ibid., p.261)

In a critique of Peter Okera's book *East-West/North-South*, which posits three basic cultural configurations: Dionysian (Asia/Africa); Apollonian (Mediterranean); and Thorian (modern Europe and America), Wilson thinks more of Joyce's sigla along these lines, especially the symbols that indicate mixtures of two or more people/places. Wilson thinks the West might need to integrate the long-repressed Dionysian holistic values, while perhaps the East needs to recognize individual liberties like the West does. "Maybe then, as both sides approach Apollonian balance neither will perceive the other, any longer, as lop-sided to the point of perversity and madness." Wilson interleaves these and preceding sentences with Joycean sigla from *FW*. (*The New Inquisition*, pp. 270-275)

Natural Law Or Don't Put a Rubber on Your Willy, in which Wilson logically and rhetorically near-eviscerates the claims of some fellow anarcho-libertarian thinkers who employed "natural law" as a foundation for their arguments, was a slim book put out by Loompanics Unlimited in 1987. Hilaritas Press republished it in 2022 with two added interviews, nine additional essays, and one short story. In a discussion of ideology, Wilson cites John Adams, who looked at ideology's effects and said he couldn't consider human history without laughing or weeping. "Most of us, these days (except the Ideologists), feel that way; like James Joyce we regard history as a nightmare from which we are trying to wake. Like Joyce, we have learned to 'fear those big words that make us so unhappy.' We have looked at the victims of 'moral passion' and 'deep belief' (which we are more likely to call fanaticism) and we have become agnostic, somewhat cynical and very, very cautious about that kind of passion and that kind of belief." (*Natural Law*, Hilaritas Press ed, p.9)

In a 1987 essay in Critique, "Art as Black Magick and Moral Subversion," published under the pseudonym "Heinrich von Hankopf", Wilson jumps off from a previous issue's long review of a book on the secret power of music, and here Wilson, in full-on satirical mode, argues that pretty much all the great artists and thinkers and writers were moral degenerates and/or members of monstrous secret societies like the Freemasons or Illuminati. Or they are Jews! Or aligned with them, or they were homosexuals!, etc. Joyce gets the treatment: "Joyce admired Wilde, was also an anarchist and lived in sin with a peasant girl for 27 years before he grudgingly married her (only to ensure that his bastard children would receive the royalties to his books after his death). Like

Yeats, Joyce was once associated with the Theosophical Society, founded by the hashish-fiend Blavatsky, who despised Christian orthodoxy and espoused ecumenicism and World Government. Ezra Pound, a friend of both Yeats and Joyce, was a fascist and lived in a *menage a trois* with a wife and mistress; he collected books on magick and shows an unwholesome sympathy for Gnostic immanentalism. The influence of the non-linear, relativistic, non-Aristotelian and therefore un-American experiments in prose and poetry by these two arch-conspirators, Joyce and Pound – who blatantly promoted each other's works and sneeringly satirized the simple and decent literature of more wholesome minds – has been poisonous and omnipresent ever since. Joyce and Pound can be found as major influences in the poetry of homosexual Jazz fan Allen Ginsberg, New Deal 'liberal' Charles Olson . . ." (As far as I know this article hasn't been reprinted in a book.)

1988 saw Wilson's article, "Synchronicity, Isomorphism and the Implicate Order: Notes on Jung and Quantum Mechanics" in *Gnosis* magazine, Winter 1988-89, issue #10, pp. 46-50. The entire article informs much of Wilson's explications of *FW* sigla/system functions and *I Ching*, quantum mechanics, DNA, Leibniz's binary system and computers, etc., but here Joyce is on the periphery. In a series of collected synchronicities, he includes the backstory to the Weiss/Schwarz white/black symbolism in *FW*. 1915, Switzerland: a man named Schwarz introduced Joyce to a man named Weiss, and it was through this coincidence that Joyce met Jung. Wilson, with more of his satirical tone: "This is the kind of thing that drives CSICOP to froth at the mouth. Joyce, as we all know, had ruined his mind by reading too much hermetic philosophy and it was absurd of him to find meaning in a coincidence of names." Later Wilson discusses Dr. David Bohm's interpretation of quantum mechanics, quoting Bohm: "It may mean that everything in the universe is in a kind of total rapport, so that whatever happens is related to everything else; or it may mean that there is some kind of information that can travel faster than the speed of light; or it may mean that our concepts of space and time have to be modified in some way that we don't now understand." Wilson notes that Bohm's first item, that everything may be in total rapport, "seems like a clear formulation of what Joyce was getting at in *Finnegans Wake*, where he links everything in Dublin with everything else in the space-time continuum." (p.49) Bohm also posits a possible holographic model of the universe. Wilson: "In other words, one day in Dublin may contain the information of the whole human odyssey, as Joyce tried to demonstrate. The peculiarities of Joyce's style result from his attempts to convey this vision by creating holographic prose. Blake asserted he could see 'infinity in a grain of sand,' but Joyce tried to *show* it to us. Got it? Bloom in *Ulysses* is not the 'reincarnation' of Odysseus and Hamlet's father; he is merely, like them, another local manifestation of one nonlocal (hidden) variable in the implicate order. Our unconscious, like that of Joyce's creatures, is not 'an area within our brains' but 'a network of connections through time and space.'" (p.49)

This line of thought about Joyce in general reaches its apex in 1988, with *Coincidance*, about which, see below.

Return to the U.S: Los Angeles and Santa Cruz: 1987-2007

In 1988 Wilson gave a radio interview with David J. Banton and Banton asked a good question: "What is your fascination with Joyce?" Wilson responded thus:

"I could talk all day about that! Joyce was more interested in synchronicity – more than any other writer before me – and he influenced me a great deal. My fascination with synchronicity grows more out of Joyce than out of Jung. *Ulysses* and *Finnegans Wake* are all about synchronicity, and they came out long before Jung ever wrote anything on the subject. Joyce fascinates me because of many other things. In *Ulysses*, he was the first person to write a relativistic novel, the first Einsteinian novel. Every other novel before *Ulysses* had one point of view, which was supposed to be the objective point of view, and in *Ulysses*, Joyce refuses to give you an objective point of view. He gives you about 54 different points of view, and leaves it up to you to decide which of the various narrative voices you're going to believe. And I find that a very appropriate style for the 20th century, it's entirely compatible with relativity and quantum mechanics . . . the amount of deception and propaganda in the 20th century, where you can't take anything at face value. It's compatible with modern philosophy, everything from Nietzsche and Wittgenstein on, we've learned more and more about how the mind creates its own reality-tunnel; it's entirely compatible with modern psychology and neurology and cultural anthropology. I don't see why anybody is writing Victorian novels. I think everybody should be writing Joycean novels, to be contemporary, to be compatible with modern science, modern philosophy and modern civilization in general. People who are writing pre-Joycean novels, it seems to me like they're riding around in a stagecoach instead of using a car or a plane."

    This was a take on Joyce that Wilson often referred to, which linked with Wilson's intellectual aesthetics: that arts and sciences should stay in constant dynamic current with each other in significant, mostly structural ways. Artists often seem to prefigure the scientific breakthroughs of the following generation, so why had writing in general fallen behind the other arts? Or are we just not looking closely enough? Have genuinely relativistic novels been ghettoized by academia? Or are they mostly only read by academics? Why does *Ulysses*, not to mention *FW*, still seem "too difficult" in 2024 for most people? Is there something about reading and mass education that militates against "difficulty" and has the current best-seller lists to this day filled with "Victorian" novels in the third decade of the 21st century? If so, why has this occurred? Has this aspect of Wilson's aesthetics been marginalized? If so, why? Answering these questions is beyond the scope of the present article, and are meant only as Ginsbergian interrogatives: Dear Reader: Think about this, please?

Coincidance: A Head Test (1988)

In a wide-ranging 1983 Bloomsday interview of Wilson conducted by John van der Does, conducted at Wilson's place within sight of Martello Tower, Wilson said he was "working on a book on synchronicity in *Finnegans Wake*, which I suspect is very non-commercial . . ." (*Coincidance: A Head Test*, Hilaritas Press, pp.324-325)

We've seen (above) the passage in the letter to Kurt Smith May 31st, 1983; that he had been very much engaged in this theme, although it would seem safe to guess the first inklings of ideas around synchronicity, isomorphism and *FW* were from at least around the time *Illuminatus!* was finally published in 1975. That is: if we simply analyze his statements about *FW* in prior interviews, ideas in his books, and essays. However, there seems a critical difference between this sort of textual analysis and actual statements of intent to cover these themes, and these begin in 1983. In Spring 1983 Wilson published "Synchronicity and Isomorphism in Finnegans Wake" in *Fortean Times*. The 1985 "Coincidance" magickal ritual that appears in *Semiotext[e] USA* (1987), but written starting on May 6th, 1985 seems to be the true ur-text for this mode of approach: FW, its sigla, interpretations of quantum mechanics, Jung and synchronicity, the I Ching/Leibniz's binary code idea/DNA, and Crowleyan Cabala methods: they all come to fruition in the book, *Coincidance: A Head Test* (1988). In 1991 he was asked by *Fifth Path* magazine if the 1985 "Coincidance" was a "shortened form of the book;" Wilson responded, "No, it was almost entirely different – some of the same material, but it contained some that wasn't in the book and vice-versa. They were sort of independent productions with an overlapping theme." (http://rawilsonfans.de/en/the-fifth-path-magazine-interview/)

But first, at this point, something should be said about Robert Anton Wilson as a type of intellectual. He was not an academic. He was a freelance writer, raising a family as such, and knew poverty intimately. He supplemented his sales of books and articles with lecture tours. He was one of the great Generalist intellectuals: trained in mathematics and the physical sciences at Brooklyn Polytechnic High School. He later earned a PhD in Psychology from an alternative university. (See *Prometheus Rising*'s origins, supra.) He chronicled his prodigious reading from an early age in his autobiographical work, *Cosmic Trigger, vol.2: Down To Earth*, and in many other places. He was erudite in the physical and social sciences, the Humanities, and in surrealism, drugs, sex, the occult and gnostic/hermetic/kabbalistic history and thought. It seems exceedingly rare to read a writer who is so well-read in classics, the physical sciences, mathematics, literature, philosophy, psychology, mythology, poetry, the history of film, and the Marginalized Discourses – those areas that academia has always shunned – magick and the occult, the history of secret societies and conspiracy theories, and "lowbrow" literature. Like Joyce, he thought the artificial separation of "High and Low" was to miss out on the booming, buzzing confusion of life and Mind outside the groves of academe. Wilson not only read the tabloids from an anthropological standpoint, he had written for "schlock" tabloids, in the early 1960s.

He told interviewers his reading had long been "omnidirectional" and that, as a high schooler he had "been a monster of erudition." Isaiah Berlin had once defined intellectuals as people "who want ideas to be as interesting as possible." The sociologist of knowledge, Peter Berger, wrote that, "'Intellectuals' (religious or otherwise) sometimes spin out very strange ideas – and very strange ideas sometimes have very important historical effects." (*The Sacred Canopy*, p.42) In addressing the use of rhetoric towards eloquence, Donald Verene wrote that eloquence "must delight in the sense that it is more important that a proposition be interesting than it be true." (*Art of Humane Education*, p.3) We suspect that at times a writer can become so enthralled by his topic that the ideas become "true" in some sense, via their initial formation and final fruition in books. The ideas that interest us most intensely really ought to be true, even if they are not demonstrably true, yet. Whether we can say this same thing about Wilson's most extravagant ideas about *FW* being "true" along these lines seems indeterminate, because of his almost Pyrrhonic skepticism, which he had fashioned into Model Agnosticism (about everything) and later, "maybe logic." This seems perfectly in keeping with the speculative generalist intellectual caste of mind that Wilson had, and as a freelancer, his need to engage and entertain readers. That his ideas were "interesting" seems obvious, but perhaps all such things are aesthetic preferences.

Finally, it must be said that Wilson thought his particular role as a writer-intellectual was in taking the ideas most interesting to him and finding similarities of structure over seemingly disparate domains of thought, which is a speculative enterprise that might indeed, to paraphrase Berger, yield "important historical effects." He was forever interested in finding structures in one domain of thought that looked similar to other structures in another area of knowledge, because there might be something very important in that search: why do disparate ideas or concepts from far-flung areas of thought appear to contain a similarity of structure? Or if not historically significant, at least such isomorphisms fired the imaginations of his readers and provoked similar trains of ideation. In this is the Artist-Novelist area of intellectuality that was Robert Anton Wilson. His form of "structuralism" was not of the French variety, but was more like Alfred Korzybski's and Buckminster Fuller's "structuralism."

NB: This search for and finding of similar structures also looks like a definition of paranoia, which is ironic in all of Wilson's work, in which paranoia is rampant, but his liberatory message was to transcend this sort of *interpretation* of speculative thought and use it more toward irony, hilaritas, delight, and mystical states of mind. He often noted that we all forget we are making artistic connections between phenomena, perception and ideas. It's up to us to notice this, and proceed in a way that makes our world larger and funnier and more interesting, and not paranoid and miserable. (By the way: Eric Wagner has shown, above, a similar not-inconsiderable level of virtuosity with cabala. Note how his life, reading and history link to almost everything in existence, not from his personal ego, but his ability to find correspondences and a cosmic giggle echoing everywhere. He trained his mind this way: 'tis the hallmark of kabbalah/cabala/qabala. This seems an unmistakable mark of the mystic, of most of our creative, artistic Weird Brothers and Sisters. These methods of imagination-generation are available to all of us, with significant effort.)

In the extravagant, wonderful, and at-times florid speculative work on Joyce in *Coincidance*, Wilson seems to want us to catch a glimpse of transcendent Intelligence, which is not artificial, but which builds up from interpretations and suppositions which had already been made by prior Joyceans. These were then treated by Wilson with a virtuosic display of isomorphic extraction based on *Finnegans Wake*, Joyce's sigla, Crowlyean cabala and magick, Wilson's survey of 20th century physics, etymology, hermeticism, binary mathematics and the *I Ching*, and ideas about the DNA-RNA-central nervous system feedback loops and other areas of knowledge.

Wilson limns speculative ideas of intelligence and consciousness in ourselves, in Nature at large, and the (or merely our local?) Universe. From an epistemological standpoint, this enterprise by Wilson is not of the type of "discovering what was already there", as when detectives find out who committed a murder, or when Watson, Crick and

Franklin discovered the structure of DNA, but an articulation of creative thought based on pre-existing structures of human knowledge. Whereas epistemologically our intuitions tell us that all knowledge had to be discovered and then its discovery procedures described and finally represented to the larger community, some knowledge represents novel patterns of reasoning and modes of perception. Wilson was absorbed by novel breakthroughs in thought, and perhaps his depiction of Einstein's thinking processes in *Masks of the Illuminati* is a good example: there were seemingly intractable problems in physics, so Einstein moved away from language by creating pictures in his mind of what the world might look like if he was, say, riding on a beam of light. This "daydreaming" indeed did yield "very important historical effects."

Wilson was fascinated by epistemological questions, and was quite adept and candid about his intellectual role as producer of "what if?" ideas and speculation in general. Those who are familiar with Kuhn's ideas about the initial formation of disciplines – physics or geology, for example – know that there were perceived phenomena among the larger community and many hypotheses about what was going on, what was causing phenomena, why and how, etc. Recall the earliest pre-Socratics: everything was water, or air, or things trying to return to where they belonged, or fire, always transient, etc. Gradually, ideas were tested, the language of mathematics developed, and other hypotheses faded, and a discipline's first theories and "paradigm" was established, always with unanswered, seemingly intractable questions that loomed. With Wilson's creation of knowledge around *FW*, Joyce and especially the non-local mind and possible Intelligence inherent in the universe, he's creating knowledge via patterns of reasoning that are themselves creative.

Wilson's lifetime work shows that thinkers who employed a novel framing technique in order to question pre-existing dogma were often branded as heretics. His combination of *FW* sigla, modern physics and Crowleyan cabala would seem ripe for charges of heresy, but very few seem to have read *FW*, and it's "only literature" so the stakes are low here. But not for us!

While many writers address ideas around the topic of what Aldous Huxley once called Mind At Large, here is a unique, artistic take on what It Might Look Like. And it has quite a lot to do with James Joyce's "vision."

The first long essay, "Synchronicity and Isomorphism in *Finnegans Wake*" (*Coincidance: A Head Test*, Hilaritas Press, pp.5-34) is an expanded version of an essay first published in 1983 in *Fortean Times*. Wilson thought no thinker – not even Carl Jung – had ever been as fascinated in synchronicity as Joyce, who even made provision in case he died before finishing *FW* that fellow Irish writer James Stephens should complete it, because he and Stephens shared the same birthday, and because "Stephen" had been a "self-caricature" of Joyce as a young man in *Portrait* and *Ulysses*.

"*Finnegans Wake* is in many ways an extension and enlargement of the forbidden and 'unthinkable' areas of human experience first explored in *Ulysses*. It is more 'difficult' than the earlier book, much more 'obscene,' more experimental in styles, much funnier, and contains many, many more synchronicities." Wilson thought the *FW* scholarship before 1983 had erred in assigning the protagonist HCE as only the Ego, when the "E" sigla Joyce used (turn that E 90 degrees until you have four versions of it) also at times functioned as not only the personal ego/self of Earwicker, but the Freudian unconscious of HCE, his relation to the Jungian unconscious/ Rupert Sheldrake's morphogenetic fields, and – most interestingly – the non-local "mind" of the universe, which Wilson finds isomorphic to Buddha Mind, the Taoist's *wu-shin*/ no mind, and Timothy Leary's 8th circuit of consciousness, or disembodied mind. ("Mind"?)

"Like Joyce, Vico believed that poetry arose out of creative etymology ('incorrect etymology' in Academese). Like Joyce – and like Whorf and Korzybski – Vico believed a radical change in language could radically alter our perceived reality-tunnels. (Is that happening yet, Dear Reader?)" (ibid., p.27) The present writer thinks of Wilson's creative etymology – not only Wilson's, but many of those (Vico, Joyce, Norman O. Brown, Nietzsche) who practiced creative etymology – is not only an interesting skill, but expands the ideas of etymology and how it might be more open to interpretation, not only given the deep psycho-archaeology of the discipline, but because *the word never was "the thing"*: we should be perhaps more open to creative etymology, or at least those interpretive schemes we might call the Poetic Faculty in all of us. Another way to frame this: *all etymology was always creative*, and a poetic interpretation of prior texts.

For *FW* exegetes, this first essay in *Coincidance* should seem fairly within the bounds of academic Joyce scholarship: it's capacious, learned and playful.

Wilson explained in verse "Why Do You Live In Ireland, Dr. Wilson?" and juxtaposed Yeats and Joyce, viz: "Yeats looked for faeries in the hills;/Joyce contemplated unpaid bills;/ Yeats, the realist, wrote in fire/The alchemical heart's desire;/ Joyce, the mystic, kept his head/Concerned with coin, and booze and bread . . ." Wilson tells us that at age 17 in Brooklyn he saw "the river Liffey dance" in a "mad trance" and that "I was damned by Yeats and Joyce:/I swear I never had a choice." And he moved to Dublin at age 50. (ibid., pp.89-92)

The second major essay on Joyce, "Death and Absence in James Joyce" (ibid., pp.99-120) covers material in *Dubliners*, *Ulysses* and *FW*. Wilson addresses Joyce's audacity in illustrating and defending the ideas of "timid courage" and "absence: the highest form of presence" and the looming presence of the long-dead Parnell over a room of political hacks in "Ivy Day in the Committee Room" (ibid., pp.99-101), and the presence of Michael Furey/Michael Bodkin in "The Dead" (ibid., pp.101-102). Wilson writes that in *Ulysses*, "the dead and absent are not only present but omnipresent" – Stephen's guilt over his dead mother, Leopold remembering his father and son, and the "absent" Blazes Boylan haunting Leopold's thoughts all day long. Homer's times are dead yet alive again and recapitulated via possibly Sheldrake's morphogenetic resonance, and Stephen as Hamlet, Leopold as the ghost of Hamlet's father and Molly as Gertrude is an exhibition by Joyce, speculates Wilson, of R. Buckminster Fuller's *"coherent synergy* or *knot . . .* a pattern that co-exists in many places and times. The dead and absent will be again live and present, in this context, because history repeats the same stories endlessly, just changing the names of the players." (ibid., p.105)

What of the relationship between Leopold Bloom and Stephen Dedalus? Is Bloom looking for a substitute son in Stephen? Does he have homosexual urges, as some critics have guessed? Was he trying to procure a young lover for Molly? Wilson thinks the answer to the relationship between Stephen and Leopold was given when Bloom confronted The Citizen, and offered as an alternative to politics and nationalistic hatred: "Love, says Bloom. I mean the opposite of hatred." Earlier Stephen admitted he'd left out of his theory of *Hamlet*: "Love, yes. Word known to all men." And Molly says in her soliloquy: "they don't know what love is" when running down all the answers to the question: What's Wrong With Men. (ibid., see p.107) All of this only revs up Wilson's energies to bolster his thesis of death, absence, rebirth, and recurrence in *FW* (ibid., 112-120)

For those Joyceans interested in Wilson's ideas about quantum physics and the synchronicities in Joyce, see "The Physics of Synchronicity," (pp.169-178, ibid.). Joyce is not even mentioned there, but this article provides background for those who seek it.

The third major essay about Joyce is "Semper As Oxhousehumper" (ibid., pp.181-202) and this is where Wilson separates himself from what had gone before in *FW* scholarship, with a long excursus on ALP and cabala, yin/yang and names in FW, including Joyce's name, in which a clerical error had his middle name recorded as "Augusta" instead of what his parents wanted, "Augustine." A female name in the middle of a male name: there are feminine (yin) aspects in males; masculine (yang) properties in females. Everything interpenetrates everything else, to some degree, and it's easy to see, for example, how Charles Dodgson merges with "Lewis Carroll" in the same body.

Furthermore, *I Ching* startled the mathematician Leibniz, who saw the first translation in Europe: it had the same binary code he thought he'd discovered, but this was an ancient book. Was Leibniz tapping into the non-local Mind of the universe? Were the early Chinese sages eavesdropping on a party circuit that connected to some eternal, transcendent Mind? In thinking about ideas such as Artificial Intelligence and the medieval history of Rabbi Loew of Prague, who invented the Golem and animated it by putting the Torah in its mouth, giving rise to our current ideas about "sentient" AI, and earlier, Frankenstein and the Sorcerer's Apprentice, here Wilson expresses ideas about intelligence that had been created: "Leibniz predicted modern computers after the isomorphism between his binary numbers and *I Ching* became clear to him; it was obvious to his fine mathematical mind that such a symbolism could be mechanically reproduced and we would then have something like a 'thinking machine.'" Wilson notes that it seems amusing that those who think computers can "think" call themselves "materialists" while those who assert the *I Ching* can think are "mystics."

But if "thinking" requires a binary code – and every introductory textbook on neurobiology describes the firing of a neuron as an all-or-nothing event – then "both computers and

I Ching must be considered to be thinking." (ibid., p.191) In Joyce's system functions/sigla for *FW* there are symbols that would transmute active yang into passive yang, and passive yin into active yin, which was not in *I Ching* or Leibniz's binary system. Wilson notes that Joyce's sigla seemingly allows for every possible transmutation to occur. That Leibniz's binary seems to have posited a "universal logical language below all consciousness" (ibid., p.190), which in turn predated Jung's "collective unconscious": here is an entry point for much further speculation on the deepest possible histories of AI, but it seems to require Joyce's sigla that allow for more flexible mutations, which is addressed further in the final major Joyce essay in *Coincidance*, about which see below.

In "Semper as Oxhousehumper" Giordano Bruno and Wilhelm Reich, Joseph Needham and the "Four Old Men" and Freemason symbols make their appearance, along with Schönberger's *The I Ching and the Genetic Code*, Lamarckian evolution, the Book of Kells, etc. This would be speculative Wilson at his most virtuosic. Apart from what is speculated here, the *method* seems as dazzling as anything else.

A fourth and final major Joyce essay, "The Hidden Variables" (ibid., pp.283-299) attempts to get to the heart of Joyce's creation of holographic prose-poetry by relying on Dr. David Bohm's interpretation of quantum mechanics: there is an Implicate Order that unfurls into our phenomenal ("funnanimal" in *FW*) world and becomes Explicate. In holograms, the entire structure is found in the smallest parts, which is isomorphic to the hermetic "as above, so below." But Bohm had been a student of Oppenheimer and had been endorsed by Einstein and had written one of the standard textbooks of quantum mechanics. As for monism, around age 18 Wilson had read Erwin Schrödinger's *What Is Life?*, in which Schrödinger's monism – influenced by Vedantism – was on copious display. Schrodinger had argued there that "mind does not exist in the plural." Did Joyce somehow tap into this monistic Universal Mind in *FW*?

Taking up the sigla that allows for more flexible and dynamic mutations between other aspects of archetypal disembodied "mind" characters in an intelligent universe, Wilson has more to say (in 1988!) about AI: "The absence of these evolutionary functions in binary may explain the fact that those computer scientists working on AI (Artificial Intelligence) continually promise mountains and deliver molehills. Perhaps they need to break out of a static binary and into a moving binary as dynamic as *I Ching*? (ibid., p.285) This seems argumentative and compelling even in 2024, but note that Wilson has already argued that Joyce's system functions/sigla allowed for even more dynamism in mutation than *I Ching* or Leibniz. As Wilson writes, "In genetics, the dynamic factor is a combination of mutation and natural selection (Joyce's 'hatch-as-hatch-can')." In 2024, we're only now seeing how the RNA-DNA dynamism is constantly being further modified in *epigenetic* actions, which either switch genes on or off, or modulate their expression as if a rheostat, all in response to environmental factors. It would seem we need not only more than a dynamic binary of Leibniz or *I Ching* to concoct a true AI, but more of something like Joyce's sigla/system functions and the deep structure of their evolutionary permutations. Carbon still ousts silicon, as of summer 2024, and AIs only "know" what humans know, because all the AIs so far have been trained by human knowledge, thought, style, etc. As I write this, a new study shows that AIs trained by other AIs go horribly wrong. They do compute freakishly fast, though.

Apart from an interpretation about non-local intelligence immanent in our universe, there also seems to be a gesture toward the infinite, and would seem to indicate something of Wilson's gnostic-flavored religious leaning. He composed these pieces on the historical doorstep of what the philosopher Timothy Morton called the age of "hyperobjects": "things that are massively distributed in time and space relative to humans," and seem beyond our ability to comprehend, much less control.

(see *Hyperobjects: Philosophy and Ecology After the End of the World*, 2013, U. of Minnesota Press, p.1) It now seems as if we've entered a No Way Back period with global warming, proliferation of WMDs, cheap tabletop-in-garage synthetic biology, pandemics, massive inequalities, deforestation (including the burning of the planet's "lungs", the Amazon rainforest), plastic, black holes, oil spills, tectonic plates, capitalism, Internet, droughts, fascism, etc.: we live inside these things and they tax, or exhaust, or confound our ability to find conceptual frames to think about them adequately. In the aggregate, these Things are demonic, monstrous, horrifying, humiliating, traumatic and menacing. Something out of H.P. Lovecraft but very real.

Other than that, we're fine. (The present writer suggests Wilson's 1959 essay, "Joyce and Daoism", discussed below, to combat any symptoms of Existential Dread.)

Wilson's extrapolations from the non-local "mind" in Joyce and *FW*, to genetics and such "things" as Bohm's Implicate Order might be among the last of the "theories of everything" (or *toward* a TOE) before humans entered this posited End of History. And thus we cannot help but read, in 2024, his dazzling cabalistic display in *Coincidance* in any other way but as ironic.

In this final analysis many of the items that came out of the May 6th, 1985 occult experiment (supra) recur in this final essay on *FW*. The overall effects seem spellbinding. These effects may be considered a function of his intellectual caste of speculative writers: addressing the numinous, or gesturing toward "infinity." Writers like Wilson keep cosmic wonder alive for those well steeped in critical/empirical/rational/logical modes as professional knowledge workers or erudite artists working off campus. More specifically, his ideal audience may have always been the stoned intelligentsia.

The present writer hasn't even tried to adequately summarize the arguments about Joyce and especially

Finnegans Wake made by Robert Anton Wilson in *Coincidance*, as they are far too dense and nuanced against the terrain of summarization and The Reader is strongly encouraged to see for herself. Again, the methods of knowledge creation here seem boundless and are perhaps the central message of this type of speculative writing.

Finally, the interested Joycean or Wilson reader who seeks out more ideas about Joyce should read the long Bloomsday interview with Wilson conducted by John van der Does, from June 16th, 1983, which was included in the Hilaritas edition but not in prior editions of *Coincidance*. (ibid., pp.303-352)

Robert Anton Wilson helped edit *Semiotext (e) SF* (1989), with Peter Lamborn Wilson and Rudy Rucker. In his Preface he recalled, "Back in 1957, when I was young – to give you an idea of the kultur of the period – the Feds had just burned the scientific books of Dr. Wilhelm Reich in an incinerator, I had the cosmic *chutzpah* to give a lecture, at the New York Academy of Sciences, in which I solemnly argued, with my bare face hanging out, that the only truly contemporary literature was that of surrealism, James Joyce and science fiction, since the so-called mainstream 'realistic' novel was based entirely on refuted Newtonian-Victorian Idolatry and should be classified with the Bible and fairy tales. I might as well have killed a cat in the sacristy. Many in the audience did not merely think I was eccentric; they were sure I was a certifiable nut-case. (I am rather proud that even now, at the age of 54, I can still provoke that response in some audiences.)" (*Semiotext (e) SF*, pp. 17-18) This is the same general theme we've seen from Wilson, for example, in the introduction to Regardie's *Eye In The Triangle*: the early 20th century revolutions in epistemology in scores of areas in the Sciences, and stylistic breakthroughs in the Arts, and how, according to Wilson's aesthetics: Sciences should keep up with Arts; Arts should keep up with Sciences. When Stephen Dedalus talks about standing upon the incertitude of the void, this was avant . . . in 1922. Why does it seem like it's *still* avant? From 1900 to 1970 we saw revolutions in "Anthropology, perception psychology, neurology, phenomenological sociology, ethnomethodology . . ." not to mention Relativity and the proliferation of quantum models of "reality." Wilson gives the Garry Owen example (there are at least three Garry Owens, etc.) once more, then writes, "This is the kind of attention to existential, phenomenological relativity that makes Joyce contemporary, whereas 'realistic' writers are still living in Aristotelian myth. Joyce's multi-valued dog is as paradigmatic of our age as Schrödinger's dead-and-alive cat." (ibid., p. 19) (The line about being 54 "now" makes this piece written in 1986, though the book was published in 1989.)

Quantum Psychology arrived in 1990 and seems to function as another "textbook" on epistemology, as a companion to *Prometheus Rising*, and as a rare book of intensely intellectual yet imminently readable interrogation of his particular field of expertise in Transactional Psychology. Here Wilson is making even more articulate many of his bailiwicks (with Wilson's heady generalist intellectual bent we must pluralize here), and there are a few riffs on Joyce and almost zero mention of psychedelic drugs, which he possibly thought would attract a readership too naive to appreciate his Joyce musings and too sensitive to enthusiastic writing about psychedelics and cannabis. Although with cannabis, in the "Introductory Note" Wilson tells us about his formal ordering of topics: that it's based on the "scatter" techniques of Sufi writers. This has always functioned as code for cannabis-influence in his writing. When psychedelics are mentioned, they are within a broad discussion of information theory and bodily processes in which endogenous "neuropeptides" allow us to break out of our reality-tunnels and allow us to "spontaneously feel-think in the manner of the 'model-agnosticism' of post-Copenhagen physics." (*Quantum Psychology*, Hilaritas Press, p.122)

The Joyce material here opens up chapter 4, where Wilson suggests *Ulysses* as a model for his advocacy of developing one's own "reality labyrinths" in that there are "nearly a hundred narrators" who report different versions of what happened. (*Quantum Psychology*, Hilaritas Press, p.27) He elaborates on the relativity in *Ulysses* a page later but noting how quaint "realistic" one point-of-view 1930s literature looks to us after Joyce's novel: "his multiple narrator technique gives multiple points of view – just as post-Copenhagen physicists escape [the single POV – RMJ] by what they call "model agnosticism," not accepting any one model as equal to the whole universe." (ibid., p.29) Wilson addresses the uncertainty around Bloom's Jewishness here (ibid., pp.87-88), which will be fleshed out in an essay in *TSOG: The Thing That Ate the Constitution*, below.

In chapter 16, "Moon Of Ice" Wilson argues that Joyce's eye problems, first addressed in *Portrait of the Artist as a Young Man,* but archival research from Cornell's Joyce Collection reveals were rooted in a very early fragment in which Joyce felt threatened by eye-devouring eagles as a boy. And this was ultimately rooted in Catholic Ireland. The omnipresent beliefs in a society are unconsciously learned from an earlier age, and Wilson places this within his readings in cultural anthropology and critical periods of imprint vulnerability. This paideuma, or semantic unconscious in late 19th/early 20th century Ireland, may have given rise to Joyce's ocular maladies and in turn resulted in Joyce's 11 eye operations, "And it may also indicate Joyce's awareness of the pain his books caused to pious Catholics. (He never did apologize . . .)" (see pp. 125-126, *Quantum Psychology*, Hilaritas, pp.113-114.)

We feel compelled to add that at this period in his writing life Wilson was heavily invested in another avant-garde writing experiment, one which is infused in *Quantum Psychology*: he used E-Prime, which "is" writing in English without the copulae (am/is/are/was/were/"be"), in order to avoid unconscious ontological statements both in himself and for his readers. Using this hack/gadget it prevents the writer from saying anything literally equals anything else, which, in the age of the quantum, seems literally true. The aim is a quality of liberation and opening of other possibilities of thought by rendering the Taoist "process" in the writing of sentences. This practice was born of a hypothesis of one of Korzybski's students, D. David Bourland, who took his teacher literally. (Much as Freud's student Wilhelm Reich took Freud's sexual theories to one of their possible logical ends.) Wilson was at the forefront of E-Prime, publishing essays on its use, but he was particularly interested in the psychological effects derived from the eschewal of the copulae, with the "is of identity" being a primary culprit to avoid. Wilson uses E-Prime throughout this book, and Joyce, Pound and Korzybski were far and away his primary influences in the philosophy of language, with Joyce and Pound's imperative to push language as far as it can go, here meeting with Korzybski's inculcation of the calculus writ large. Only the reader can judge the effects, within her own nervous system.

 1991 witnessed the release of Wilson's *Cosmic Trigger vol. II: Down To Earth*. He discusses his maternal grandfather Anton Milli from Trieste. Wilson replaced his given middle name, Edward, with Anton for his *nom de plume*. And he "inherited" Milli's cynical pacifism, an unashamed lack of patriotism. In a section on his reading from ages 18-20 he relates how he became deeply enthralled by Alfred Korzybski's General Semantics, and how it has dovetailed so well with his readings of Wittgenstein, Bohr, Bridgman, Whitehead, Poincaré, Shannon, Whorf, McLuhan and Bateson. But Wilson continually re-read Korzybski while stoned on cannabis, which "made it easy to understand that allegedly 'raw' perception contains as much inference and organization-or-orchestration as our more obviously brain-generated mathematical formalisms or religious dogma." (*Cosmic Trigger vol II*, Hilaritas ed., p.174) This practice of noticing different perceptual grids or "reality tunnels" influenced his readings of Joyce: "I went through my annual re-reading of Joyce's *Ulysses*. To my astonishment, it now appeared that Joyce had not only written a great Freudian-Jungian 'psychological novel,' but had also written the first novel based entirely on Relativity." (ibid., p.174) Wilson then gives his Garry Owen theme, with variations: Joyce's use of Garry Owen is comparable to the multiperspectivalism seen in *Citizen Kane* and *Rashomon*. In an interview with ROC magazine he says Joyce taught him to see the same scene from multiple angles. (ibid., p.158) Later in the same interview he says he regards Joyce as a "premature postmodernist." (ibid., p.160)

In "She Had The Eyes of a Saint" Wilson describes landing in Dublin on Bloomsday, 1982 and "everything seemed 'high-lighted', luminous, 'psychedelic,' *more real than real*, because I already knew all the store names and streets from Joyce's novels, and because I couldn't stop thinking that *statistically* I must have been walking at least part of the time in the *exact* footsteps of my grandfather, who had left there and gone to Brooklyn one hundred years earlier in 1882." He recalls The Invincibles, Joe Brady, the Phoenix Park murders, and Siobhan McKenna's 30 hour radio broadcast of the reading of *Ulysses*. Wilson describes the "Wandering Rocks" chapter and its 19 episodes overlapping in space-time. Wilson tells of the unveiling of Joyce statues and the supreme irony of such a tourist attraction about a man Dublin was angry at for so long, Joyce having exposed Ireland's dirty laundry, and who had set his novel on the day in which Nora Barnacle had eventually given him a hand-job. (ibid., pp.49-50)

In the essay "Another Bloomsday . . . The Pookah Returns", Wilson describes 1985's Bloomsday in Dublin and his own synchronicities around the "Sirens" chapter and the Herald Building and the Ormonde, then cites and quotes Joyce scholar Sheldon Brivic, a fellow expert on Joyce and synchronicity. At the end of the piece Wilson meets one of Joyce's grand nephews at the Joyce/Martello Tower. He tells Wilson his hobby is collecting photos of Joyce. Wilson asks if there's a photo of Joyce in a brown mackintosh, and is told no. "If he had said yes I would have a new solution to another of the Bloomday puzzles that Joyce scholars love to mull. Who was the 'lanky galoot' in the brown mackintosh who appears at Paddy Dignam's funeral at 10 a.m., ducks across the street just before the royal procession at 3 p.m., reappears at Burke's pub at 11 p.m., and leaves the whorehouse just as Bloom is entering it at midnight? I still think it's Joyce but I can't prove it yet." (ibid., pp.196-198; c.f. the July 3rd, 1986 letter to Smith, above.)

In another short autobiographical essay Wilson recalls the terror of Catholic school and a nun's story about God dropping ground glass in the eyes of a man for the Sin of Pride, which worked like black magic on Wilson. In this he finds empathy for Joyce: "I still have more chronic eye problems than any other writer I know. It gives me a deep sense of empathy with Joyce." (ibid., pp. 90-92) There is a brief discussion of hypnosis and its ubiquity, and how Murray Gell-Mann lifted "quark" from *FW*, and how so many scientists seem to forget their models started out as metaphors. (ibid., pp.96-97; an obvious echo to Roger Jones's *Physics As Metaphor*) In a remembrance of teenage reading, Wilson recalls his discovery of Joyce, "who seemed to me so earth-shaking that I have now devoted 41 years to the study of his works," at around age 18 and 1950, though elsewhere he recalls buying his first copy of *Finnegans Wake* at age 16 -- see notes under *The Illuminati Papers* and "Coex! Coex! Coex" above -- let us keep in mind Wilson's autobiographical memory as to exactly when. It seems safe to say Wilson began his readings in *Ulysses* and *Finnegans Wake* by age 18 at the latest. Wilson kept no personal archive, probably due to the itinerant life of the freelancer. He had written about "magickal" and "dream" diaries, but these seem to have been lost.

Wilson returns to the theme of arts and sciences being current with each other: "I think Pound influenced me almost as much as Joyce. Together, they convinced me that our century was going through so many radical changes simultaneously that the techniques of literature, like the other arts, had to become 'experimental' in order to capture the orders and magnitudes of the breakdowns and breakthroughs we were experiencing – breakdowns of old reality-tunnels, breakthroughs to new ways of orchestrating our perceptions." What Joyce and Pound did was break down linear order into "luminous fragments – quanta – which they reassembled into synergetic wholes . . ." This made them contemporary with quantum theory and films that Wilson loved. Reading Pound and Joyce involved "stepping outside the subject-predicate order into the modes of thought you find in differential calculus or in the montages of directors like Welles, Eisenstein, Kurosawa." (ibid., pp.123-124)

When reading Philip Wylie's *An Essay On Morals* in 1948 (age 16), he recalls Wylie asking many questions about why the structures of fairy tales and myths had so many recurring themes: why all the dead gods rising again? Why is it always the weakest of the three brothers who slays the dragon?, etc. What is the meaning of the thousands of "beauty and the beast" stories? When recalling this reading, he remembers a physical "tingly" feeling and likens it to Stephen Dedalus's "My soul swoons softly." Wilson had had a profound experience – an epiphany – as a child, watching *King Kong*, with the effect of the final lines: "No, it wasn't the airplanes – it was Beauty that killed the Beast . . ." (*King Kong* was a recurring theme for much of Wilson's almost 50 year writing career) Other epiphanies: Wilson worked as an ambulance attendant in New York and notes how "obstetric cases" made everyone feel good, even the "tough, mean and suspicious" cops. This feels a tad reminiscent of "Oxen of the Sun." (ibid., pp. 205-206) His trip to the Boyne Valley and Newgrange and the ancient megaliths resonates many times with his obsession with *FW*. (ibid., pp. 201-204)

Wilson wrote a long Introduction to Wayne Saalman's *The Illuminati of Immortality: Alchemy, Dreams and the Cybersonic Quest* (1992, New Falcon) in which he uses his cabalistic prowess to discuss the 7/28 system in *Genesis* and the seven day week and lunar month, ALP, the symbol for *delta*, rivers in *FW*, then twelve-ness in *FW*, links to Jungian archetypes, morphogenetic fields, the RAYNBOW girls, etc. After the magickal working starting on May 6th, 1985, this sort of writing probably felt like Bud Powell taking a solo on some tune he'd played many times. At this point he had become an Adept at this kind of thing. (see *Illuminati of Immortality*, pp.20-22)

Wilson published his own magazine/newsletter for many years, *Trajectories: The Journal of Futurism and Heresy*, with the aid of his friend D. Scott Apel, and his wife, Arlen. It was mostly futurology, "weird news," book reviews, and the latest news about libertarian ideas. Mostly written by himself, his wife and a few friends – George Carlin, Timothy Leary and Peter Russell contributed – there was no mention of Joyce in the "best of" book *Chaos and Beyond: The Best of Trajectories* (1994)

However, in pieces that did not get reprinted in that compendium, there was a long review of *The Silence of the Lambs* by Wilson in issue number 12, Spring 1993, "Fearful Symmetry: Reflections on "The Silence of the Lambs" in which Wilson links Clarice Starling's Jungian "underground initiation" to the archetypes Osiris, Dionysus and Tim Finnegan. Hannibal Lecter is also a cannibal, and Wilson reminds us of the cannibal that appears very early in *FW*. Wilson's friend Apel saw fit to include this piece in his 2019 compendium, *Beyond Chaos and Beyond*. (Impermanent Press, see, pp. 308-319)

In issue #14, Spring 1995, "Apologies and Divagations: Theology, Demonology and Codology," Wilson had a few words on Joyce and "codology" in a 1902 speech by Joyce and in "The Dead." He archly defines "codology" as a "rarer study" than demonology or theology, and it's "mostly confined to Dublin, and even the rest of Ireland knows little about it, or knows it only in an amateur way." It's "the scientific study of Irish Facts in a ludic context", and "operates under the banner of Metaphors 'R Us." Wilson links this "study" to Hugh Kenner's *A Colder Eye*, where "an Irish Fact is unlike an English or American fact in possessing the elasticity of a rubber inch." It's also alluded to in Anthony Burgess's *Re: Joyce*, where Irish use of English is "totally ludic," where the Anglo-Australian-American use of English is "pragmatic." At the end of Joyce's 1902 speech, "Death, the highest form of life" qualifies as "undergraduate codology" but the next day a parody of this appeared, "Absence, the highest form of presence": this is post-graduate codology. Advanced Codology would be Swift, still insisting that Partridge had died, despite Partridge's vehement claims otherwise. And Oscar Wilde's question: Are the commentators of *Hamlet* really mad or just pretending to be mad? Rationalists can address demonology and theology, but they don't know what to do with Codology, and the Rationalists only "stand glumly" and mutter about "Celtic whimsy" or "poetic terrorism" or "guerrilla ontology." Among the non-Celtic Codologists, Wilson lists Derrida, Charles Fort, Borges, Dali, Pynchon, J.R. "Bob" Dobbs, and the filmmaker Alex Cox. (*Trajectories*, issue #14, Spring 1995, p.3)

Cosmic Trigger vol III: My Life After Death (1995) has a Prologue in which he names influences who have improved his perceptions/conceptions: Buckminster Fuller, Marshall McLuhan, Timothy Leary, Barbara Marx Hubbard, and Alfred Korzybski. "I would like to acknowledge specially a few who played a major role in shaping and inspiring the present work: Moses Horowitz, Orson Welles, James Joyce, Jean Cocteau, Harold Garfinkel, and the man who called himself Elmyr." (*Cosmic Trigger vol III*, Hilaritas, 1995, p.xi-xii. "Moses Horowitz" was AKA "Moe" of the Three Stooges.)

After someone announced Wilson's death on the Internet, he got philosophical and wondered about ontology in a literal way: "The result of all this was beginning to make me wonder if I only exist in some semiotic or metaphoric sense myself, sort of like an elderly male Madonna. I mean, like, man, do I exist the way Howth Castle in Dublin exists, or the way Howth Castle and Environs in *Finnegans Wake* exists?" (ibid., p.7) Wilson had also begun spoofing the fundamentalist materialists at CSICOP by inventing "Timothy F.X. Finnegan, of Trinity College, Dublin" founder of the Committee for Surrealistic Investigation of Claims of the Normal, or CSICON. They would award $10,000 to anyone who could produce a "normal" person, place, thing, sunset, or day. (ibid., p.19)

In remembering his friend and co-author of *Illuminatus!*, Robert Shea, Wilson recalled that Shea said he'd stayed a Catholic until age 28, or maybe 27 or 29: "Having quit Rome at 14, like James Joyce, I had assumed all intelligent people got out around that age . . ." (ibid., p.41)

A discussion of Orson Welles's pseudo-documentary, *F For Fake*, Wilson cites *Ulysses* as a precursor: "The classic of our century's literature [. . .] in which the surface 'realism' contains a thousand spooky jokes, and critics have, in 70 years, learned that every narrative voice that originally seemed to speak 'objective truth' has an element of quantum uncertainty about it." (ibid., p.67) Wilson then waxes on about how interpretations of *Ulysses* had changed over those 70 years, with specific examples -- especially dubiousness about Molly's alleged "rampant promiscuity" – from *Ulysses* and a citation from Hugh Kenner's *Joyce's Voices*. (ibid., pp.67-68)

That Ezra Pound made a new calendar that began at "Midnight 30 October 1921 (Gregorian) – the date Joyce wrote the last words of *Ulysses*. (The 'p.s.U' means *post scriptum Ulysses*, 'after the writing of *Ulysses*.')" is something not a lot of us knew. (ibid., p.105) Reviewing a book on postmodernism, *A Higher Form of Superstition*, Wilson notes that far too many academic postmodernist critics see relativity everywhere, except their own dogma, and he confesses he hopes he hasn't fallen into the same trap. He's not interested much in solving puzzles, and his *Weltanschauung* was stated thus: "I see the world as a Puzzle to Work On, Joyce-Welles fashion, and not as a Puzzle Solved." (ibid., p.205) When discussing Philip K. Dick's *VALIS* novel and gnostic ideas around such, Wilson likens it to Joyce's "nightmare of history" but Dick's ontology goes further: we erred in taking the illusion of the phenomenal world as "real." (ibid., p.230)

In a piece on the intersection of Art, Magick and hoaxes and that puzzles often linger when a hoax has collapsed, Wilson uses Joyce: "Here, said Mr. James Joyce to the Paris intelligentsia of 1922, *I offer you a shockingly realistic novel.* And everybody nodded sagely, appreciating the genius of Joyce's prose, and swallowing the realism claim like art dealers grabbing up Elmyrs before 1968." In what "realistic" novels before 1922 had the main characters menstruate, defecate, urinate, masturbate and fornicate? Soon after its appearance, critics wondered about the label "realism" and novels. Had they been taken in by Joyce? "In the 72 years since then, we have gradually noticed that the ultra-realistic *Ulysses* parodies every other realistic novel, parodies romantic novels and epics also, even parodies itself, and contains 102 synchronicities, three cases of ESP, one case of precognition, one ghost walking in the broad daylight of a Spring afternoon and more uncertainty than quantum equations." (ibid., p.162; italics in original)

Wilson ends this book by discussing the reality of "masks": once we've gone into a brain-freeing school or "path of liberation", we must come back out and once again put on our masks: "We must again see and think in masks, or we will not have the ability to communicate with and deal with others," and after we have been on a brain-change journey, it's difficult to write about it without producing gobbledygook or "incomprehensible and mind-boggling brands of philosophy normally called 'metaphysics', or some new form . . ." and here Wilson suggests Joyce's prose, Yeats's poetry, the paradoxes of Charles Fort, the 'occult' joke-books of Aleister Crowley, and, by subtextual enthymeme, his own oeuvre as among the new forms of metaphysics. (ibid., p.244)

Discussing heresy and heretical thought with *Omni* magazine's Patrick Huyghe in 1997, Huyghe asks, "Can the heretic ever win? Are there enough of them to make things change faster?"

Wilson: Heresy always wins. All establishments grow rigid and ossified and die off. The individual heretic may play a role in the new paradigm or may just serve as comedy relief, i.e., appear as nutty to the future as to the current establishment. Heresy is no game for security seekers.

Huyghe: I suppose heretics are what you also call infophiles and the establishment is run by infophobes. And it's a constant fight between the two, isn't it? Even more so these days it seems.

Wilson: I see the conflict as cosmic and recurrent. Joyce shows it that way in *Finnegans Wake*, and he's my major historical theorist. Shem and Shaun never stop their war, their comedy act, their dance, whatever you call this dialectic.

Wilson wrote an article, "Nonprophet Futurism" that was included in the book *Solstice Shift: Magical Blend's Synergistic Guide to the Coming Age*, edited By John Nelson (1997), and Wilson argued the increasing importance of listening and seeing the other's point of view:

"We will all learn to listen more and listen better, and we will value those who listen best, as we now value the most exceptional in all fields – athletes, scientists, artists and movie stars. And you hear strange, disturbing, enlightening things when you learn to listen. The novels of Joyce and Faulkner, our greatest twentieth century writers, resulted from their capacity to listen, as both of them stated clearly. When you stop talking to people and begin talking with them, they tell you as much of the truth as they know, painful and awful as this usually seems at first." (*Solstice Shift*, p.75)

In 1998 Wilson produced an encyclopedia of conspiracy theories, *Everything Is Under Control*, with Miriam Joan Hill. How does Wilson manage to work James Joyce in? In the entry on the John Birch Society, which he had been lampooning since the 1960s, a main source of Bircher conspiracy/paranoia came from testimony by an ex-Communist, who said the Communist Party in the US came not from Moscow but from three very wealthy men at the Waldorf Towers in New York. Dr. Bella Dodd testified, "I would certainly like to find out who is really running things." Wilson links "The three mystery-millionaires" here to "the three ruffians who killed The Widow's Son in Freemasonic legend, and maybe to the three men in black who haunt and vex UFO contactees (and maybe the three Soldiers – a Scotsman, and Englishman, and a Welshman — who torment the Irish dreamer all through Joyce's *Finnegans Wake*.)" (*Everything Is Under Control*, Harper, 1998, pp. 79-80) There is an entry for "Gordon Brown" followed by one for Giordano Bruno: Joyce used "Gordon Brown" as a pen name and called him "the Nolan" in his 1901 short pamphlet "Day of the Rabblement." When Dean tells Stephen that Bruno was a terrible heretic in *Portrait of the Artist as a Young Man*, Stephen replies that Bruno was "terribly burned." Bruno was burned at the stake by the Inquisition in 1600. Joyce was heavily influenced by Bruno, who combined cabala with the new science of his day. "Whatever his link with occult secret societies, he influenced Hegel, Marx, theosophy, James Joyce, Timothy Leary, Discordianism, and Dr. Wilhelm Reich." (ibid., pp. 94-95) In the entry for Thomas Pynchon, Wilson notes that in *Gravity's Rainbow*, Pynchon "uses calculus and quantum mechanics the way Joyce used Homer in *Ulysses*." (ibid., pp.137-138) Under "Golden Dawn, Hermetic Order of the," we once again see Wilson link Joyce to it: "Much of modern literary culture owes its symbolism and themes to this group; not only Yeats' poetry, but even the works of James Joyce, Ezra Pound, and T.S. Eliot, show Golden Dawn elements, which were common currency in the London of 1900-1914, where all those writers met." (ibid., pp.204-205) This same passage was inserted into Wilson's Foreword to Charles Kips's *Astrology, Aleister & Aeon* (New Falcon, 2001). Wilson's 13 page Foreword was dated 1998, though.

The penultimate book Wilson produced while he was still alive was *TSOG: The Thing That Ate the Constitution* (New Falcon ed. 2002; Hilaritas Press ed., 2022) A widower, battling Post-Polio Syndrome, Wilson turned 70 the year *TSOG* appeared. His prior life of fairly heavy lecture tours greatly attenuated due to airline travel being too unpleasant, he had turned to teaching courses online, with his Maybe Logic Academy. But his writing was still strong.

The Joyce connections here: in a piece on the psycho-archaeology of Santa Claus, Wilson links him to research by anthropologist Weston La Barre in his *Ghost Dance: The Origins of Religion*; La Barre found a primordial bear-god all the way from the tip of South America, up through North America, over the North Pole, and down into across most of Europe and some of Asia. He's in cave paintings from 30,000 BCE and has morphed into Arduina, Artemis, and King Arthur. "And I swear the same God-Bear tromps and shambles through every page of Joyce's masterpiece of psycho-archaeology, *Finnegans Wake*; and if you don't believe me, consult Adaline Glasheen's *Third Census to Finnegans Wake*." (*TSOG*, Hilaritas ed, pp. 71-72; full essay pp.70-74; the title of Glasheen's book is *Third Census of Finnegans Wake*)

Was Leopold Bloom a Jew? That's examined in "Schrödinger's Jew": Orthodox Jews say your mother must be a Jew; in this case, Bloom was not a Jew. The Nazis considered anyone with a Jewish ancestor to be a Jew; here Bloom "is" Jewish. Modern thought has anyone who practices Judaism as a Jew; here Bloom doesn't qualify as a Jew. Wilson: "Existentially or phenomenologically, a Jew 'is' somebody considered Jewish by all or most of the people he meets. By this standard, the multi-ordinal Bloom 'is' a Jew again." Wilson then discusses Bloom's run-in with The Citizen in "Cyclops" and, as soon as Bloom is pushed far enough, he tells the antisemite, "And Jesus was a Jew too. Your god. He was a Jew like me." But later Bloom recalls this scene, "And he called me a Jew, which as a matter of fact I'm not." Wilson's final analysis: "I suppose Joyce made Bloom such a tangled genetic and cultural mixture to expose the absurdities of anti-Semitism; but I also suspect that he wanted to undermine that neurolinguistic habit which postmodernists call 'essentialism' and which Korzybski claimed invades our brains and causes hallucinations or delusions every time we use the word 'is.'" (ibid., pp.83-84)

Wilson recounts the exploits of Luke Flanagan, AKA "Ming the Merciless", who had been a strong pro-cannabis activist in Ireland, and Wilson adds, "Every country gets the villain it deserves. And as Joyce would say, there's lots of fun in Flanagan's work." (ibid., p.160) (Since this book appeared the autistic Flanagan has been a member of the European Parliament from Ireland since 2014 and remains a strong proponent of cannabis legalization and against police corruption.) In "Why Hannibal Lecter Would Make A Better President Than George W. Bush" Wilson discusses his own satire: "The writers I enjoy most (Swift, Twain, Bierce, Faulkner, Joyce, Pound, Chandler, Higgins) all contain a special flavor of satire that I could not define even though I think it permeates my own books; 'acid satire' hardly seemed satisfactory." (ibid., p.172)

Joycean epiphany surrounds the subject of the essay "Copulating Currency," in which Wilson suddenly realized how often he heard some version of this line in a movie: "I want my fucking money, motherfucker!": "James Joyce defined an artistic epiphany as any 'vulgarity of language' which reveals the 'whatness' or 'radiance' of an event or of those structural systems which remain 'grave and constant in human affairs.' As biographer Richard Ellmann noted, the effect of these fragments of conversation, preserved in Joyce's novels, often appear 'uncanny.' "I myself tend to find them a combination of the tragic and the hilarious." What then follows is an essay on Joyce's development of his idea of epiphany, and Wilson's long-observed role of money and domesticated primate behavior around it. "For over 400 years now, the world has struggled over Money – working for it, swindling and robbing for it, conspiring to monopolize it, going to war over it." He notes that less than one percent of humans own 99% of the Money, so we all seem desperate for it. No wonder lines like "Gimme my motherfucking money! Shit! I want my fucking money, motherfucker!" show up in films: this reflects our at-times desperate bio-survival anxiety over the symbols that are paper money. Then Wilson tells us he was axed from a speaking gig because his own website related this epiphany from lines in a Spike Lee film. He proceeds to discuss historical etymology and the English language and phonetic sounds that emanated from certain areas of Europe, Vico and the buried history of class warfare and ethnic conflict. This language around money and "fuck" and "shit" relate to the anal-territorial circuit in our nervous systems. This is followed by a discussion of how money actually does seem to "fuck": it's called compound interest and Finance Capitalism. Aristotle, St. Ambrose, Shakespeare, Vico, Pound, and Buckminster Fuller all thought this "copulating currency" was a swindle. Most of us have forgotten it, it seems, though those who protest the WTO or IMF, while not inventing original or radical ideas have "merely rediscovered the view of most of the Western classics. (Since the classics got chucked out of Academe, this rediscovery marks a major intellectual event.)" (ibid., pp.179-186)

The end of Wilson's book (ibid., pp. 215-223) gives a preview of Wilson's next book, *The Tale of the Tribe*, which never appeared; he died before he could work it out. It would have featured not only Joyce (see p.220 for a short encapsulation of Joyce's genius/uniqueness/inventiveness), but Bruno, Vico, Nietzsche, Fenollosa, Korzybski, Pound, McLuhan, Shannon and Fuller. It was to have something to say about the alphabet and Internet. Not much is known how this treatment was going to play out.

While *The Tale of the Tribe* never appeared, Wilson had been cognizant of many of his fans dredging up old articles by him on the Internet. Due to the transient nature and omnipresent threats of precarity for the freelance writer, Wilson appears to have not kept an archive of the 1000-2000 articles he'd published since 1959, in everything from scholarly journals to mainstream periodicals to men's magazines, to tabloids. A significant portion of his work before his first book was for various "counterculture" and anarchist/libertarian little mags. He had told *Contemporary Authors* in an interview that he'd rather not see his strictly from hunger writings resurface, but apparently his fans had dredged some pieces he thought worthy of anthologizing, and these appear in the last book he published while still alive, *Email To The Universe* (2005, Hilaritas Press).

In "The Celtic Roots of Quantum Theory" (*Email To The Universe*, Hilaritas, pp. 26-36) Wilson juxtaposes American and English-English with Irish English and uses Richard Bandler's neurolinguistic programming model: American and English-English tends to have the structure of the "Meta-Model," which contains statements which we can judge logically as true or false; Irish-English seems more along the Milton Model (after master hypnotist Milton Erickson): statements which might be judged logically true or false, but tend to have the quality of seducing the listener into new perceptions. Wilson then proceeds to illustrate this by quoting an Irish farmer, Yeats, Liam O'Flaherty, Wilde, Padraic Colum, Flann O'Brien, Swift, and Bishop Berkeley. (ibid., pp.27-29)

Underlying part of this ludic use of language must be the results of a people long colonized, who learn to use subtext in addition to surface text. An example is in the short second montage in the "Wandering Rocks" chapter of *Ulysses* in which Corny Kelleher is talking to a constable and . . . what is being said? The constable says, "I seen that particular party last evening . . ." Who is the "particular party"? We can only infer.

Yeats had said Ireland had been part of Asia until the Battle of the Boyne, but "Joyce knew that Ireland remained part of Asia; *Finnegans Wake* tells us it emerged from 'the Haunted Ink Bottle, no number, Brimstone Walk, Asia in Ireland." (ibid., pp.29-31) (In the 1974 Polanski film *Chinatown*, it's cops and detectives who go into Los Angeles's Chinatown and they don't know what's going on because they can't speak the language nor do they understand the social mores there; Wilson liked to use "Chinatown" as cognate with Chapel Perilous: a metaphorical state of mind in which you are suddenly lost and have no bearings and find you don't know what to do to "get back" and become grounded again. This observation by Wilson about Joyce's "Asia in Ireland" seems congruent here.)

Along the colonizer/colonized line, the British seem to hew to "being on time;" the Irish seem suspicious that the Brits invented time in order to make them work more hours than seem reasonable, and Wilson writes that "Joyce noted that the only three world-class philosophers of Celtic genealogy, Erigena, Berkeley, and Bergson, all denied the reality of time (and only Berkeley lived under English rule)."(ibid., p.31) (You're right: Bergson was French, but – genealogy – his mother was Anglo-Irish; was Joyce maintaining the groups of Three Men?)

Wilson illustrates Irish/Gaelic grammar: "My uncle was busy feeding the pigs one night *and* I a girl of six years . . ." American and English speakers would say "My uncle was busy

feeding the pigs one night *when* I was a girl of six years . . ."
Wilson: "The Irish English retains the grammar of Irish
Gaelic, but it thereby retains the timeless or Daoist sense of
a world where every now exists but no now ever 'becomes'
another now." (ibid., p.31) This all leads to the (probably?)
greatest Irish mathematician ever, William Rowan Hamilton
(1805-1865), who invented an algebra in which, unlike the
math we were all taught, a x b = b x a (the commutative
property), Hamilton's math had a x b *not* equaling b x a,
and it took 100 years for his pure, internally self-consistent
mathematical system to find a good application in science, and
when it did: it was in quantum mechanics. "Hamilton's math
describes the sub-atomic (quantum) world, and ordinary math
does not." (ibid., p.32) (Quaternions – a non-commutative
algebra – were invented by Hamilton in 1843 as a way of
modeling 3-D geometry. Quaternions were eventually used
by physicists in modeling the "spin" of electrons in quantum
experiments.)

Further, Wilson tells us Hamilton had heard the debates
about light traveling as waves vs. particles, and Hamilton
supported *both* ideas, which was anathema at the time, until
we eventually realized, long after Hamilton's death, that it's
particles when you set up an experiment a certain way; waves
in other experimental set-ups: they are *complementary*. Which
most of us think Niels Bohr had discovered; Wilson states
there's a case for William Rowan Hamilton getting there first.

This "perspectivalism", Wilson reminds us, "haunts
postmodern literary theory, cultural anthropology, and,
especially, the Joyce Industry, as more and more Joyce scholars
realize that all of the 100+ narrative 'voices' in *Ulysses* seem
equally true in some sense, equally untrue in some sense, and
equally beyond either/or logic in any sense." (ibid., p. 32)

In 1964-65, Irish physicist John S. Bell proposed a
theorem that would later be tested and Nobel Prizes awarded:
any two particles once connected remained connected, even if

you separate than by an ungodly distance . . . which seems to violate Einstein's speed limit in the universe: nothing travels faster than the speed of light – 186,000 miles per second – but these particles (and waves) *do* violate the Law. Or seem to. We assume there must be some physical force between two bodies of matter, even if they are photons, but that doesn't seem to be the case. This might mean that *everything* is correlated. It's only gotten weirder since then. Wilson then relates how 20th century physicists have tried to explain this, and he cites David Bohm, Wolfgang Pauli, Henry Stapp, and Nick Herbert. Not to mention Fritjof Capra, who wrote a famous popularization of quantum theory called *The Tao of Physics*, which prompts Wilson to add, "I suggest physicists often explain this in Chinese metaphors because they don't know as much about Ireland as they do China, and because they haven't read *Finnegans Wake*." (ibid., p.34)

"And so we see that two Irishmen, Hamilton and Bell, have the majority of physicists arguing about issues that make them sound like a symposium among Berkeley, Swift, Yeats, O'Brien and Joyce. Through their literature, speakers raised in Irish English have transformed the printed page; now their mathematicians, raised in the same neurolinguistic grid, have revolutionized our basic notions of 'reality,' which in the light of what we have seen, badly needs the dubious quotes I just hung on it." (ibid., p.35)

In an assessment of what we can say about our "Dreams of Flying" (ibid., pp. 67-78) we're reminded that "Daedalus" meant "Artist" and flying out of the labyrinth of Ireland/ Catholicism/English imperialism/the nightmare of history would take a real Artist, we might ask, why was Daedalus an "artist" and not a scientist? Wilson reminds us that the Greeks made no significant distinction. Simply: make something that had not existed before: *texne*. (ibid., p.69) Lest we forget: Joyce named him Dedalus, not Daedalus and was also named after St. Stephen, the Protomartyr, "who reported a vision and was stoned to death for it." (ibid., p.77)

Some but not all of us loved the feeling of being tossed in the air as babies. Perhaps some of us who loved this are infophilic while those who cried out in terror are infophobic, we're not sure. But most of us know the feeling of having a dream in which we fly. Wilson quotes from p.628 of Book Four of *FW*: "My great blue bedroom, the air so quiet, scarce a cloud. In peace and silence. I could have stayed up there for always only. It's something fails us. First we feel. Then we fall... I'll see him come down on me now under whitespread wings like he'd come from Arkangels, I sink I'd die down over his feet, humbly dumbly, only to washup." Wilson unpacks this passage then adds, "Joyce primarily invokes our deep awareness that gravity 'pulls us down,' our deep yearning to break free of this 'drag' and soar back to our home above the clouds." (ibid., p. 72) Wilson seems to be drawing from memory pp.627-628 of FW here, with only the lines pertinent included.

In the last book overseen by Wilson, we see collected the piece he'd written 45 years earlier, in 1958 (published in 1959) as a 26 year old freelancer, for the *James Joyce Review*, "Joyce and Daoism." In a brief introduction he says here he's changed the Chinese spellings to reflect current post-Mao orthodoxies, and notes the piece feels like it's written by an "Acid Head" even though he wouldn't try LSD until 1962. Wilson then saw the affirmation of Molly's "yeses" as "forced" but not insincere "any more than the neurotic's desire to be cured is 'insincere'" (ibid., p.85) Also, the humor in *Ulysses* is mostly satiric, negative and Swiftian, although there are some Rabelaisian elements; *Finnegans Wake* seems completely affirmative and its humor is "not only Rabelaisian, but Carrollian: it has that element of nonsense and childishness which only the well-integrated can sustain for long." (ibid., p.91) In this Wilson sees *FW* and Joyce as a Daoist, with the "process universe" on display throughout. The very first word of the book, "riverrun," conveys the Daoist aspect of ALP throughout the novel and it never lets up.

The reason Wilson thinks Joyce hadn't yet internalized the process universe of Daoism by 1922, when *Ulysses* appeared, was because the "Hangman God" – "Gun, the Farther" – hadn't yet been exorcized, but in *FW* "the Hangman God is securely put in his place." (ibid., p.90)

There is a section on the misguided Wyndham Lewis, who charged Joyce, Einstein, Pound, Picasso, Whitehead and the Futurist painters as being part of a "Time Cult" probably started by Henri Bergson. The dichotomizing Lewis decided his own Aristotelian space cult was superior, but with Einstein's findings that ship had sailed. (ibid., 94-95)

The cavalcade of interpenetrating opposites in *FW* – such as Shem and Shaun, who contain a little of each other – seems perfectly Daoist: Shem's ying and Shaun's yang meld, as do all the complex characters, and, as they are dreamed, one character contains them all, and contains an individual Ego, his own Freudian unconscious. It is contained within the Jungian collective unconscious, and is part of the non-local, everyone everywhen everywhere everything Mind. Anna Livia Plurabelle is watery, flowing, indivisible and completely Daoist.

Wilson instantiates his thesis with quotes from the *Dao De Jing* (and *FW*'s "Laotsey taotsey," p.242), and from *Kuan Tzu*, and links this universe that doesn't care about us, which is hilarious, to the feminine, oral-matrist values he'd encountered in Ian Suttie's *The Origins of Love and Hate*, Wilhelm Reich's *The Mass Psychology of Fascism*, Gordon Rattray Taylor's *Sex In History*, and Robert Graves' *The White Goddess*.

Linked to Daoist "feminine" values of receptivity and passivity is the ideal mental stance of the Scientist, and Wilson quotes T.H. Huxley: "Science seems to me to teach in the highest and strongest manner the great truth which is embodied in the Christian conception of entire surrender to the will of God. Sit down before fact as a little child, be prepared to give up every preconceived notion, follow humbly wherever and to whatever abysses Nature leads, or you shall learn nothing." (ibid., p.87)

Wilson: "That the Dao just happens, that it has no purpose or goal, no regard for self-importance ('Heaven treats us like straw dogs', Lao-Tzu says) – this is not a gloomy philosophy at all. When one understands this fully, on all levels of one's being, the only possible response is to have a good laugh. Daoist humor results from realizing that the recognition of the most joyous truth of all seems to the egocentric man (you and me) frightening and gloomy." (ibid.,p.92) (Wilson wrote on his deathbed his last blog post: "I don't see how to take death seriously. I look forward without dogmatic optimism, but without dread. I love you all and implore you to keep the lasagna flying." – on January 6th, 2007, five days before his death, January 11, 2007. Keeping the lasagna flying was his in-group joke-code for continuing to use your brain, to keep thinking for yourself.)

The 26 year old Joycean had produced an essay that could function as a decent introduction to *Finnegans Wake*; that it finally appeared for everyone to read 45 years after it was written seems a goddess-send. (ibid., pp. 85-96)

A brief meditation on "Theotopology and Theometerorology" and Vico's thunder as the beginning of the Urvater ideas in us of course includes Joyce, who "uses this god = thunder equation repeatedly in *Finnegans Wake* (which drove me to read Vico) . . ." (ibid., pp.103-104)

An excerpt from a 1981 interview included in *Email To The Universe* tells a little more about Joyce's influence on Wilson: "Joyce taught me a great deal about how to vary the tone of a paragraph and create emotional effects which are almost subliminal, and how to convey very subtle psychological processes." (ibid., p.230)

In R.U. Sirius's book of interviews with prominent people on the edge of technology, science and consciousness, *True Mutations* (2006), Wilson admits the pace of change has become so accelerated he has a difficult time keeping up with all his interests, and that many of the earliest interpretations of what Bell's Theorem might "mean" in quantum theory and nature are no longer cutting-edge, and he lamented, "You can't keep up with everything. I can't even keep up with Joyce scholarship." (*True Mutations*, Pollinator Press, p. 248)

The 2019 book put out by Wilson friend and accomplice D. Scott Apel, *Beyond Chaos and Beyond*, is a compendia of transcriptions of Wilson talks and video appearances, fugitive interview excerpts, and an essay of personal memory of Apel's 30 year friendship with Wilson, but it's mostly articles from Wilson's and Apel's newsletter *Trajectories* that had not been included in *Chaos and Beyond: The Best of Trajectories* and thus serves as an invaluable source for the hardcore Wilson fans. Some Joycean items that appear therein:

In a 1977 interview Wilson discusses the publishing industry: "Well, by and large I am not madly in love with publishers. Publishers are businessmen, and businessmen are really not my favorite type of human beings. James Joyce went into business briefly, and after a while he said to Italo Svevo, 'You know, I think my partners are cheating me.' Svevo said, 'You only *think* they're cheating you? Joyce, you *are* an artist!'" (*Beyond Chaos and Beyond*, 2019, Impermanent Press, p. 15) In a discussion of his novel *Illuminatus!*, Wilson says that, among other things, he's "continuing something that Joyce started, which is breaking down this artificial distinction between high art and low art, between great literature and folk literature. I can't emphasize too strongly how much I despise class distinctions in literature." (ibid., p.23) The examples of Wilson combining "low and high" seem far too numerous to even mention: perhaps this use of high mixed with low has had a rhetorical effect that was most democratic in tone and nature, and was part of his overall didactic strategy.

The blurring of distinctions between High and Low was a very strong literary value Wilson attributed to Joyce's influence, but perhaps a more profound idea derived from Joyce was the idea of our lives as being in books: "That was one of Joyce's great discoveries, that everybody is living in a novel. That's why *Ulysses* is an anthology of novels. It's a novel in the form of an anthology, and each of the characters is living in a separate tunnel-reality that's a mirror of the literature that's been programmed into their neurological circuits. Marshall McLuhan learned everything about media from James Joyce." (ibid., pp.33-34) This theme – while having obviously deeply trippy implications – of characters in his fiction slowly finding out they're in a book, or being told they're in a novel by some other character – is a hallmark of Wilson's fiction. This theme writ large, for all of us, is a major rhetorical frame in his *nonfiction*, and takes the form of the discourse of "reality tunnels" and "reality labyrinths" that we all live in: most of us don't realize our brain easily "edits" our "reality" at every moment of every day. And we later override earlier editorial decisions, etc. That we "end" a piece of literature would then seem somewhat "dogmatic." So literature should contain an open-endedness, or inter-connectedness or inter-textual aspects, which would make us less dogmatic thinkers overall, and that books should go on and address other books directly.

That we are all in a book became a well-trod metaphor of much of "postmodern" literature, but the effect of mental displacement for the reader – especially if the reader is actually imagining oneself as a character in a book reading characters in a book who are arguing over some ideas in a book – might be something having a similarity of structure to the psychedelic or cannabis high . . . seems perhaps too obvious to mention. Clearly, there is a similarity to any other *mise en abyme*, at the very least. Cannabis enthusiasts and psychonauts will have opinions on this that differ from the "straight" academic. Of course!

One of Wilson's perennial lectures was about juries and the twelve-ness that forms a part of psycho-archaeology. A 1992 talk on this that Apel transcribed for *Beyond Chaos and Beyond* is on this theme and as Wilson launches into the *Finnegans*

Wake aspect of twelve-ness – "all the hoolivans of the nation, prostrated in their consternation and their duodismally profusive plethora of ululation" – he tells the audience at the Renaissance Faire, "Now I'm sure in an educated audience like this you're all familiar with *Finnegans Wake* and I don't have to explain its deep structure or its polylinguistic meanings," before immediately proceeding to hold forth in erudite glee on *FW*. That *dour* and *dismal* go into *duodismally*. That duodecimalism is found from Neolithic times, etc., up to Earwicker's jury. Eggs, the zodiac, the months of the year, Jesus's apostles, Hercules's labors. Ululation means "moaning like an owl" and Athena/Minerva, patron of juries, was a Stone Age owl goddess who later became incorporated into the Olympic pantheon, and she's linked to the owl. "So when we are making a jury out of twelve people, we are re-enacting a Paleolithic ritual involving twelve celebrants and the one who's going to be sacrificed, who appears as the defendant, in the modern form of the ritual." Defense and prosecution are Mick and Nick, Mutt and Jute, Shem and Shaun, Yin and Yang, etc. Wilson links this to Paleolithic rituals of driving out Winter and ushering in Spring and who or whatever is found guilty of Winter is sacrificed and was often burned in a mock execution. Wilson certainly knew his *Golden Bough*. (ibid., pp.231-233)

Apel transcribed "An Evening With Robert Anton Wilson" in San Jose, Oct. 9th, 1987 and it's a *tour de force* example of his intellectual stand-up style: he ranges effortlessly over subject after subject, riffing improvisationally over favorite topics, while artfully linking them in transition. After talking about Orson Welles at length, he begins on Joyce and synchronicity, his Bloomsday experience, while finally getting in his Garry Owen licks, while linking this back to Orson Welles and how indeterminacy rules over both Welles films and Joyce novels. (ibid., pp.264-267; the entire lecture pp. 249-286, including audience's questions)

In a 1996 article in *Trajectories* Wilson addressed "Brain

Books" and commented on what he considered essential reading. This is one of a few places in which he wrote along these lines, and the books aren't always the same, although there are overlaps, and of course *Ulysses* always makes the cut; Wilson provocatively thought the person who hadn't read it hadn't "really entered the 20th century . . ." (*Beyond Chaos and Beyond*, p.381)

From 2004 until sometime in 2006, a year before his death, Wilson taught courses online about his subjects: Pound's ideogrammic method, the Eight Circuit Brain, *Illuminatus!*, and The Tale of the Tribe being only four. Other Wilson-allied thinkers were brought in to teach courses. Joyce was of course quite prominent.

In September/October of 2004 Wilson gave assignments for reading and writing, and often: viewing movies. He was present and answered any questions the students had. Wilson taught students to read the first 23 lines of *Finnegans Wake* using different "filters" in one course. Of *FW* the lack of apostrophe "represented a warning to the ruling class [Read it as a sentence . . .]"

Because the class notes – forwarded to me by attendees – seem so often personal, answering students' questions in a one-to-one way but shared with all in the course, I see Wilson's writing, while at times quite insightful, especially about Joyce himself and *FW*, too informal. Perhaps one day his notes will be shared online or in some sort of anthology. Though he was never an academic, Wilson was always a Teacher.

Here are some links current as of Summer 2024 that give insight into the MLA courses:

https://maybelogic.blogspot.com/2014/06/incomplete-history-of-maybe-logic.html

http://www.hilaritaspress.com/hilaritas-press-news/interacting-processing-the-maybe-logic-academy/

https://rawilsonfans.org/maybelogic-academy/

https://propanon99.medium.com/robert-anton-wilsons-2005-crowley-101-course-bd062a3e2626

Robert Anton Wilson was a philosophical artist who went to great pains to remind his readers, over and over, that they "make" their worlds from their perceptions. I think he would not balk at the present writer reminding his Readers that Wilson's readings of Joyce were filtered through his own nervous system, and that, in a very real sense, Wilson's Joyce was his own. The very idea of a "correct" reading of Joyce would appear to Wilson as ludicrous. They are only more insightful and interesting readings than others. Furthermore, my Wilson-on-Joyce was made from what *I paid attention to* when I read Wilson on Joyce, and my perceptions were strongly shaped by my own readings of Joyce, albeit this essay was concentrated on how I see the influence of Joyce on Wilson. Wilson's constructivist views would also remind the Reader that their readings of Joyce and/or Wilson seem possibly more of their own "making" than they at times realize. This would be true to some degree also to any readings of any texts the present Reader is encountering, has encountered, or will be encountering, including history, private memos, poetry, and the backs of cereal boxes.

Wilson had told more than one interviewer that the one thing his critics seemed to have missed was how strong the influence of James Joyce was on his thinking and writing. We hope that these notes have gone some way to remedy this lacuna.

– R. Michael Johnson
Penngrove, CA
August 23, 2024

Acknowledgements from R. Michael Johnson

I'd like to thank Eric Wagner for the invitation to be included in this volume. Ever since the earliest days of alt.fan.rawilson on Usenet in the late 1990s, Eric and his compendious mind and personality has been a longstanding source of wisdom, deep informed readings, odd facts, humor, and encouragement. Thanks for the choice vibes! It's easy for writers to get the feeling that no one cares about their writing. Eric has always made me feel like my writing is worthy of readers, and for this I'm grateful.

To Christina Pearson and Richard Rasa at Hilaritas Press: you guys have been so sweet and supportive in publishing my discursive essays that were born of a genuine mania for those subjects. Danke schoen!

Certain librarians and professors have fueled my bookish ways and concern with both citation, humor, and trying to not be too much of a bore when writing, and no doubt foremost on this roster are retired professor (and now mystery novelist) Dr. L. David Sundstrand and now-retired librarian extraordinaire Lanny Swallow. I don't know where either of you are these days, but both of you had an outsized influence on me and I think of you both every day. Other fantastic librarians who have patiently nurtured me were Susan Sarno, Marjeanne Blinn, and Hillary Theyer. You have no idea how your care and professionalism affected me. Merci!

Thanks to the stalwart regulars, the original gangstas at the Petaluma Book and Brew book group, who gave me encouragement and support while writing the piece in this volume, even though they hadn't read *Ulysses*, *Finnegans Wake* or even heard of Wilson. Our years-long once-per-month meetings keep me on my toes, and besides: you guys actually laff at my jokes (sometimes) and/or at the very least: tolerate my idiosyncrasies. And we continue to read books and talk about them. A good way to live.

Frank McNerney has greatly aided and abetted my madness, by plying me with nanobrew IPAs, John Coltrane and Kenny Burrell recordings and general all-around musical and political harmonies. We have both found a deep personal relationship to the gods named "Bach" and "Bird" and "Hendrix." He often calls me "Dr. Johnson," which fuels my ego and tends to push me even further towards becoming some sorta de Selby-like thinker. I'm trying to keep that under control, but thanks!

Fellow RAW-phile and comic book artist of effulgent repute Bobby Campbell has always egged me on with his interviews and just all- 'round hail fellow well-met-ness-iosity. Excelsior! You were the rare reader of the Overweening Generalist, and I admire your patience. In the RAW-welt, I'd like to mention Oz Fritz, Brian Shields (RIP), Mike Gathers, Martin Wagner, Tom Jackson, and Marc Lutter. There are many others. Of course!

Certain women have played a huge role in keeping an impecunious freelance scholar-writer-weirdo in hard-to-find books. Most preeminent here are my sister Janet Marott and my friend and conversationalist extraordinaire Branka Krsul-Tesla. Hvala! For your enablement and indulgence of my bibliomania, you deserve both blame and my frothing gratitude.

Finally, Caroline Canada: you've been everything for me since Beethoven's birthday, 1989. Would I have been on skid row if not for you? Probably. Maybe. I may have flailed on some variant of a skid. We both shudder to think it. At this point we literally have our own private language, and quite often, telepathic communication. Like I said: everything.

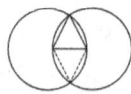

Selected Bibliography

Attridge, Derek and Marjorie Howes. Introduction. *Semicolonial Joyce*. Ed. Attridge and Howes. Cambridge UP, 2000.

Beckett, Samuel, Stuart Gilbert, Eugene Jolas, *et al. Our Exagmination*. Shakespeare and Co, 1929. Reprinted as *An Exagmination*.

Bishop, John. Introduction. *Finnegans Wake*. By James Joyce. Penguin, 1939.

– *Joyce's Book of the Dark*. U of WI P, 1986.

Campbell, Bobby. Rawillumination.net. 22 Sept. 2011.

Campbell, Joseph and Henry Morton Robinson. *A Skeleton Key to* Finnegans Wake. Harcourt, 1944.

Cheng, Vincent J. "Authenticity and identity: catching the Irish spirit." *Semicolonial Joyce*. Ed. Attridge and Howes. Cambridge UP, 2000.

"Dorothy Gale." Wikipedia. 14 July 2012. Web. 18 July 2012.

Ellmann, Richard. *James Joyce*. Oxford UP, 1959, 1982.

García Márquez, Gabriel. *One Hundred Years of Solitude*. Perennial classics, 1970.

Gifford, Don. *Joyce Annotated*. U of California P., 1982.

Hayman, David. *Ulysses: The Mechanics of Meaning*. U of Wisconsin P., 1970, 1982.

Hyatt, Christopher. *Undoing Yourself with Energized Meditation,* Third Edition. Falcon P, 1987.

Joyce, James. *Finnegans Wake.* Penguin, 1939.
– *The Portable James Joyce.* Penguin, 1946.
– *A Portrait of the Artist as a Young Man.* Signet, 1991. Originally published 1916.
– *Ulysses.* 1922. New York: Vintage, 1961.

Kenner, Hugh. Introduction. *James Joyce and the Making of Ulysses.* By Frank Budgen. Indiana U P, 1960. P
– "Joyce's *Portrait* – A Reconsideration." Reprinted in the Norton Critical Edition of *A Portrait of the Artist as a Young Man.* Norton, 2006.
– *Ulysses* Revised Edition. Johns Hopkins U. Pr., 1987.

Kirk, Russell. "Ten Conservative Principles." Kirkcenter.org, 1993.

Leary, Timothy. *Flashbacks*, Tarcher, 1983.
– *Musings on Human Metamorphoses.* Ronin, 1988, 2003.
– and Robert Anton Wilson. *The Game of Life.* Peace Press-Starseed, 1979.

McHugh, Roland. *Annotations to* Finnegans Wake. Johns Hopkins P, 1980.

Maddox, Brenda. *Nora: A Biography of Nora Joyce.* Minerva, 1988.

Powers, Michael J. "Issy's Mimetic Night Lessons: Interpellation and Resistance in *Finnegans Wake.*" *Joyce Studies Annual* Vol. 11, Summer (2000): 102-123.

Rabaté, Jean-Michel. "Joyce and Jolas." *Journal of Modern Literature* XXII.2 (Winter 1998-99): 245-252.

Shea, Robert and Robert Anton Wilson. *Illuminatus!* Dell, 1975, reprinted by MJF Books.

Sterling, Clarence. Various articles. 19 July 2012. http://rosenlake.net/fw/index.html.

Terrell, Carroll F. *A Companion to the Cantos of Ezra Pound.* U of CA P, 1980.

Tindall, William York. *A Reader's Guide to Finnegans Wake.* Noonday P, 1969.

Twain, Mark. *The Annotated Huckleberry Finn.* Ed. Michael Patrick Hearn. Norton, 2001.

Wagner, Eric. *An Insider's Guide to Robert Anton Wilson.* New Falcon P., 2004.

Wilde, Oscar. *The Complete Works of Oscar Wilde.* Collins, 1966.

Wilson, Robert Anton. *Coincidance.* Falcon P., 1988.
– *Cosmic Trigger.* Falcon P., 1986.
– *Cosmic Trigger III: My Life After Death.* New Falcon P., 1995.
– "Diagonal Relationship 9, The." *RAW Illumination.* 25 Nov. 2010. 30 Nov. 2010.
– *Earth Will Shake, The.* 1982. Hilaritas Edition, 2018.
– *email to the universe.* New Falcon P., 2005.
– *Everything Is Under Control.* Harper Perennial, 1998.
– *The Illuminati Papers.* And/Or P., 1980.
– *Masks of the Illuminati.* Dell, 1981.
– *Nature's God.* Hilaritas, 1991, 2018 (Hilaritas edition).
– *Prometheus Rising* (Second Edition). Hilaritas, 1983, 1997 (Second Edition), 2016 (Hilaritas edition).
– *Robert Anton Wilson Website, The.* 19 July 2012.
– "Re: Masks of the Illiffinati." E-mail to the author. 20 Oct. 2001.
– *Sex, Drugs & Magick.* New Falcon, 2000. Ut Originally published as *Sex and Drugs* by Playboy Press in 1973.
– *TSOG: The Thing That Ate the Constitution.* New Falcon P., 2002.

Yared, Aida. "Joyce's Sources: Sir Richard F. Burton's *Terminal Essay* in *Finnegans Wake.*" *Joyce StudiesAnnual* 11, Summer (2000): 124-166.

Zardoz. "*Finnegans Wake.*" Forums of the Aleister Crowley Society. 5 Dec. 2008. 19 July 2012 . http://www.lashtal.com/forum/index.php?topic=3285.0.

Zukofsky, Louis. *Bottom: On Shakespeare*. Wesleyan UP. 2002.

HILARITAS PRESS

Publishing the Books of Robert Anton Wilson
and Other Adventurous Thinkers

www.hilaritaspress.com

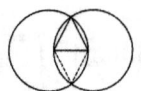

www.ingramcontent.com/pod-product-compliance
Lightning Source LLC
Chambersburg PA
CBHW070047080526
44586CB00013B/948